cccmaps.com

Contents

City Area Maps

City Centre Maps

Map Tips

❯ The **map page number** and **grid reference** found next to the title on the city area and city centre map pages represent the location of that community on the provincial map pages.

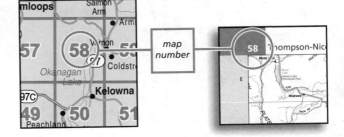

City Area Map Page 132

Richmond can be found on page 6 in grid reference K-16

Locator Maps

❯ Turn to the Locator Maps found on pages iii - v. Each of the small squares outlined on this map represent a different map page in the atlas.

❯ Locate the specific part of the atlas coverage area that you're interested in.

❯ Note the appropriate page number.

❯ Turn to that map page.

map number

© Copyright 2013

Canadian Cartographics Corporation

70 Bloor Street East • Oshawa, Ontario • L1H 3M2
phone: 905-436-2525
email: feedback@cccmaps.com

Front Cover Photo ©Copyright Kathleen Andersen

Creative Team
Norm Adam • Karen Dyer • Steve Fillinger • Lorne Franklin • Peter Gunter • Kelly Lawrence • Lisa McGhie • Meghan Miller • Salina Morrow • Lars Tegtmeyer • Michelle White

British Columbia Distance Chart

A triangular road-distance matrix (in kilometres) between the following locations (listed in chart order):

Banff, AB · Calgary, AB · Campbell River, BC · Courtenay, BC · Cranbrook, BC · Dawson Creek, BC · Edmonton, AB · Fort Nelson, BC · Fort St. John, BC · Hope, BC · Jasper, AB · Kamloops, BC · Kelowna, BC · Nanaimo, BC · Nelson, BC · Penticton, BC · Port Alberni, BC · Powell River, BC · Prince George, BC · Prince Rupert, BC · Princeton, BC · Quesnel, BC · Revelstoke, BC · Salmon Arm, BC · Smithers, BC · Terrace, BC · Vancouver, BC · Vernon, BC · Victoria, BC · Whistler, BC · Whitehorse, YT · Williams Lake, BC

Distances from **Williams Lake, BC** (bottom row of the chart), to:

To	Distance
Banff, AB	779
Calgary, AB	907
Campbell River, BC	702
Courtenay, BC	656
Cranbrook, BC	893
Dawson Creek, BC	644
Edmonton, AB	904
Fort Nelson, BC	1058
Fort St. John, BC	697
Hope, BC	396
Jasper, AB	543
Kamloops, BC	287
Kelowna, BC	447
Nanaimo, BC	553
Nelson, BC	741
Penticton, BC	469
Port Alberni, BC	631
Powell River, BC	670
Prince George, BC	238
Prince Rupert, BC	962
Princeton, BC	404
Quesnel, BC	120
Revelstoke, BC	497
Salmon Arm, BC	395
Smithers, BC	609
Terrace, BC	815
Vancouver, BC	540
Vernon, BC	404
Victoria, BC	583
Whistler, BC	660
Whitehorse, YT	1877

How to Use the Distance Chart

Find the first location you want to find a distance from. Find the second location. Follow the row of numbers across from the first location until it comes to the column of numbers going up from the second location. This is the distance between the two locations.

Detail view (zoom) of the upper-left portion of the chart:

	Campbell River, BC	Courtenay, BC	Cranbrook, BC	Dawson Creek, BC	Edmonton, BC	Fort Nelson, BC	Fort St. John, BC	Hope, BC	Jasper, AB	Kamloops, BC	Kelowna, BC
AB	46	1002	1346	1312	1751	1399	312			951	512
Campbell River, BC		956	1300	1266	1714	1353	266			905	466
Courtenay, BC			1181	698	1641	1254	695		**504**		606
Cranbrook, BC				590	460	1040	677				931
Dawson Creek, BC					1050	663	361	1005			800
Edmonton, BC						387	1454	1137	1345		
Fort Nelson, BC							1093	750	984		
Fort St. John, BC								644	205		
Hope, BC									439		
Jasper, AB											

In the example above, the distance between Cranbrook and Jasper (highlighted in red) is 504 kilometers.

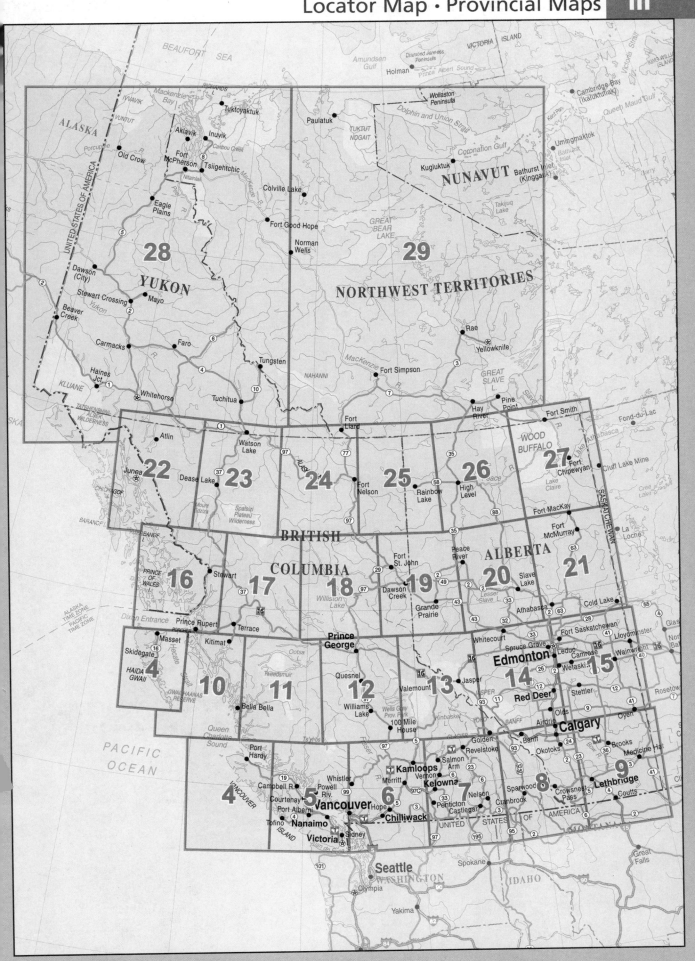

BRITISH COLUMBIA

PACIFIC OCEAN

VANCOUVER ISLAND

Prince Rupert
PORCHER I.
Hecate Strait
BANKS I.
PITT ISLAND
Terrace
Kitimat
Douglas Chan.
Kimsquit
Ocean Falls
Bella Bella
KING I.
HUNTER I.
Namu
Queen Charlotte Sound
CALVERT I.
Good Hope
Rivers Inlet
Bella Coola
Hagensborg
Dean Chan.

YELLOWHEAD HY.
Smithers
Telkwa
Granisle
Babine Lake
Topley
Houston
Burns Lake
Morice Lake
Francois Lake
Fraser Lake
Grassy Plains
Stuart Lake
Fort St. James
Nechako
Vanderhoof
Prince George
Bear Lake
McGregor River
Nechako R.

Eutsuk Lake
Ootsa Lake
Tweedsmuir Provincial Park
Itcha Ilgachuz P.P.
Nazko
Quesnel
Anahim Lake
Chilanko Forks
Chilcotin
River
Williams Lake
150 Mile House
Tatla Lake
Nunsti P.P.
Nemaiah Valley
Chilko L.
Ts'yl-os P.P.
Big Creek P.P.
Clinton
Gold Bridge
D'Arcy
Lillooet
Ashc...
Stein Valley P.P.
Lytton
Boston Bar
Harrison Lake
Hope
Chilliwack
Abbotsford
Manning P...
UNITED STATES
Bellingham
Port Angeles
Everett
Seattle
Tacoma
WA

Kingcome Inlet
Knight Inlet
Thompson Sound
Bute Inlet
Queen Charlotte Strait
Holberg
Winter Harbour
Port Hardy
Port McNeill
Port Neville
Sayward
Woss
Port Alice
30
Brooks Peninsula Prov. Park
Tahsis
31
Gold River
Campbell River
28
Black Creek
Strathcona P.P.
Courtenay
Cumberland
32
Qualicum Beach
Powell River
Saltery Bay
33
Egmont
Sechelt
Gibsons
Lions Bay
Whistler
Garibaldi P.P.
Squamish
Vancouver
Richmond
36
Pt. Coquitlam
37
38
39
Tofino
34
Ucluelet
Bamfield
PACIFIC RIM NAT'L. PK.
Port Alberni
Nanaimo
34
Youbou
N. Cowichan
Duncan
Port Renfrew
35
Sidney
Sooke
Victoria
Juan de Fuca Strait

Strait of Georgia

ALBERTA

WASHINGTON

Tumbler Ridge · Beaverlodge · Wembley · Grande Prairie · Valleyview · Lake · Hondo
Murray R. · Wapiti River · Smoky R. · Athabasca · Lac La Bic
Swan Hills · Athabasca · Smoky Lake
Kakwa Rec. Area · Fox Creek · Whitecourt · Westlock · Redwater · North
Fraser River · Grande Cache · Little Smoky R. · Barrhead · Morinville · Gibbons · St Saskatchewan
Willmore Wilderness Park · Edson · Mayerthorpe · Pembina River · St. Albert · Fort Saskatchewan · Veg
YELLOWHEAD HIGHWAY · McBride · Entrance · Hinton · YELLOWHEAD HWY. · McLeod R. · Edmonton · Sherwood Park · Beaumont
Bowron Lake P.P. · Mt. Robson 3954 m. · Robb · Drayton Valley · Calmar · Leduc · Camrose · 14
arkerville · Mount Robson · Cadomin · River · Winfield · Wetaskiwin
kely · Valemount · Mt. Robson P.P. · JASPER · Jasper · NATIONAL · Brazeau River · Ponoka · Rimbey · Stettler
Quesnel Lake · 86 · 87 · PARK · Saskatchewan · Rocky Mountain House · Lacombe · Red Deer
Wells Gray Provincial Park · Kinbasket Lake · 84 · Bighorn · Wildland · Innisfail · Drumheller
Blue River · Mt. Columbia 3747 m. · 85 · Rec. · Clearwater R. · Olds · Three Hills · Han
100 Mile House · YELLOWHEAD HY. · Mica Creek · Saskatchewan River Crossing · 82 · 83 · Area · Sundre · Red Deer · Airdrie · Drumheller
N. Thompson R. · GLACIER NAT'L PARK · BANFF · NAT'L · Ghost River Wilderness · Calgary · Strathmore
Adams Lake · Rogers Pass · 76 · 77 · 78 · YOHO NAT'L PK. · 79 · PARK · Lake Louise · Banff · Canmore
Barriere · MT. REVELSTOKE NAT'L PARK · Golden · Columbia R. · 95 · 81 · Redwood Meadows · Bow River
Shuswap L. · Revelstoke · Bugaboo P.P. · 80 · KOOTENAY NAT'L PK. · Okotoks · High River · Vulcan
Cache Creek · Savona · Chase · Sicamous · 68 · 69 · 70 · 71 · Radium Hot Springs · Turner Valley · Enchant
64 · 65 · 66 · 67 · 68 · Galena Bay · Invermere · 72 · 73 · 74 · 75 · Nanton
Kamloops · Salmon Arm · Upper Arrow Lake · Goat Range P.P. · Elk Lakes P.P. · Claresholm
56 · 57 · 58 · Vernon · 59 · 60 · Nakusp · 61 · 62 · 63 · Canal Flats · Elkford · 23 · 25
Lower Nicola · Merritt · Coldstream · Okanagan Lake · New Denver · Purcell Wilderness · Sparwood · Crowsnest Pass · Fort Macleod
97C · Kelowna · Valhalla P.P. · Kaslo · Kootenay Lake · Kimberley · Fernie · Pincher Creek · Stand Off
48 · 49 · 50 · 51 · Granby P.P. · 52 · 53 · 54 · 55 · Cranbrook · Elko · Twin Butte · Cardston
Peachland · Naramata · Lower Arrow Lake · Winlaw · Nelson · WATERTON LAKES NAT'L. PK. · Carway · Del B
Summerland · Penticton · Gladstone P.P. · Castlegar · Salmo · MONTANA
40 · 41 · 42 · 43 · 44 · 45 · 46 · 47 · Creston
Keremeos · Oliver · Trail · Rossland · Fruitvale
Cathedral P.P. · Osoyoos · Midway · WASHINGTON · IDAHO
TES OF AMERICA · 395 · Spokane · Coeur d'Alene
Franklin D. Roosevelt Lake · Lake Pend Oreille · Kalispell
Wenatchee · 97A · Flathead Lake

1:1 500 000

0   15   30
km

PARKS LOCATED IN
AND ON VAN
(South of

13a. Hardy Island Marine Prov. Pk.
14. Garden Bay Marine Prov. Pk.
15. Skookumchuck Narrows Prov. Pk.
16. Sandy Island Marine Prov. Pk.
17. Filomgley Prov. Pk.
18. Boyle Point Prov. Pk.
19. Tribune Bay Prov. Pk.
20. Helliwell Prov. Pk.
21. Sabine Channel Prov. Pk.
22. Jedediah Island Marine Prov. Pk.
23. Squitty Bay Prov. Pk.
24. Smuggler Cove Marine Prov. Pk.
25. Buccaneer Bay Prov. Pk.
26. Simson Prov. Pk.
27. Sargeant Bay Prov. Pk.
28. Roberts Creek Prov. Pk.
29. Plumper Cove Marine Prov. Pk.
30. Gabriola Sands Prov. Pk.
31. Sandwell Prov. Pk.
32. Drumbeg Prov. Pk.
33. Hemer Prov. Pk.
34. Pirates Cove Marine Prov. Pk.
35. Roberts Memorial Prov. Pk.
36. Whaleboat Island Marine Prov. Pk.
37. Dionisio Point Prov. Pk.
38. Wallace Island Marine Prov. Pk.
39. Bodega Ridge Prov. Pk.
40. Montague Harbour Marine Prov. Pk.

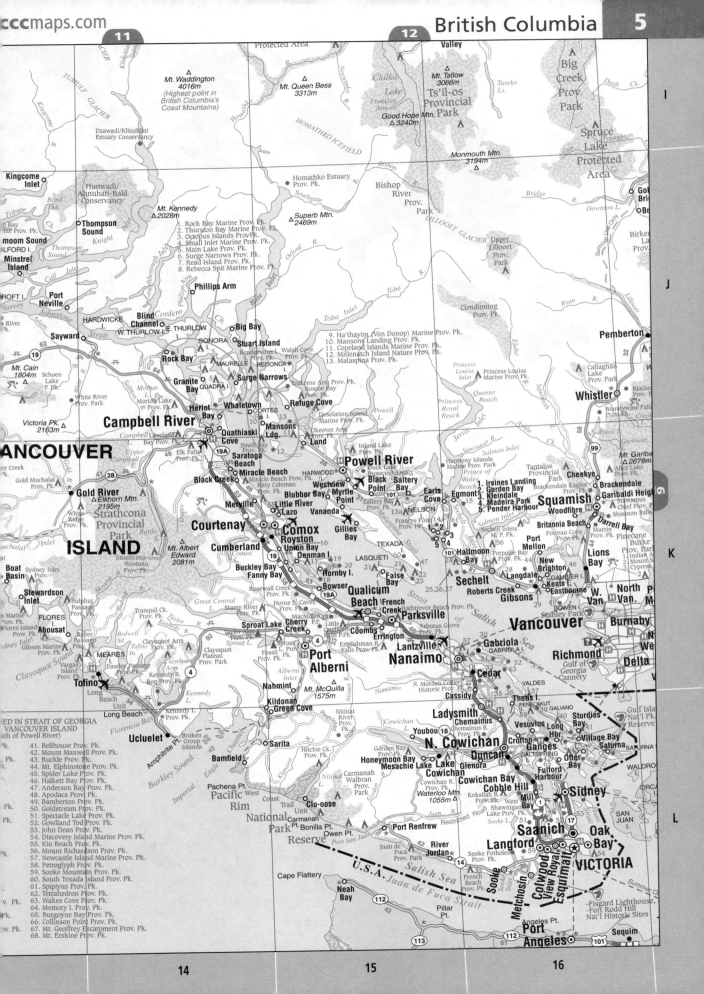

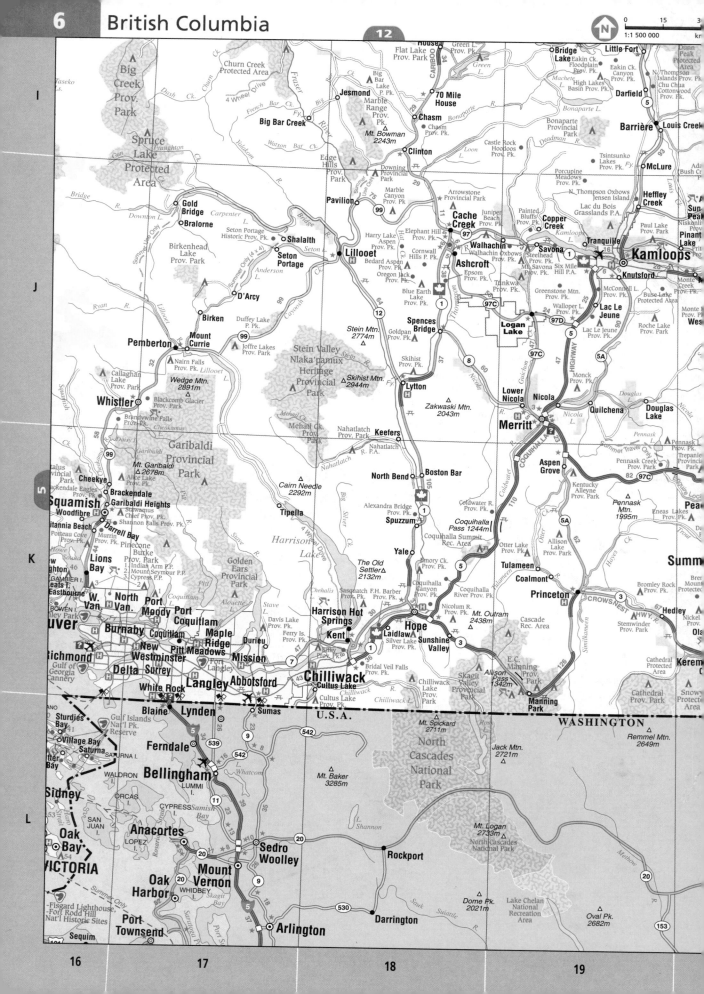

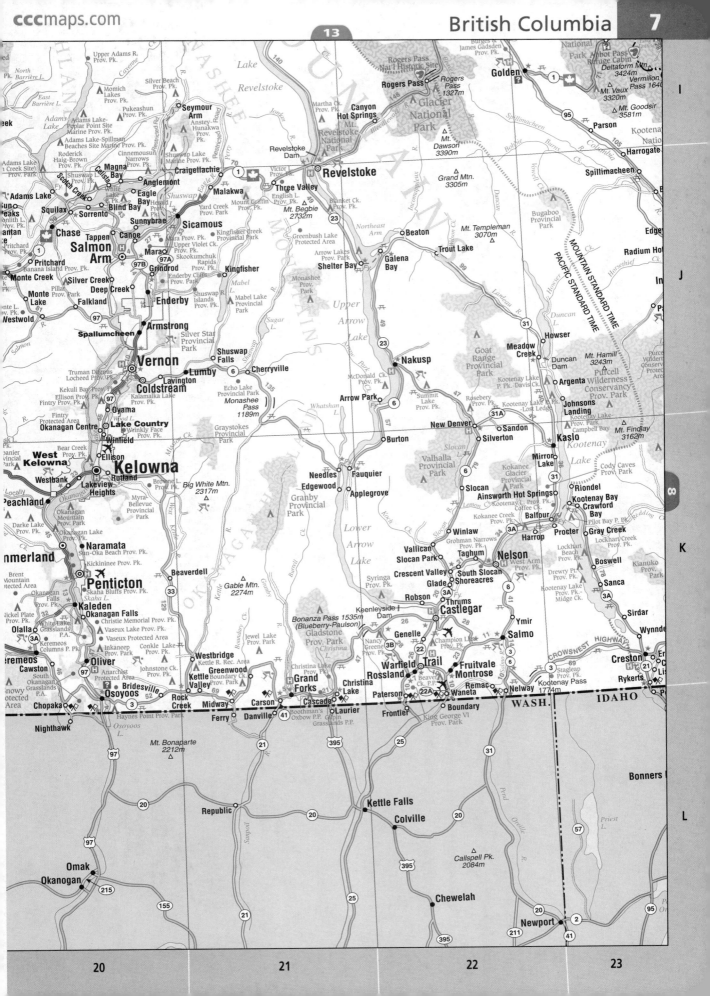

1:1 500 000

0   15   30
km

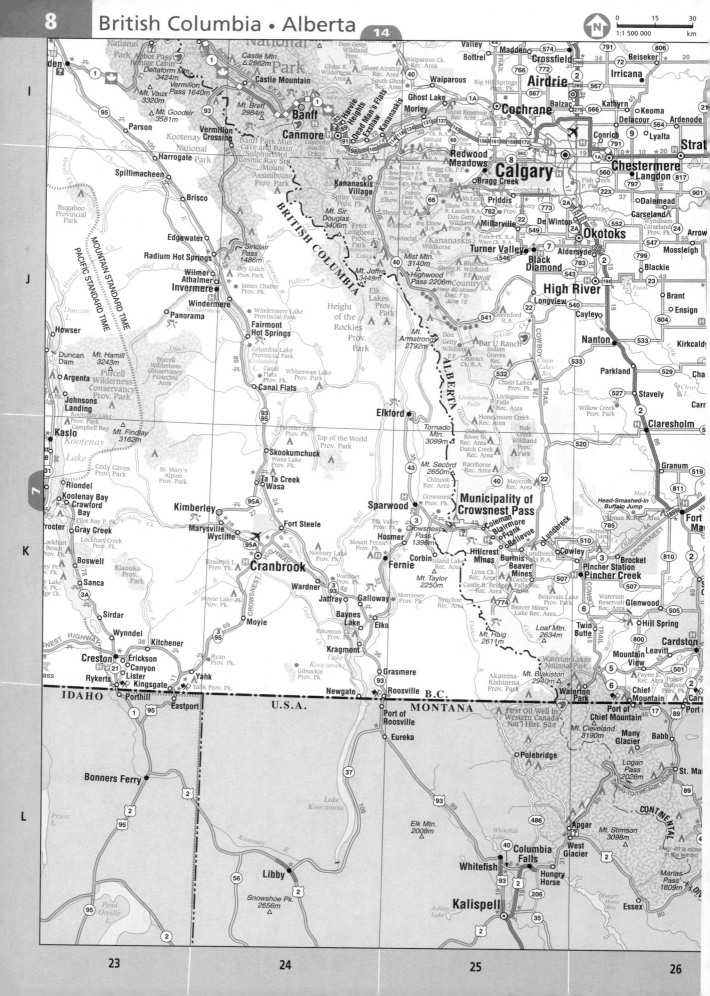

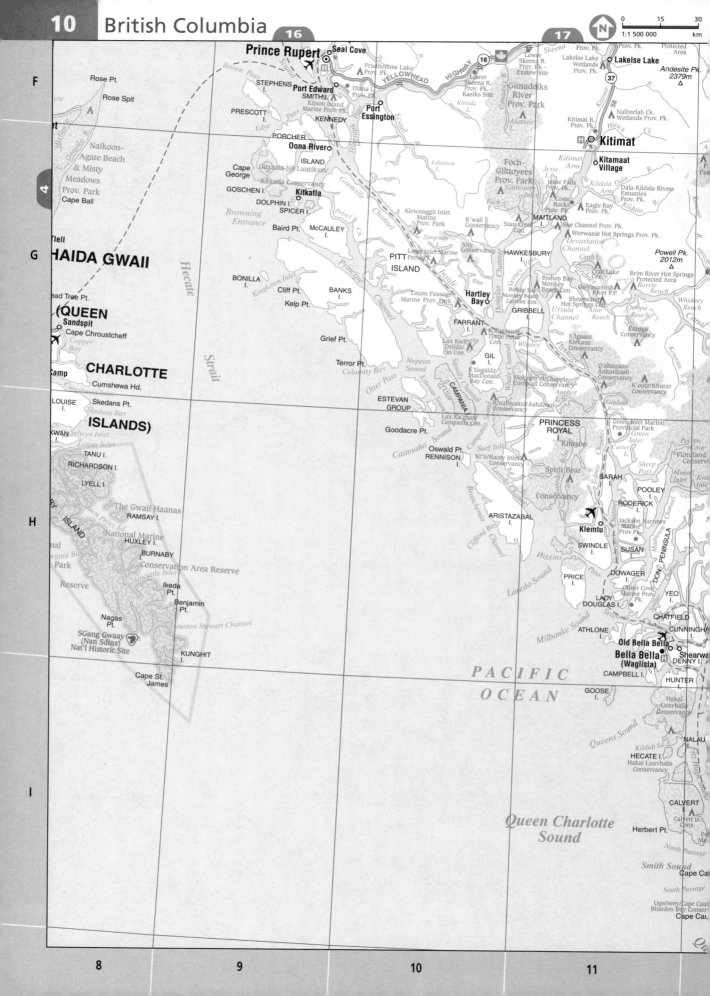

1:1 500 000

0   15   30
km

F

Rose Pt.
Rose Spit

Naikoon-
Agate Beach
& Misty
Meadows
Prov. Park
Cape Ball

4

G **HAIDA GWAII**

Tlell

Sandspit
Cape Chrouscheff
Copper
Bay

Camp **CHARLOTTE**
Cumshewa Hd.

(QUEEN
LOUISE
I.
Skedans Pt.
Skedans Bay

KWAN
Selwyn Inlet
Logan Inlet

ISLANDS)

TANU I.
RICHARDSON I.
LYELL I.

Juan Perez Sd.
The Gwaii Haanas
RAMSAY I.
H National Marine
HUXLEY I.

BURNABY
Conservation Area Reserve
Park

Reserve
Ikeda
Pt.
Benjamin
Pt.
Nagas
Pt.
SGang Gwaay
(Nan Sdins)
Nat'l Historic Site
KUNGHIT

Cape St.
James

I

Hecate
Strait

Prince Rupert
Seal Cove
STEPHENS
I.
Port Edward
SMITH
PRESCOTT
I.
Port Essington
KENNEDY
I.
PORCHER
Oona River
ISLAND
Cape
George
Kitkatla Conservancy
GOSCHEN I.
Kitkatla
DOLPHIN I.
SPICER I.
Baird Pt.
McCAULEY
BONILLA
I.
Cliff Pt.
BANKS
Kelp Pt.
I.

Grief Pt.

Terror Pt.
ESTEVAN
GROUP

Goodacre Pt.

Oswald Pt.
RENNISON

ARISTAZABAL
I.

PRINCESS
ROYAL

SARAH

RODERICK

SWINDLE
I.
SUSAN
I.

PRICE
I.
DOWAGER

LADY
DOUGLAS I.

ATHLONE

Old Bella Bella
Bella Bella
(Waglisla)
CAMPBELL I.

GOOSE

PACIFIC
OCEAN

Queen Charlotte
Sound

Smith Sound

8   9   10   11

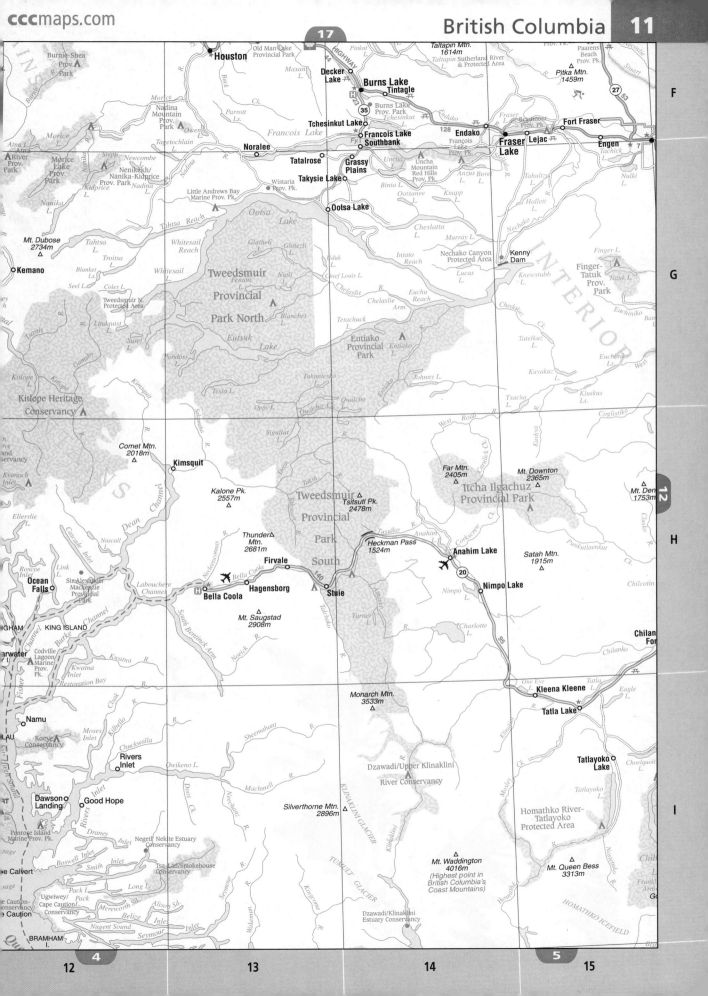

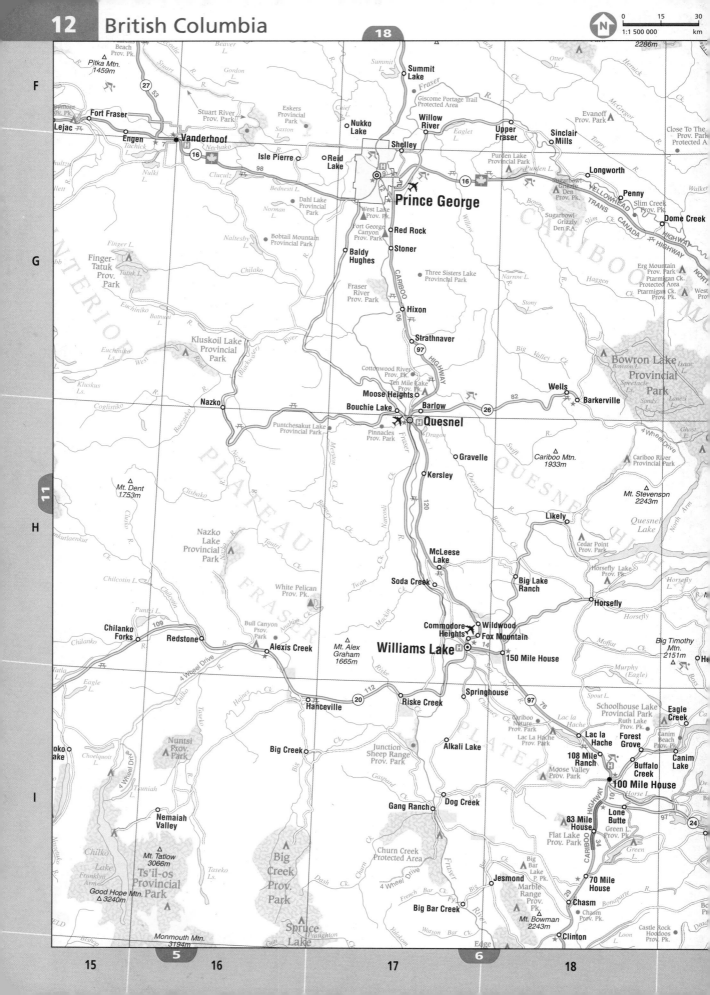

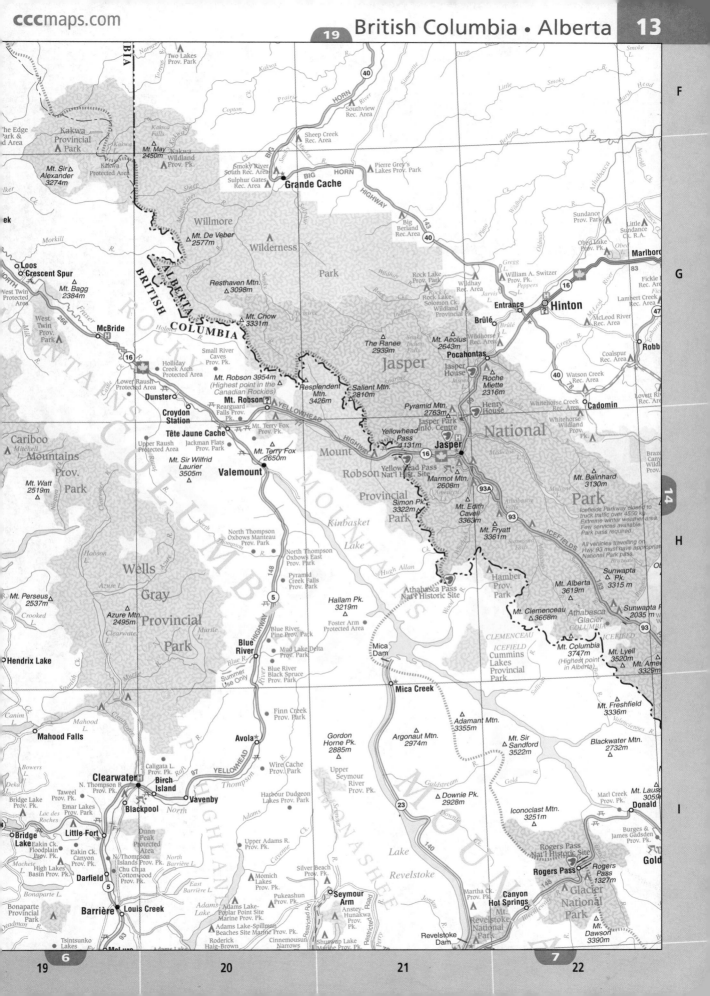

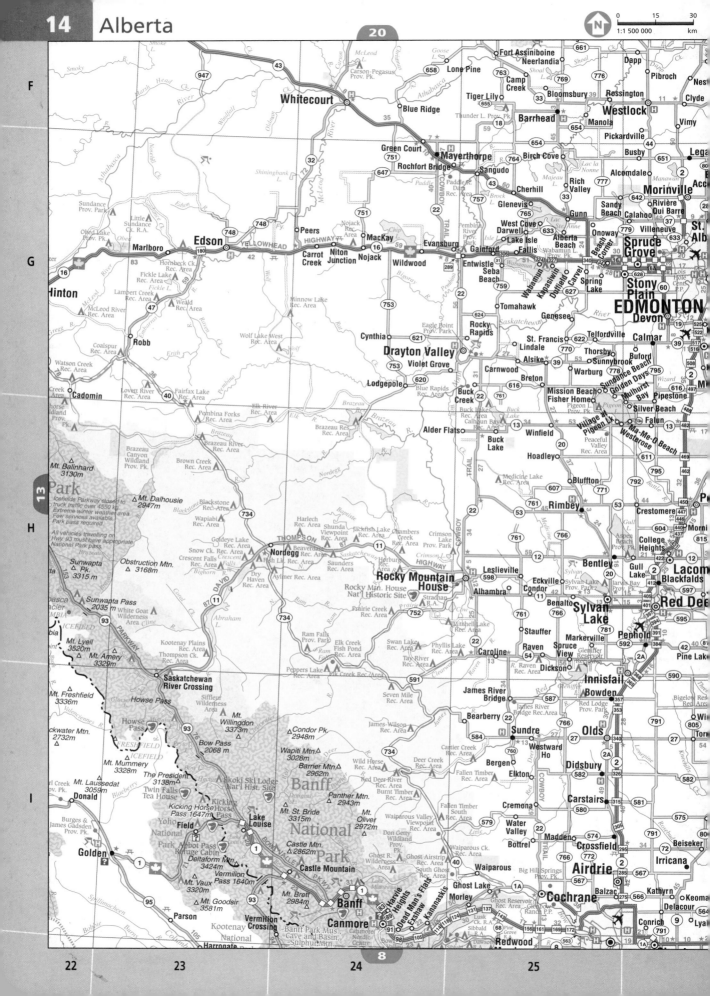

0   15   30
km
1 : 1 500 000

C

Fanshaw

Thomas Bay

BAIRD GLACIER

Devils Thumb
2767m

KUTCHUM

KUPREANOF
ISLAND

PATTERSON GLACIER

Great
Glacier
Prov. Park

Mt. Robertson
△

Porcupine   *Sphaler Ck.*

Iskut River
Hot Springs
Prov. Park

Bob Quinn Lake

CASSIAR HIGHWAY

Burnie R.

Tumeka L.

Brown Cove

Petersburg

LINDENBERG PEN.

Tonka

Cosmos
Pt.

(7)

MITKOF
I.

DRY FARM

RYNDA

SOKOLOF

VANK
I.

Choquette
Hot Springs
Prov. Park

Mt. Gallatin
1554m

Stikine

Iskut

Katete R.

More R.

Ck.

Ningunsaw
Prov. Park

△

Ningunsaw R.

Bell II

48

Delta Pk.
2298m
△

WOEWODSKI
I.

*Wrangell
Narrows*

Duncan Canal

D

ZAREMBO
I.

WORONKOFSKI
I.

Wrangell

Clarence

Pt.
Nesbitt

KASHEVAROF
ISLANDS

STEVENSON
I.

*Zimovia
Strait*

WRANGELL
I.

ETOLIN
I.

Strait

*Blake
Channel*

Bradfield Canal

ALASKA

Craig
Headwaters
Protected
Area

△ Lava Forks
Prov. Park

Mt. Lewis
Cass
2092m △

Unuk R.

Border Lake
Prov. Park

Craig R.

Bell - Irving R.

94

Bowser
L.

LEDUC GLACIER

Mt. Willibert
2067m △

Mt. Pattullo
2729m
△

65

37A

Mezia

Me

*Meziadin
L.*

Bear Glacier
Prov. Park

E

TUXEKAN
I.

Ernest Sound

ONSLOW
I.

CLEVELAND PENINSULA

Mt. Tyee
1430m
△

*Burroughs
Bay*

Bell Island
Hot Springs I. BELL

HASSLER

Bell

Behm Canal

PRINCE
OF
WALES
ISLAND

SAN
FERNANDO

Klawock

Salt Chuck

Kasaan

Craig

Kasaan Bay

Meyers
Chuck

BETTON
I.

Loring

REVILLAGIGEDO
ISLAND

Neets Bay

Carroll Inlet

Walker Cove

Rudyerd B.

SMEATON

Smeaton B.

Misty
Fjords
National
Monument

Treble Mtn.
△

Kinskuch R.

Lavender Pk.
2323m
△

Alice Arm

Hastings Arm

Alice Arm

Gated Restric

Waterfall

GOAT
I.

Hydaburg

SUKKWAN
I.

Cholmondeley Sds.

Hetta Inlet

Wacker

Ketchikan
Mountain
Point

GRAVINA
I.

Clarence

Metlakatla

ANNETTE
I.

Nichols Pass

Tongass Narrows

Thorne Arm

MARY
I.

Revillagigedo Channel

Boca de Quadra

*Nakat
Inlet*

Observatory Inlet

Portland Canal

Kingcolith R.

Ksi Xts'at'kw/
Stagoo
Conservancy

Gitwinksihlkw
(Canyon City)

113

Laxgalts'ap
(Greenville)

Gingolx (Kincolith)

Alder Pk.
2220m
△

F

Cape
Lookout

DALL
I.

Cape
Augustine

LONG
I.

Cape
Cornwallis

Pt.
Marsh

Cape
Muzon

*Cordova
Bay*

Kaigani Strait

Nichols Bay

Moira Sound

DUKE
I.

PEARSE
I.

WALES
I.

Cape Fox

Nakat Bay

ALASKA
U.S.A.   **ALASKA STANDARD TIME**

PACIFIC STANDARD TIME

SOMERVILLE
I.

Pearse Canal

*Nasoga
Gulf*

*Nass
Bay*

Khutzeymateen Inlet

Khutzeymateen
Grizzly Bear
Sanctuary

Khutzeymateen
Inlet Conservancy

Nass R.

Ishkheenickh R.

ZAYAS
I.

Whitby
Pt.

Lax Kw'alaams

FINLAYSON

Caamaño Pass

DUNDAS
I.

Lax Kwaxl/
Dundas &
Melville Is.
Con.

BARON
I.

DUNIRA I.

MELVILLE I.

Big Bay

Chatham Sound

Work Channel

Quottoon
Inlet

*Union
Inlet*

TSIMPSEAN PEN.

Exchamsiks
Prov. Park

Exchamsiks R.

Ecstall R.

G

Langara
Pt.

McPherson Pt.

LANGARA
I.

Parry Pass

Knox

te Pt.

Pt.

Klashwun Pt.

Masset Harbour

Wiah Pt.

Virago Sound

McIntyre Bay

Naden R.

Hiellen R.

Masset

*Naden
Harbour*

*Christie
Pt.*

Yakoun R.

Pure

Mamin R.

Naikoon-

Rose Pt.

Rose Spit

Prince Rupert

Seal Cove

Prudhomme Lake
Prov. Pk.

YELLOWHEAD HIGHWAY

16

STEPHENS
I.

Port Edward

SMITHI.

Kitson Island
Marine Prov. Pk.

Diana L.
Prov. Pk.

Port
Essington

Skeena R.

Lower
Skeena R.
Prov. Pk.-
Kasiks Site

Khtada
L.

PRESCOTT
I.

KENNEDY
I.

PORCHER

Brown Pass

Ogden Channel

Telegraph Pass

Oona River

ISLAND

Johnston

Gunboat Pass

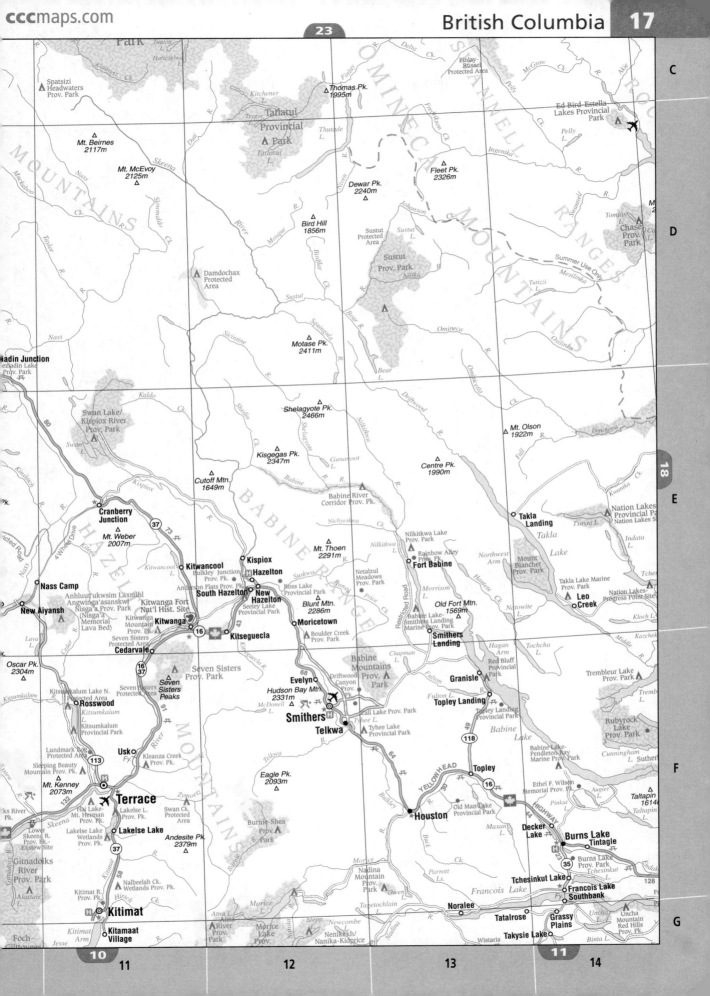

C

Spatsizi
Headwaters
Prov. Park

Thomas Pk.
1995m

Ed Bird-Estella
Lakes Provincial
Park

Mt. Beirnes
2117m

Tatlatui
Provincial
Park

Mt. McEvoy
2125m

Dewar Pk.
2240m

Fleet Pk.
2326m

D

Chase
Prov.
Park

Bird Hill
1856m

Sustut
Protected
Area

Damdochax
Protected
Area

Sustut
Prov. Park

Motase Pk.
2411m

Omineca

Nadin Junction
Meziadin Lake
Prov. Park

Summer Use Only

Shelagyote Pk.
2466m

Mt. Olson
1922m

Swan Lake/
Kispiox River
Prov. Park

18

Kisgegas Pk.
2347m

Centre Pk.
1990m

Nation Lakes
Provincial Pa
Nation Lakes S

E

Cutoff Mtn.
1649m

Babine River
Corridor Prov. Pk.

Cranberry
Junction

Mt. Weber
2007m

Takla
Landing

Nass Camp

Mt. Thoen
2291m

Nilkitkwa Lake
Prov. Park

Rainbow Alley
Prov. Pk.

Mount
Blancher
Prov. Park

Takla Lake Marine
Prov. Park

Kispiox
Kitwancool
Hazelton
Fort Babine

Nation Lakes
Progress Point Site

Anhluut'ukwsim Laxmihl
Angwinga'asanskwl
Nisga'a Prov. Park
(Nisga'a
Memorial Lava Bed)

South Hazelton
New
Hazelton

Netalzul
Meadows
Prov. Park

Leo
Creek

New Aiyansh

Kitwanga Fort
Nat'l Hist. Site

Ross Lake
Provincial Park

Blunt Mtn.
2286m

Old Fort Mtn.
1569m

Kitwanga

Moricetown

Babine Lake-
Smithers Landing
Marine Prov. Park

Oscar Pk.
2304m

Kitseguecla

Boulder Creek
Prov. Park

Smithers
Landing

Cedarvale

Seven Sisters
Prov. Park

Babine
Mountains
Prov. Park

Granisle

Trembleur Lake
Prov. Park

Rosswood

Seven Sisters
Peaks

Evelyn

Driftwood
Canyon
Prov. Pk.

Topley Landing

Rubyrock
Lake
Prov. Park

Kitsumkalum
Provincial Park

Hudson Bay Mtn.
2331m

McDonell

Tyhee Lake Prov. Park

Topley Landing
Provincial Park

F

Usk

Smithers
Telkwa

Tyhee Lake
Provincial Park

Babine
Lake

Babine Lake-
Pendleton Bay
Marine Prov. Park

Mt. Kenney
2073m

Eagle Pk.
2093m

YELLOWHEAD

Topley

Ethel F. Wilson
Memorial Prov. Park

Taltapin
1614

Terrace

Lakelse L.
Prov. Park

Houston

Old Man Lake
Provincial Park

Decker
Lake

Burns Lake
Tintagle

Lakelse Lake
Wetlands Prov. Pk.

Lakelse Lake

Andesite Pk.
2379m

Nadina
Mountain
Prov. Park

Burns Lake
Prov. Park

Sleeping Beauty
Mountain Prov. Pk.

Burnie-Shea
Prov. Pk.

Tchesinkut Lake

Gitnadoiks
River
Prov. Park

Francois Lake
Southbank

Kitimat

Noralee

Tatalrose

Grassy
Plains

Uncha
Mountain
Red Hills
Prov. Pk.

Kitamaat
Village

Morice
Lake
Prov.

Nenikekh/
Nanika-Kidprice

Takysie Lake

128

G

10   11   12   13   11   14

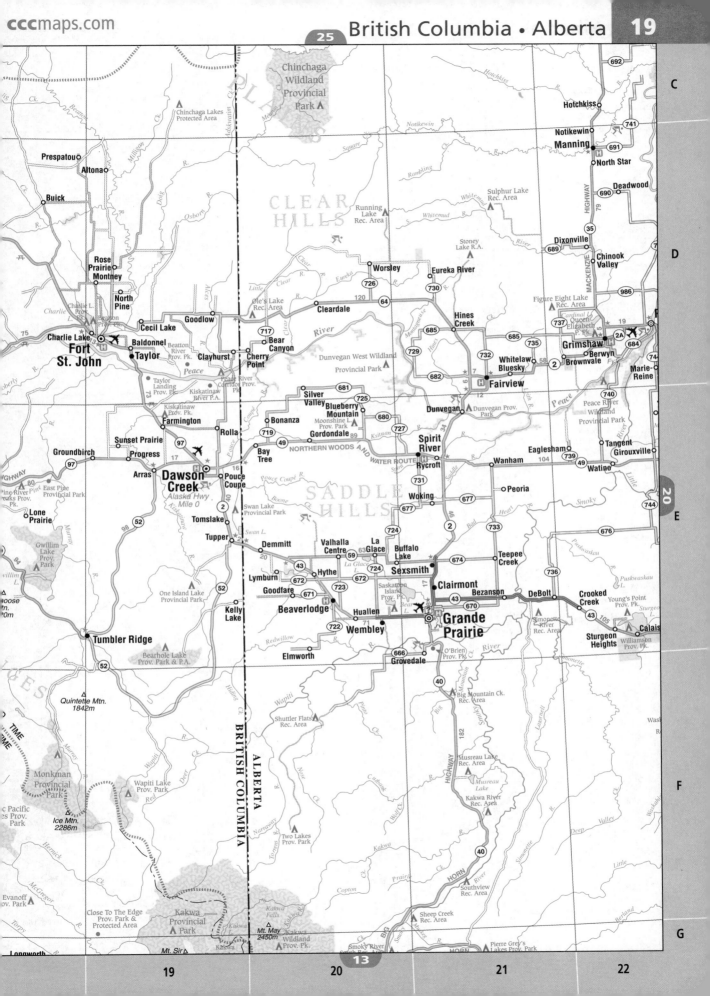

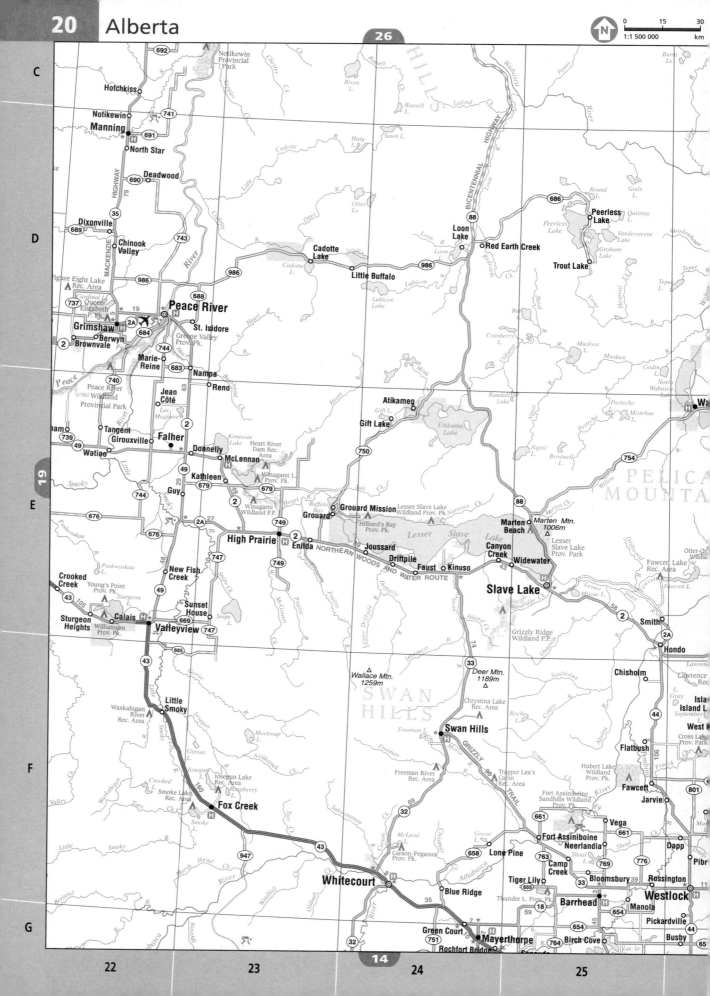

1:1 500 000

0   15   30
km

C

Notikewin Provincial Park

Hotchkiss

Notikewin
Manning
North Star
691

690
Deadwood

MACKENZIE HIGHWAY 79

35
Dixonville
689
Chinook Valley
743

D

Figure Eight Lake Rec. Area
737
Queen Elizabeth P.P.
986
688
Peace River
684
Grimshaw
Berwyn
2A
Brownvale
2
744
Marie-Reine
683

740
Jean Côté
Peace River Wildland Provincial Park
Lac Magloire

739
49
Tangent
Girouxville
744
Watino
676
676

E
2A
27

New Fish Creek
747
749

Crooked Creek
43 105
Young's Point Prov. Park
Sturgeon Heights
Williamson Prov. Pk.
Calais
Valleyview
747
665

43

Little Smoky

Waskahigan River Rec. Area
160
Smoke Lake Rec. Area

F
Iosegun Lake Rec. Area

Fox Creek

947
43
8

Whitecourt
35
Blue Ridge

G
32
751
Green Court
Rochfort Bridge
Mayerthorpe
764 Birch Cove

692

Chester Ck.

Russell L.
Bison L.

Lafond L.

BICENTENNIAL HIGHWAY

Cadotte
Cadotte Lake
986

88
Loon Lake
986
Red Earth Creek

Little Buffalo

Lubicon Lake

686
Peerless Lake
Peerless Lake
Vandersteene Lake
Graham Lake
Trout Lake

Round L.
Gods L.
Quitting L.

Woodenhouse L.

Tepee L.
Tepee L.

St. Isidore
Greene Valley Prov. Pk.
Nampa
Reno

Atikameg
Gift L.
Gift Lake
750

Utikuma Lake
754
PELICAN MOUNTAIN

Donnelly
McLennan
Winagami L. Prov. Pk.
49
Kathleen
679
Guy 29 679
2
Winagami Wildland P.P.

Grouard Mission
Grouard
749
Lesser Slave Lake Wildland Prov. Pk.
88
Marten Beach
Marten Mtn. 1006m

High Prairie
2
Enilda
Joussard
Driftpile
Faust Kinuso
Canyon Creek
43
Widewater

NORTHERN WOODS AND WATER ROUTE

Lesser Slave Lake
Lesser Slave Lake Prov. Park

Slave Lake
58
2
Smith
2A
Hondo

Grizzly Ridge Wildland P.P.

33
Deer Mtn. 1189m

Wallace Mtn. 1259m

SWAN HILLS

Chrystina Lake Rec. Area

Chisholm

44
Island L

West

GRIZZLY TRAIL

Swan Hills

Freeman River Rec. Area

Trapper Lea's Cabin Rec. Area

Hubert Lake Wildland Prov. Pk.

Flatbush
106

Fawcett
Jarvie
801

Fort Assiniboine Sandhills Wildland Prov. Pk.

661
Vega
661

32
McLeod
Carson-Pegasus Prov. Park
69

658 Lone Pine
Fort Assiniboine
Neerlandia
763 Camp Creek
33
769 Bloomsbury 39
776 Rossington
Dapp

Tiger Lily
855
Thunder L. Prov. Pk.
18
Barrhead
654
59

Pibr

Westlock
Manola
Pickardville
654
Busby
85

14

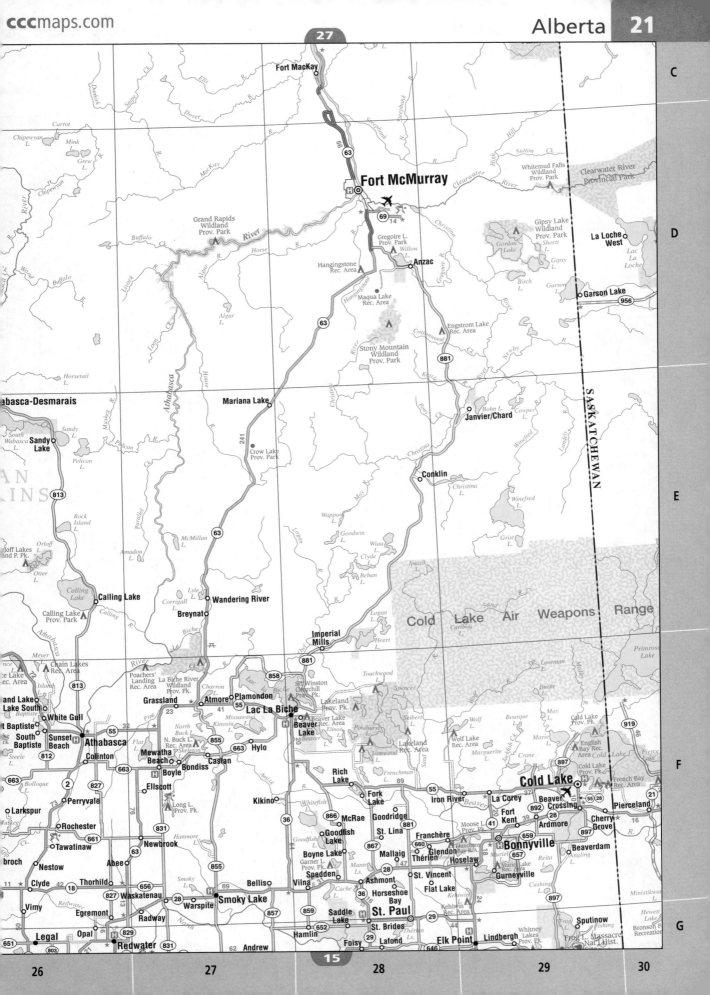

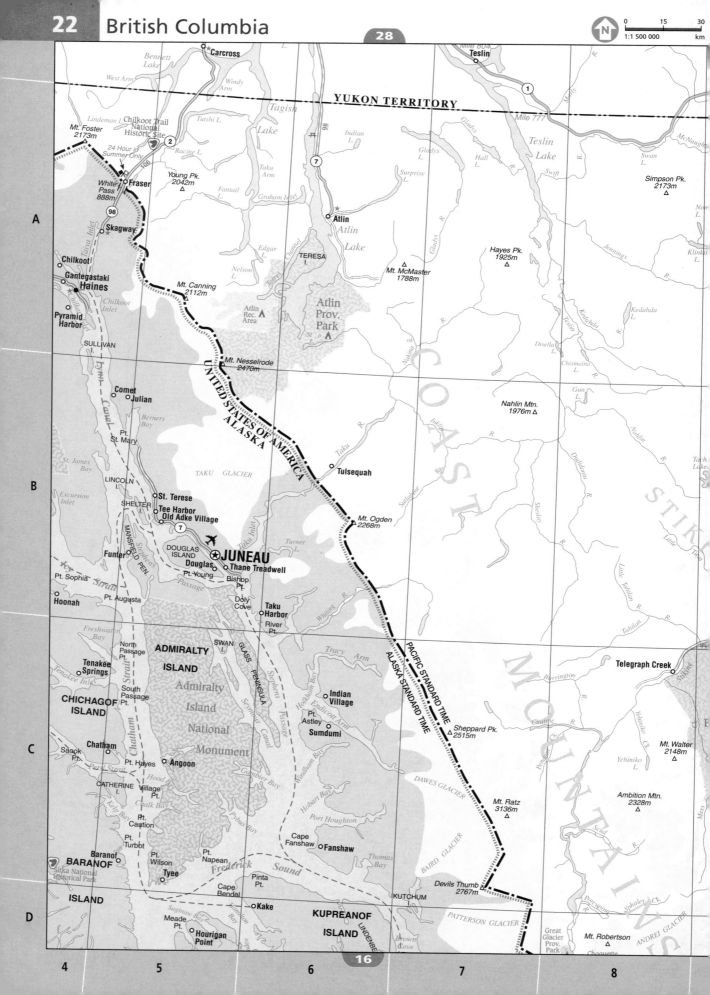

0 15 30
1:1 500 000 km

YUKON TERRITORY

Carcross

Teslin

Mile 804

Mile 777

Teslin Lake

Bennett Lake

West Arm

Windy Arm

Tagish Lake

Tutshi L.

Simpson Pk. 2173m △

Lindeman L.

Chilkoot Trail National Historic Site

Mt. Foster 2173m

24 Hour in Summer Only

Young Pk. 2042m △

Taku Arm

Indian L.

Gladys L.

Hall L.

Swan L.

Fraser

White Pass 888m

Skagway

A

Atlin

Atlin Lake

TERESA I.

Hayes Pk. 1925m △

Mt. McMaster 1788m △

Edgar L.

Nelson L.

Kedahda L.

Chilkoot!

Gantegastaki **Haines**

Pyramid Harbor

Mt. Canning 2112m

Atlin Rec. Area △

Atlin Prov. Park

Kedahda

SULLIVAN I.

Chilkoot Inlet

Disella L.

Mt. Nesselrode 2470m

B

Comet Julian

Berners Bay

UNITED STATES OF AMERICA

Nahlin Mtn. 1976m △

Chismaina

Pt. St. Mary

ALASKA

St. James Bay

TAKU GLACIER

Taku L.

Gun L.

Excursion Inlet

LINCOLN I.

SHELTER I.

St. Terese

Tee Harbor Old Adke Village

Tulsequah

C O A S T

S T I K I

Nakina

Inklin R.

Sutlahine R.

Sheslay R.

Nahlin R.

Funter

DOUGLAS ISLAND

JUNEAU

Douglas Thane Treadwell

Mt. Ogden 2268m

Pt. Sophia

Hoonah

Pt. Augusta

Bishop Pt.

Pt. Young

Doly Cove

Taku Harbor

River Pt.

Turner L.

Whiting R.

Telegraph Creek

C

Freshwater Bay

North Passage Pt.

SWAN I.

ADMIRALTY ISLAND

Tracy Arm

PACIFIC STANDARD TIME

ALASKA STANDARD TIME

Barrington R.

Mt. Walter 2148m △

Tenakee Springs

South Passage Pt.

Admiralty Island National Monument

Hoktaheen Bay

Indian Village

Pt. Astley

Sumdumi

Sheppard Pk. 2515m △

Yehiniko

CHICHAGOF ISLAND

Chatham

Pt. Hayes

Angoon

Gambier Bay

Windham Bay

Yehiniko Ck.

Sagook Pt.

Peril Strait

CATHERINE I.

Village Pt.

Hood Bay

Chalk Bay

Pybus Bay

Hobart Bay

Port Houghton

DAWES GLACIER

Ambition Mtn. 2328m △

Pt. Caution

Pt. Turbot

Kelp Bay

Cape Fanshaw

Fanshaw

Mt. Ratz 3136m △

BARANOF

Baranof

Sitka National Historical Park

Pt. Wilson

Pt. Napean

Tyee

Frederick

Sound

Thomas Bay

BAIRD GLACIER

Cape Bendel

Pinta Pt.

KUTCHUM I.

Devils Thumb 2767m

ISLAND

Kake

KUPREANOF ISLAND

PATTERSON GLACIER

Great Glacier Prov. Park

Mt. Robertson

ANDREI GLACIER

D

Meade Pt.

Hourigan Point

Saginaw Bay

Brown Cove

4   5   6   16   7   8

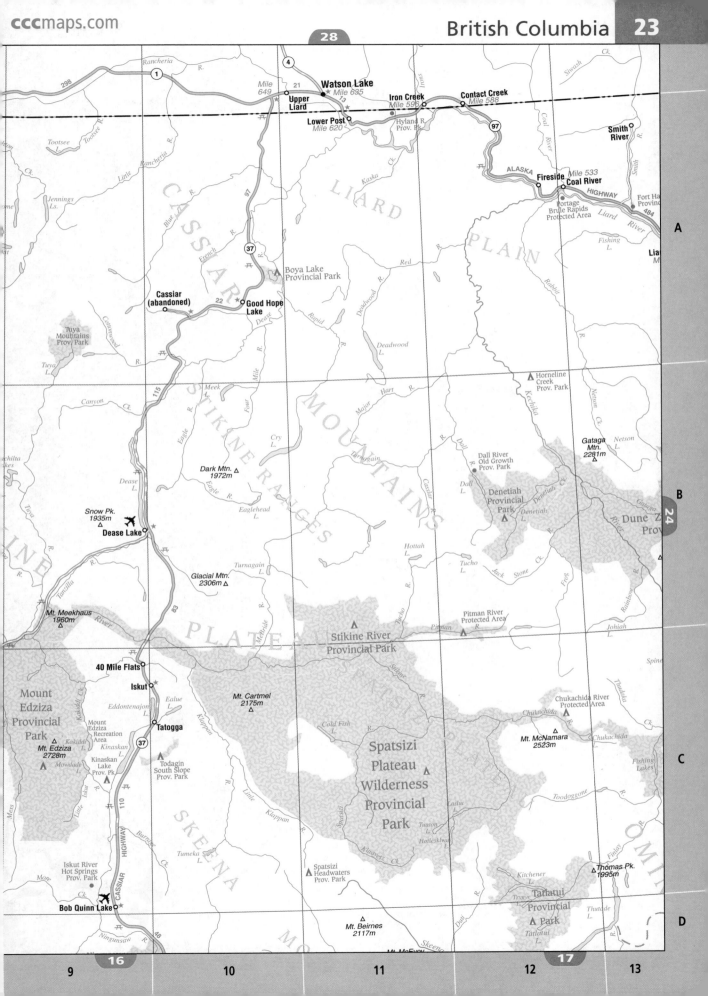

Rancheria R.

298

1

Mile 649

4

Watson Lake
Mile 635

21

13

Upper Liard

Iron Creek
Mile 595

Contact Creek
Mile 588

97

Smith River

Lower Post
Mile 620

Hyland R.
Prov. Pk.

Kaska R.

Coal River

ALASKA

Mile 533

Fireside   Coal River

HIGHWAY

Fort Ha
Provin

484

Lia
M

A

Tootsee L.

Jennings Ls.

CASSIAR

Little Rancheria R.

97

Blue R.

French R.

37

Boya Lake Provincial Park

Red R.

Deadwood R.

Rapid R.

LIARD   PLAIN

Liard River

Portage Brule Rapids Protected Area

Fishing L.

Cassiar (abandoned)

22

Good Hope Lake

Dease R.

Deadwood

115

Tuya Mountains Prov. Park

Tuya L.

Cottonwood R.

STIKNE RANGES

Meek R.

Four R.

Canyon Ck.

Eagle R.

Cry L.

Hart R.

Dall R.

Dall River Old Growth Prov. Park

Dall L.

Horneline Creek Prov. Park

Kechika R.

Nelson R.

Netson L.

Gataga Mtn. 2281m

B   24

Dark Mtn. 1972m

Eagle R.

Eaglehead L.

Turnagain R.

MOUNTAINS

Cassiar R.

Denetiah Provincial Park

Denetiah Ck.

Denetiah L.

Dune Z Prov

Snow Pk. 1935m

Dease Lake

Dease L.

Turnagain R.

Glacial Mtn. 2306m

Hottah L.

Tucho L.

Jack Stone Ck.

Frog R.

Gataga River

Rainbow R.

Mt. Meekhaus 1960m

Tanzilla R.

83

PLATEAU

McBride R.

Pitman R.

Stikine River Provincial Park

Pitman River Protected Area

Johiah L.

Spine

40 Mile Flats

Iskut

Tatogga

37

Mount Edziza Provincial Park

Mt. Edziza 2728m

Kakiddi Ck.

Mount Edziza Recreation Area

Kinaskan Lake

Mowdade L.

Kakiddi L.

Kinaskan Lake Prov. Pk.

Todagin South Slope Prov. Park

Ealue L.

Eddontenajon L.

Klappan R.

Mt. Cartmel 2175m

SPATSIZ

Cold Fish L.

Stikine R.

Spatsizi R.

Chukachida R.

Chukachida River Protected Area

Mt. McNamara 2523m

Chukachida R.

Fishing Lakes

C

SKEENA

Little Klappan R.

Spatsizi Plateau Wilderness Provincial Park

Laslui L.

Tuaton L.

Hotlesklwa L.

Toodoggone R.

O M I

Iskut River Hot Springs Prov. Park

110

Burrage Ck.

Tumeka L.

Klappan R.

Kl-uavetz Ck.

Spatsizi Headwaters Prov. Park

Dall R.

Kluayaz L.

Finlay R.

Thomas Pk. 1995m

Kitchener L.

Tatlatui Provincial Park

Bob Quinn Lake

CASSIAR HIGHWAY

48

Ningunsaw R.

MO

Mt. Beirnes 2117m

Mt. McEvoy

Skeen

Tatlatui L.

Thutade L.

D

1:1 500 000

0 15 30 km

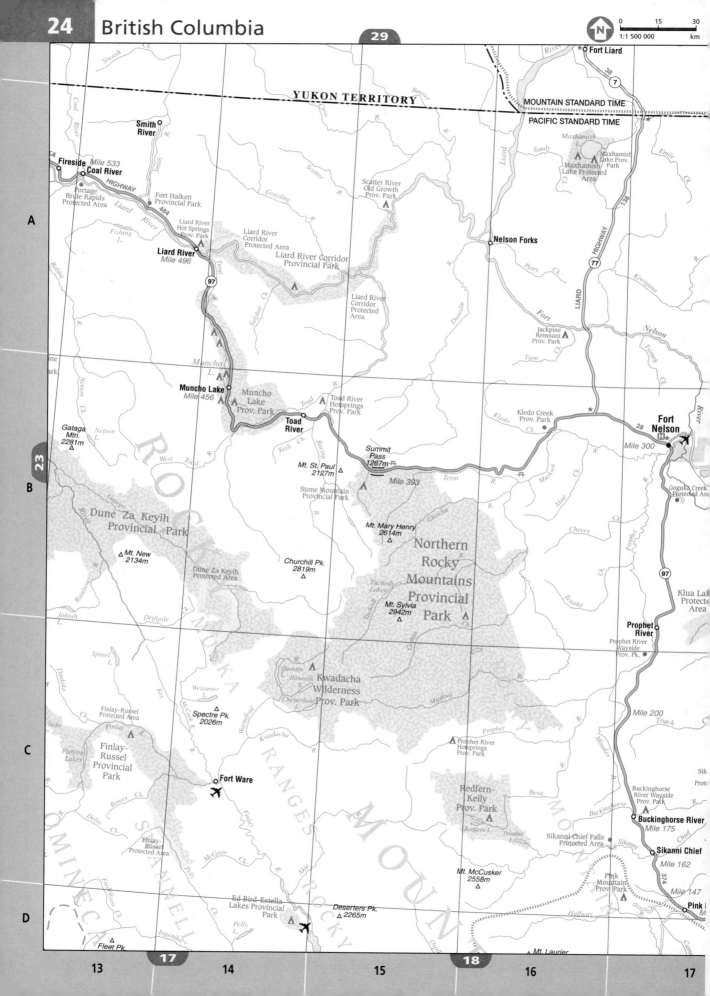

YUKON TERRITORY

MOUNTAIN STANDARD TIME

PACIFIC STANDARD TIME

★ Fort Liard

Smith River

Fireside
Coal River Mile 533

Portage
Brule Rapids
Protected Area

Fort Halkett
Provincial Park

HIGHWAY 484

Maxhamish
Lake Prov.
Park
Maxhamish
Lake Protected
Area

Scatter River
Old Growth
Prov. Park

Nelson Forks

Liard River
Hot Springs
Prov. Park

Liard River
Corridor
Protected Area

Liard River Corridor
Provincial Park

Liard River
Mile 496

97

Liard River
Corridor
Protected
Area

HIGHWAY 77

Jackpine
Remnant
Prov. Park

Muncho
L.

Muncho Lake
Mile 456

Muncho
Lake
Prov. Park

Toad River
Hotsprings
Prov. Park

Kledo Creek
Prov. Park

Fort
Nelson

Mile 300

Toad
River

Gataga
Mtn.
2281m

Summit
Pass
1267m

Mt. St. Paul
2127m

Mile 393

Goguka Creek
Protected Area

Stone Mountain
Provincial Park

Dune Za Keyih
Provincial Park

Mt. New
2134m

Churchill Pk.
2819m

Mt. Mary Henry
2614m

Northern
Rocky
Mountains
Provincial
Park

Tuchodi
Lakes

Mt. Sylvia
2942m

Klua Lake
Protected
Area

Dune Za Keyih
Protected Area

Prophet
River

Prophet River
Wayside
Prov. Pk.

Finlay-Russel
Protected Area

Spectre Pk.
2026m

Kwadacha
Wilderness
Prov. Park

Quentin
L.
Haworth
L.
Chesterfield
L.

Mile 200

Finlay-
Russel
Provincial
Park

Fishing
Lakes

Fort Ware

Prophet River
Hotsprings
Prov. Park

Redfern-
Keily
Prov. Park

Buckinghorse
River Wayside
Prov. Park

Buckinghorse River
Mile 175

Finlay-
Russel
Protected Area

Redfern L.

Trimble
L.

Sikanni Chief Falls
Protected Area

Sikanni Chief
Mile 162

Mt. McCusker
2558m

Pink
Mountain
Prov. Park

Mile 147

Ed Bird-Estella
Lakes Provincial
Park

Deserters Pk.
2265m

Pink

Fleet Pk.

Mt. Laurier

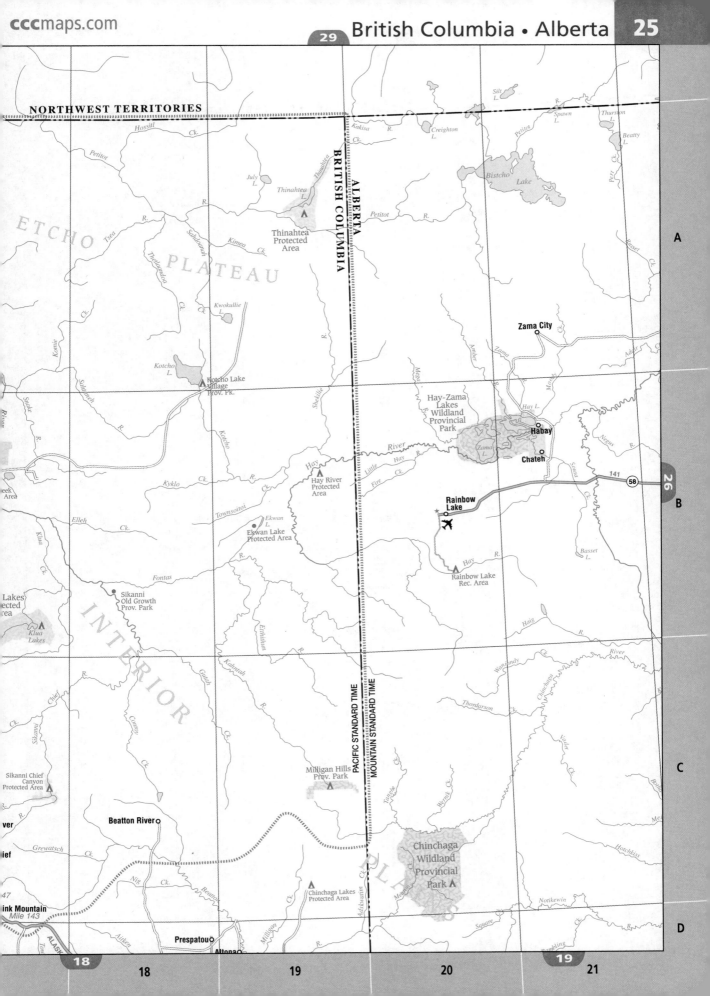

NORTHWEST TERRITORIES

ALBERTA

BRITISH COLUMBIA

ETCHO PLATEAU

INTERIOR PLAINS

Hossitl Ck.

Petitot R.

July L.

Thinahtea L.

Thinahtea Protected Area

Kakisa R.

Creighton L.

Silt L.

Spawn L.

Thurston L.

Bistcho Lake

Beatty L.

Petitot R.

Petitot R.

Tsea R.

Sahtaneh R.

Kimea Ck.

Thelindaa R.

Konie Ck.

Kwokullie L.

Sahtaneh R.

Kotcho L.

Kotcho Lake Village Prov. Pk.

Shekilie R.

Kotcho R.

Snake River

Zama City

Megai R.

Amber R.

Zama R.

Zama R.

Hay-Zama Lakes Wildland Provincial Park

Hay L.

Moody R.

Habay

Zama L.

Negus R.

Chateh

141

58

26

Elleh Ck.

Kyklo Ck.

Townsottol

Hay R.

River

Hay R.

Little R.

Fire Ck.

Hay River Protected Area

Ekwan L.

Ekwan Lake Protected Area

Rainbow Lake

Rainbow Lake Rec. Area

Hay R.

R.

Basset L.

Klua Ck.

Fontas R.

Lakes ... ected Area

Klua Lakes

Sikanni Old Growth Prov. Park

Etthithun R.

Haig R.

Sikanni R.

Conroy Ck.

Kahntah R.

R.

R.

Wentzel ...

Wentzel Ck.

Chuchaga R.

Valda R.

Chief R.

PACIFIC STANDARD TIME

MOUNTAIN STANDARD TIME

Wanlundy R.

Thordarson R.

Sikanni Chief Canyon Protected Area

Milligan Hills Prov. Park

Tataple R.

Wembi Ck.

Bouba ...

Mertz ...

...ver

...ief

Grewatsch Ck.

Beatton River

Beatton R.

Nig Ck.

Ck.

Chinchaga R.

Chinchaga Lakes Protected Area

Meikle R.

Adskwatim R.

Chinchaga Wildland Provincial Park

Hotchkiss R.

Notikewin R.

...47

...nk Mountain Mile 143

ALASKA ...

Aitken Ck.

Milligan Ck.

Prespatou

Altona

Square R.

Rumbling ...

A

B

C

D

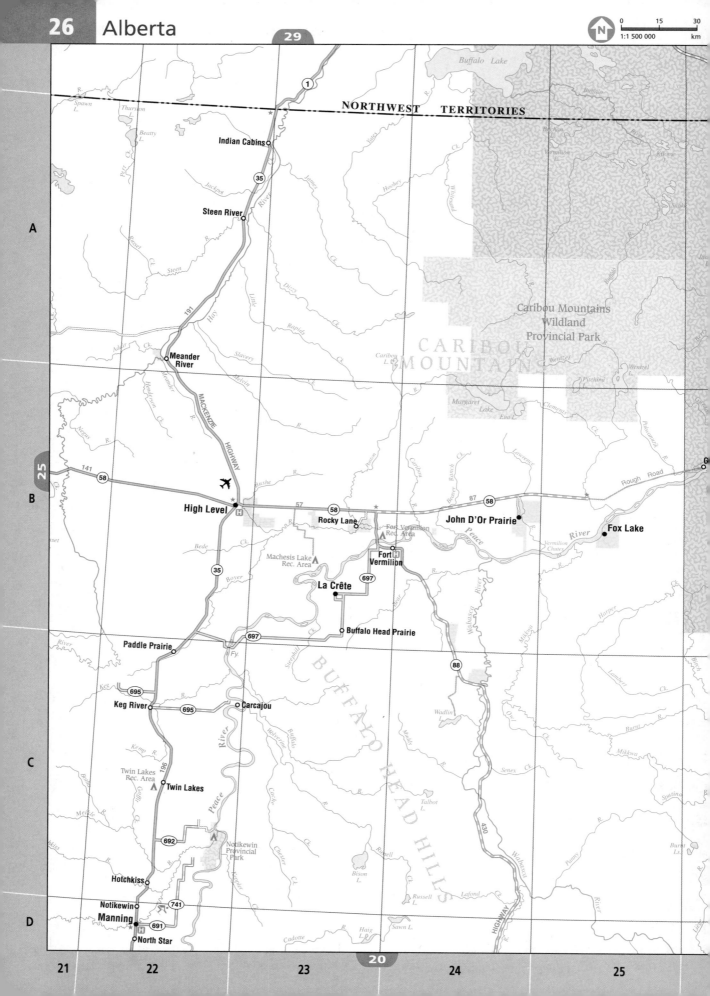

29

1:1 500 000

0 15 30
km

1

NORTHWEST   TERRITORIES

Indian Cabins

35

Steen River

A

191

Hay River

MACKENZIE   HIGHWAY

Meander
River

Caribou Mountains
Wildland
Provincial Park

CARIBOU
MOUNTAINS

Margaret
Lake

Eva L.

141

58

Rough Road

G

25

High Level

57

58

Rocky Lane

Fort Vermilion
Rec. Area

87

58

John D'Or Prairie

Peace   River

Fox Lake

B

35

Machesis Lake
Rec. Area

Fort
Vermilion

Boyer

La Crête

697

Buffalo Head Prairie

697

Paddle Prairie

88

695

Keg River

695

Carcajou

Wadlin
L.

BUFFALO   HEAD   HILLS

C

196

Twin Lakes
Rec. Area

Twin Lakes

Peace   River

Talbot
L.

430

HIGHWAY

692

Notikewin
Provincial
Park

Bison
L.

Hotchkiss

Notikewin

741

D

Manning

691

North Star

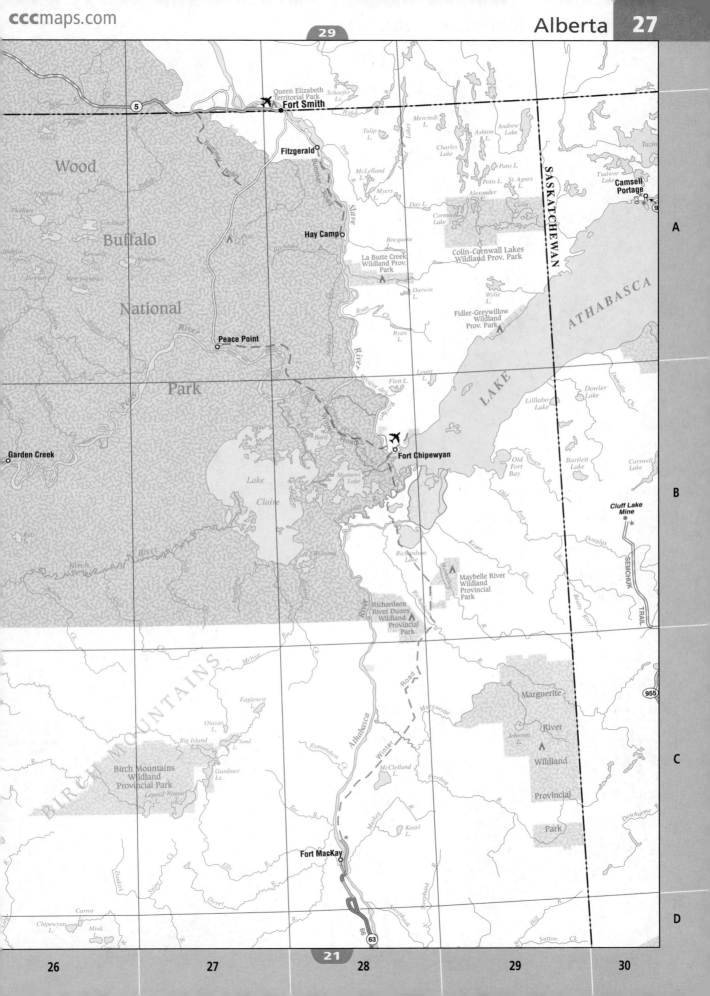

1:4 500 000

0   45   90
km

ALASKA

YUKON

BEAUFORT SEA

D

Arctic Village

Fort Yukon

Circle

E

Eagle

Boundary

TOP OF THE WORLD HY.
(Summer traffic only)

Tetlin Junction

Northway Junction

Beaver Creek

Kluane Wildlife Sanctuary

Burwash Landing

Destruction Bay

Ghost Town of Silver City

Mt. Wood 4840 m.

Mt. Lucania 5226 m.

Table Mtn. 2853 m.

Mt. Logan 5959 m.

Mt. Queen Mary 3886 m.

Mt. Augusta 4289 m.

Mt. Vancouver 4785 m.

Mt. St. Elias 5489 m.

Mt. Cook 4194 m.

Mt. Seattle 3072 m.

Mt. Hubbard 4577 m.

Mt. Armour 2673 m.

KLUANE NATIONAL PARK & RESERVE

UNITED STATES OF AMERICA

Yakutat Bay

Yakutat

Haines Junction

Champagne

Kathleen L.

Kluksho

Kusawa Lake T.P.

Million Dollar Falls T.P.

Tatshenshini Alsek Prov. Park

Canyon Ck. Bridge

Takhini Hot Springs

Whitehorse

Wolf Creek T.P.

Pine Lake

Fox Lake T.P.

Marsh Lake

Tagish

Carcross

Jake's Corner

Teslin

Teslin Lake T.P.

Johnson's Crossing

ALASKA HY.

Old Crow Flats Special Mgmt. Area

Old Crow

IVVAVIK NATIONAL PARK

VUNTUT NATIONAL PARK

HERSCHEL I.
Herschel Island Territorial Park

Kendall Island Migratory Bird Sanctuary

RICHARDS I.

Tuktoyaktuk

Aklavik

Inuvik

Winter roads

Happy Valley T.P.

Jak T.P.

Fort McPherson

Nitainlaii T.P.

Tsiigehtchic

Gwich'in T.P.

Tetlit Gwinjik T.P.

Rock River T.P.

Eagle Plains

ARCTIC CIRCLE

DEMPSTER HY.

Peel River

Blackstone R.

Hart River

Wind River

Snake River

Bonnet Plume River

ARCTIQUE
Ni'iinlii Njik (Fishing Branch) Territorial Park

Tombstone Territorial Park

Dawson City

Klondike River T.P.

Yukon River T.P.

Stewart Crossing

Moose Creek T.P.

Stewart

Elsa

Keno City

Mayo

Mayo L.

Pelly Crossing

Minto

Carmacks

Tatchun Lake T.P.

Little Salmon L.

Faro

Ross River

Ddhaw Groh Habitat Protection Area

Macmillan R.

Hess R.

Horn Peak 2515 m.

Keele Peak 2975 m.

Macmillan Pass

Keele R.

Twitya R.

Canol Heritage Trail

CANOL RD.

DIVIDE

Frances Lake T.P.

Frances L.

East Arm

CAMPBELL HY.

Quiet Lake (N. & S.) Territorial Parks

Tuchitua

NAHANNI RANGE RD.

Mt. Sir James MacB 2773 m.

Tungsten

BEAUFORT SEA

McKinley Bay

Liverpool Bay

Anderson River Delta Migratory Bird Sanctuary

Reindeer Grazing Reserve

Eskimo Lakes

Sitidgi L.

Mackenzie River

Carnwath R.

Colvill

Fort Good Hope

Hare R.

Ramparts River

Arctic Red River

Mountain River

Carcajou River

Winter road

Frances R.

Hyland R.

Liard R.

Coal R.

Coal River Territorial P

Watson Lake

Upper Liard

Lower Post

Iron Creek

Contact Cre

Wolf L.

F

G

H

2   3   22   4   5   23   6

Whitehorse

Tanana River

Yukon River

Nisling River

White R.

Donjek R.

Aishihik R.

Klondike HY.

Teslin River

Porcupine River

Cheenjek River

Peel River

Porcupine River

Mackenzie Bay

Tuktut

Ross River

Klondike R.

Stewart River

Questen R.

Pelly R.

NUNAVUT

NORTHWEST TERRITORIES
TERRITOIRES DU NORD-OUEST

Cape Parry

Franklin
Bay

Darnley
Bay

Parry
Peninsula

Paulatuk

TUKTUT NOGAIT
NATIONAL PARK

Wollaston
Peninsula

Simpson
Bay

Dolphin and Union Strait

Dease Strait

Stapylton Bay

Coronation Gulf

Arctic
Sound

Croker R.

Bluenose
L.

Rae   River

Kugluktuk

Dismal
Lakes

Kugluk/
Bloody
Falls T.P.

Kikerk L.

Hood   River

ARCTIQUE

POLAIRE

CERCLE

Coppermine   River

Napaktulik
Lake

Burnside   River

Horton   River

Aubry
L.

Lac Maunoir

Colville L.

Iville Lake

Lac
Belot

Lac
des Bois

Horton L.

Dease Arm

Hornby
Bay

Itchen
Point

Contwoyto

Anderson   River

Hare Indian   pe

GREAT BEAR
LAKE

Smith Arm

McTavish Arm

Deerpass
Bay

Keith Arm

McVicar Arm

Sawmill
Bay

Hottah
L.

Gamet
R.

Lac de Gras

Norman Wells
McKinnon
Territorial Park

Déline

Great Bear R.

Winter   roads

Hardisty
L.

Wekweèti

MacKay

Tulita

Keele   R.

Redstone   R.

Blackwater
Lake

Keller L.

Lac
Taché

Lac
Grandin

Faber L.

Gamètì

Yellowknife   River

Winter
roads

Wrigley

Lac
la Martre

Whatì

Marian L.

Behchokò

North Arm
T.P.

North   Arm

-Prosperous Lake
-Madeline Lake
-Prelude Lake
Territorial

Fred Henne
T.P.

④

-Hidden Lake
-Powder Point
-Cameron Falls Trail
Territorial Parks

-Cameron River Crossing
-Reid Lake
Territorial Parks

Yellowknife

Dettah

Pontoon
Lake T.P.

Yellowknife
River T.P.

GREAT SLAVE
LAKE

Willowlake   River

Horn   River

Willow L.

MacBrien

North Nahanni   River

MacKenzie   River

Fort Simpson
Territorial Park

Fort Simpson

Jean Marie
River

Mills

Chan
Lake T.P.

Mackenzie
Bison
Sanctuary

Fort Resolution

NAHANNI
NATIONAL
PARK
RESERVE

eth Nahanni

River

Liard   River

Sambaa Deh
Falls T.P.

Fort Providence
Fort Providence
T.P.

Dory
Point T.P.

Hay River
Territorial
Park

Little Buffalo
River Crossing T.P.

Pine
Point

⑥

Blackstone
T.P.

LIARD   TRAIL

①

Kakisa
River T.P.

Kakisa
Lady Evelyn
Falls T.P.
Kakisa L.

MACKENZIE
HY.

McNallie
Creek T.P.

Hay
River

②

Slave   River

Little Buffalo
River Falls T.P.

Nahanni Butte

⑦

Trout R.

Winter road

Trout L.

Trout Lake

Tathlina
L.

Enterprise

Twin Falls
Gorge T.P.

⑤

Beaver   River

er Springs
rial Park

Creek

Fort
Liard

①

Sixtieth
Parallel
T.P.

Bistcho
L.

Buffalo   L.

Indian Cabins

WOOD BUFFALO

NATIONAL PARK

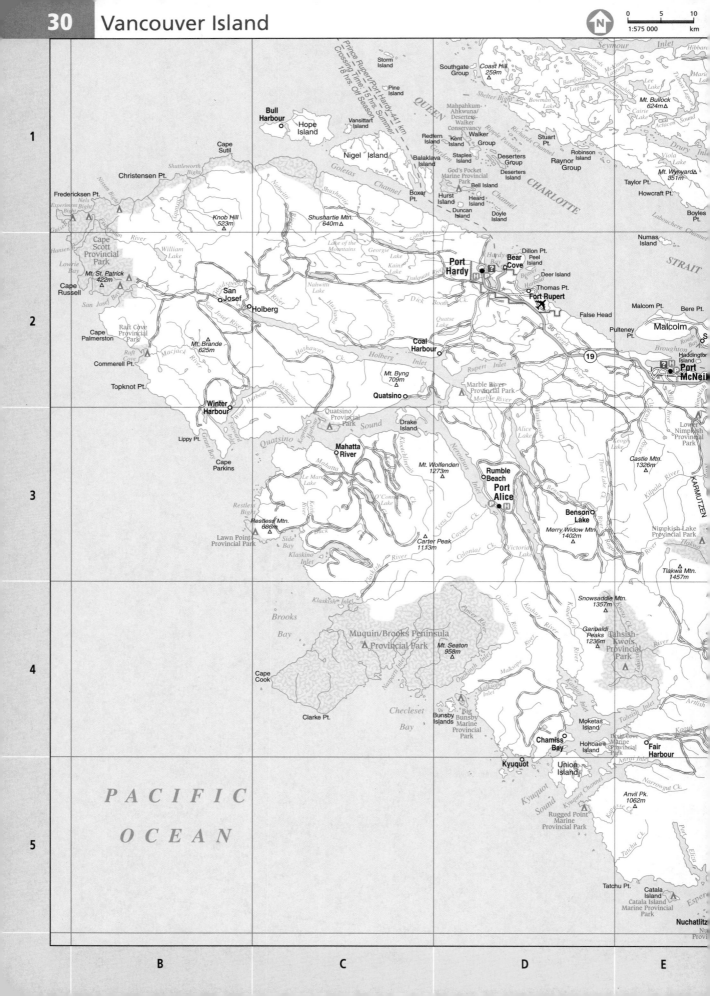

Island
Sointula
Donegal
Head
Midsummer Island
Owl Island
Swanson Island
Village Island
Gilford Pt.
Steep Head
Protection Pt.
Mt. Scriven 1318m
Knight Inlet
Call Inlet
Fulmore Lake
Port McNeill
Alert Bay
Cormorant Island
Haddington Island
Cormorant Channel Provincial Marine Park
Pearse Island
Hanson Island
Harbledown Island
Crease Island
Mamalilaculla
Turnour Island
Minstrel Island
Batt Bluff
Mt. Summerfield 1296m
Mt. Berkeley 1214m
Telegraph Cove
Beaver Cove
Kokish
Cracroft Pt.
Qwiquallaag
Boat Bay Conservancy
Boat Bay
Robson Bight
Cracroft Islands
Port Neville
Lapan Lake
Seabird Lake
Sunderland Channel
Mt. Royston 901m
Mt. George 1154m
Blackfish Sound
FRANKLIN RANGE
Mt. Sir John 1430m
Lower Tsitika River Provincial Park
Johnstone Strait
Hardwicke Island
Hardwicke Island
Salmon Bay
Mt. Hoy 1418m
BONANZA RANGE
Tsitika Mtn. 1657m
Mt. Derby 1646m
Mt. Peel 1547m
Mt. Palmerston 1763m
Kelsey Bay
Sayward
Hkusam
West Thurlow Island
Nimpish
Whiltilla Mtn. 1693m
Bonanza Lake
RANGE
Claud Elliott Provincial Park
Hkusam Mtn. 1671m
Mt. Roberts 1479m
Mt. Ashwood 1745m
Claud Elliott
Mt. Elliott 1584m
Jagged Mtn. 1701m
Mt. Juliet 1637m
Mt. Markusen 1435m
Mt. Cain
Mt. Romeo 1662m
Woss
19
Hoomak Lake
Schoen Lake Provincial Park
Schoen Lake
Mt. Schoen 1863m
Mt. Nora 1684m
White River Provincial Park
Zeballos Pk. 1577m
Woss Lake
Klaklakama Lake
Maquilla Pk. 1845m
Mt. Adam 1730m
SUTTON
Woss Mtn. 1595m
Woss Lake Provincial Park
Victoria Pk. 2163m
Kaouk Mtn. 1309m
Rugged Mtn. 1875m
Sutton Pk. 1852m
RANGE
Zeballos
Mt. McKelvie 1631m
Waring Pk. 1601m
Mt. Evelyn 1387m
Mt. Judson 1748m
Crown Mtn. 1847m
Tahsis
Weymer Creek Provincial Park
Mt. Flannigan 1570m
Esperanza
Mt. Bate 1703m
Big Den Mtn. 1777m
Trio Mtn. 1733m
Tahsis Mtn. 1326m
Muchalat Lake
28
Mt. Filberg 2036m
Nuchatlitz
Mt. Rosa 747m
Santiago Mtn. 1291m
Conuma Pk. 1482m
Gold Muchalat Provincial Park
Puzzle Mtn. 1828m
Elkhorn Mtn. 2210m
Nootka Island
Mt. Walker 1154m
Gold River
White Ridge Provincial Park
Mt. Colonel Foster 2130m
Strathcona
Santa Cruz de Nucu Mtn. 941m
Bligh Island Marine Provincial Park
Big Baldy Mt. 1611m
Mt. Donner 1813m
Golden Hinde 2201m
Provincial
Nootka
Santa Gertrudis-Boca del Infierno Provincial Marine Park
Yuquot
Maquinna Pt.
Mt. Albemarle 1082m
Mt. Rufus 1134m
Matchlee Mtn. 1845m
Park
Escalante Pt.
Splendor Mtn. 1766m
Moyeha Mtn. 1805m
Boat Basin
Hesquiat Lake Provincial Park
Sydney Inlet Provincial Park
Mt. Bourke 890m
Lone Wolf Mtn. 1480m
Mariner Mtn. 1778m
Hesquiat Peninsula Provincial Park
Hesquiat Peninsula
Stewardson Inlet
Shelbert Mtn. 1200m
Abco Mtn. 1481m
Ursus Mtn. 1509m
Estevan Point
Hesquiat
Maquinna Marine Provincial Park
Sulphur Passage Provincial Park

E   F   G   H

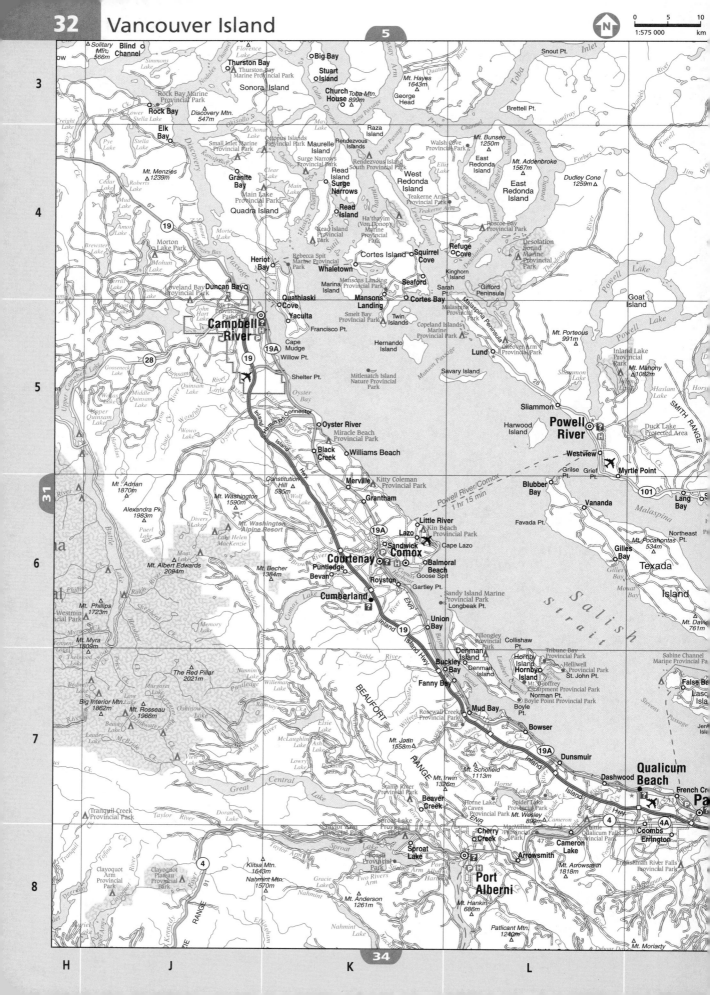

1:575 000

0   5   10
km

3

Solitary Mtn. 566m
Blind Channel
Thurston Bay
Thurston Bay Marine Provincial Park
Big Bay
Stuart Island
Sonora Island
Church House
Toba Mtn. 899m
Mt. Hayes 1643m
George Head
Snout Pt.
Toba Inlet
Brettell Pt.

Rock Bay Marine Provincial Park
Rock Bay
Discovery Mtn. 547m
Raza Island
Walsh Cove Provincial Park
Mt. Bunsen 1250m
East Redonda Island
Mt. Addenbroke 1567m
Dudley Cone 1259m

4

Elk Bay
Mt. Menzies 1239m
Granite Bay
Small Inlet Marine Provincial Park
Octopus Islands Provincial Park
Surge Narrows Provincial Park
Maurelle Island
Read Island
Rendezvous Islands
Rendezvous Island South Provincial Park
West Redonda Island
Teakerne Arm Provincial Park
East Redonda Island
Roscoe Bay Provincial Park
Desolation Sound Marine Provincial Park

19

Morton Lake Park
Main Lake Provincial Park
Quadra Island
Read Island Provincial Park
Read Island
Surge Narrows
Ha'thayim (Von Donop) Marine Provincial Park
Squirrel Cove
Refuge Cove
Kinghorn Island
Gifford Peninsula
Goat Island

Heriot Bay
Rebecca Spit Marine Provincial Park
Whaletown
Cortes Island
Seaford
Sarah Pt.
Inland Lake Provincial Park

Loveland Bay Provincial Park
Duncan Bay
Elk Falls Provincial Park
Quathiaski Cove
Mansons Landing Provincial Park
Manson Island
Mansons Landing
Cortes Bay
Malaspina Peninsula
Mt. Porteous 991m

5

28
Campbell River
John Hart Lake
Yaculta
Francisco Pt.
Smelt Bay Provincial Park
Twin Islands
Copeland Islands Marine Provincial Park
Lund
Okeover Arm Provincial Park
Mt. Mahony 1082m

19
19A
Cape Mudge
Willow Pt.
Hernando Island
Manson Passage
Savary Island
Sliammon
Inland Lake Provincial Park

19
Shelter Pt.
Oyster Bay
Mitlenatch Island Nature Provincial Park
Harwood Island
Powell River
Westview
Duck Lake Protected Area
SMITH RANGE

Oyster River
Miracle Beach Provincial Park
Williams Beach
Grilse Pt.
Grief Pt.
Myrtle Point

31

Mt. Adrian 1870m
Black Creek
Kitty Coleman Provincial Park
Powell River/Comox 1 hr 15 min
Blubber Bay
Vananda
101
Lang Bay

Alexandra Pk. 1983m
Mt. Washington 1590m
Constitution Hill 595m
Merville
Grantham
Favada Pt.

Mt. Washington Alpine Resort
Little River
Kin Beach Provincial Park
Lazo
Cape Lazo
Mt. Pocahontas 534m
Northeast Pt.
Gilles Bay

6

Mt. Albert Edwards 2094m
Mt. Becher 1384m
Courtenay
Sandwick
Comox
Balmoral Beach
Goose Spit
Texada Island

Mt. Phillips 1723m
Puntledge
Bevan
Royston
Gartley Pt.
Sandy Island Marine Provincial Park
Longbeak Pt.
Gilles Bay
Mt. Davie 761m

Mt. Myra 1809m
Cumberland
Mt. Rosseau 1966m
Big Interior Mtn. 1862m
The Red Pillar 2021m

7

Union Bay
Denman Island
Fillongley Provincial Park
Collishaw Pt.
Hornby Island
Tribune Bay Provincial Park
Helliwell Provincial Park
St. John Pt.
Sabine Channel Marine Provincial Park

Buckley Bay
Denman Island
Mt. Geoffrey Escarpment Provincial Park
Norman Pt.
Boyle Point Provincial Park

Fanny Bay
Boyle Pt.
False Be...

Rosewall Creek Provincial Park
Mud Bay
Bowser
BEAUFORT
RANGE
19A
Dunsmuir

Mt. Joan 1558m
Mt. Schofield 1113m
Dashwood
Qualicum Beach
French Cre...

Mt. Irwin 1326m
Stamp River Provincial Park
Beaver Creek
Horne Lake Caves Provincial Park
Spider Lake Provincial Park
Mt. Wesley 899m
MacMillan Provincial Park
Little Qualicum Falls Provincial Park
4
4A
Coombs
Pa...
Errington

8

4
Tranquil Creek Provincial Park
Clayoquot Arm Provincial Park
Klitsa Mtn. 1643m
Nahmint Mtn. 1570m
Sproat Lake
Sproat Lake Provincial Park
Cherry Creek
Cameron Lake
Mt. Arrowsmith 1818m
Arrowsmith
Englishman River Falls Provincial Park

Clayoquot Plateau Provincial Park
Mt. Anderson 1261m
Port Alberni
Mt. Hankin 686m
Patlicant Mtn. 1240m

H   J   K   L

Nanaimo

Wellington 19A
East Wellington
Neck Pt.
Arbutus Grove Provincial Park
ENR

Gabriola Island
Newcastle Island
Gabriola Sandwell Provincial Park
Gabriola Island

Chase River
Cedar
Extension
South Wellington
Flat Top Islands
Drumbeg Provincial Park
Wakes Cove Provincial Park
De Courcy Island
Pirates Cove Marine Provincial Park

Cassidy
Valdes
Whaleboat Island Marine Provincial Park
Roberts Memorial Provincial Park
Island Gulf
Yellow Pt.

Mt. DeCosmos 1355m

Iona Island
Vancouver International Airport
Sturgeon Bank

Richmond Lulu Island
Delta
Ladner

Westham Island
Roberts Bank
Tsawwassen

Gulf of Georgia Cannery National Historic Site

8

Vancouver (Tsawwassen)/Nanaimo (Duke Point)
2hr

Boundary Bay
Beach Cove
Boundary Bay
Point Roberts

Mt. Landale 1537m
Mt. Whymper 1550m

Ladysmith
PH
Saltair
Mt. Hall 1311m

Thetis Island
Reid Island
Thetis Island
North Galiano
Secretary Islands
Penelakut Island
Wallace Island
Wallace Island Marine Provincial Park
Bodega Ridge Provincial Park
Galiano Island

Chemainus
Osborn Bay
Vesuvius Bay
St. Mary Lake

Youbou
Lake Cowichan
Honeymoon Bay
Mesachie Lake

North Cowichan
Crofton
Westholme
Maple Bay
Salt Spring Island
Ganges
PH

Parker Island
Montague Harbour
Sturdies Bay
Long Harbour
Bellhouse Provincial Park
Collinson Point Provincial Park
Prevost Island
Mayne
Mayne Island
Port Washington
Pender Island
North Pender Island
Saturna
Saturna Island

Montague Harbour Marine Provincial Park

Gulf Islands National Park Reserve

Patos Island State Park
Tumbo Island
East Pt.

9

Paldi 18
Hillcrest
Hayward
Duncan
Koksilah 1

Sahtlam
Cowichan Station
Cobble Hill

Mt. Prevost 787m
Mt. Maxwell Provincial Park
Mt. Sullivan 703m
Burgoyne Bay Provincial Park
Fulford Harbour
Portland Island

South Pender
South Pender Island
Moresby Island
Waldron Island

Stuart Island State Park
Johns Island
Spieden Island
Flattop Island
Jones Island
Deer Harbour

10

Mt. Bolduc 1204m
Mt. Modeste 1124m
Mt. Todd 968m

Waterloo Mtn. 1055m
Survey Mtn. 938m
Mt. Wood 625m
Mt. Sullivan

Shawnigan Lake
Mill Bay
Cowichan Bay

Deep Cove
North Saanich
Swartz Bay
Sidney
Bazan Bay

Piers Island
Coal Island
Sidney Island

Henry Island
Roche Harbor
Stuart Island State Park

San Juan Island
Friday Harbour
Lime Kiln Point State Park
San Juan Island National Historical Park

SAN JUAN RIDGE
Valentine Mtn. 957m

Malahat
Memory Island Provincial Park
Spectacle Lake Provincial Park
Saanichton
17A
Central Saanich
Brentwood Bay
James Island
D'Arcy Island

Prospect Lake
Royal Oak 17
Cordova Bay
Gordon Head
Cadboro Pt.
Chatham Island
Discovery Island

Mt. Angeles

11

Mt. Muller 1143m

Botfort Pt. de Fuca Provincial Park 14 38
Jordan River
San Simeon Pt.

French Beach Provincial Park
Sheringham Pt.
Orveas Bay
Otter Pt.

Milnes Landing
Saseenos 14
Happy Valley
Colwood
Glen Lake
Langford
Belmont Park
Lagoon
Esquimalt

Fisgard Lighthouse, Fort Rodd Hill National Historic Sites

Saanich
Gordon Head
Oak Bay
Gonzales Pt.
Discovery Island Marine Provincial Park

VICTORIA
Port Angeles U.S.A.
Victoria/Seattle U.S.A. Summer Only
Victoria (Swartz Bay) 1hr 35 min

Sooke
Metchosin
East Sooke
Rocky Point
William Head
Christopher Pt.
Beechey Head

Salish Sea
Juan de Fuca Strait

CANADA
UNITED STATES OF AMERICA

BRITISH COLUMBIA
WASHINGTON

Clallam Bay
Slip Pt.
Sekiu
Clallam Bay 112
Pillar Pt.

Ellis Mtn. 815m
Low Pt.
Tongue Pt.
Observatory Pt.
Angeles Pt.
Ediz Hook
Freshwater Bay

Dungeness Split
Dungeness Bay
Dungeness

12

Sappho 101
16 113
Mt. Muller 1143m
Joyce
Piedmont
112
Fairholm 101
Elwha
Lake Aldwell
Lake Sutherland
Lake Crescent

Port Angeles
Port Angeles Harbor

Green Pt.
Agnew
Carlsborg
101
Sequim
Sequim Bay State Park

Blyn

Olympic National Park
Mt. Angeles 1967m

13

M | N | P | Q

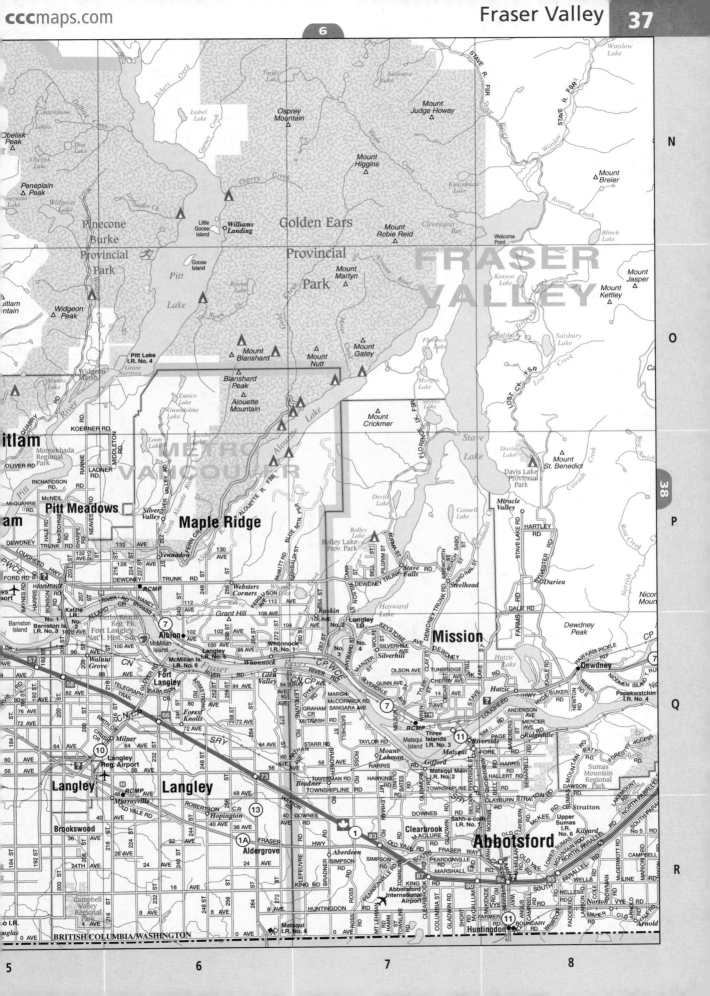

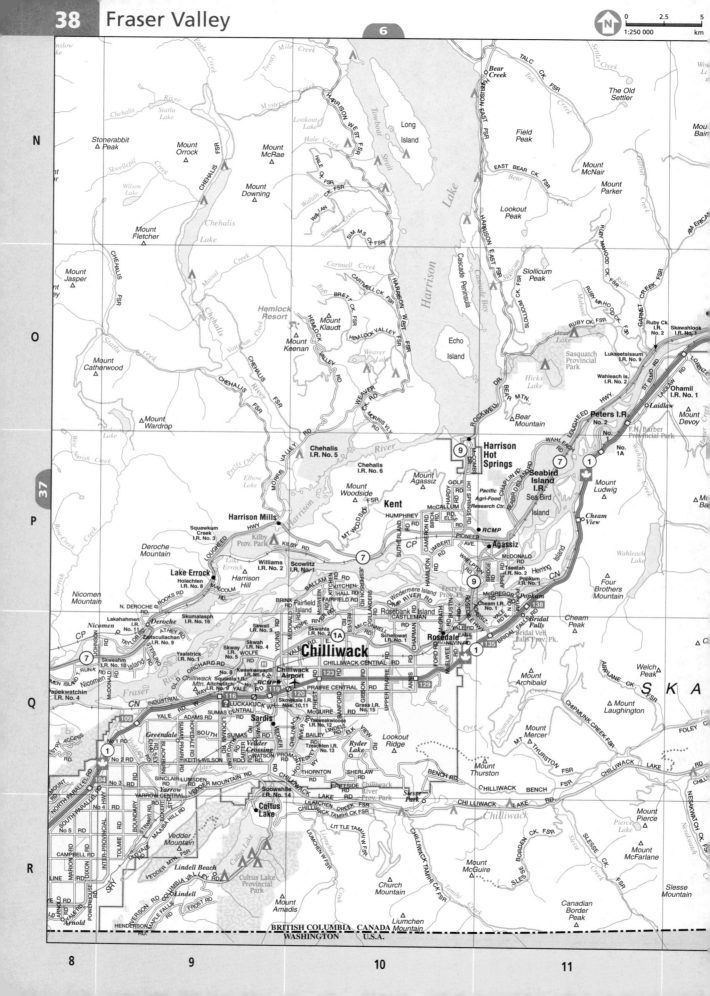

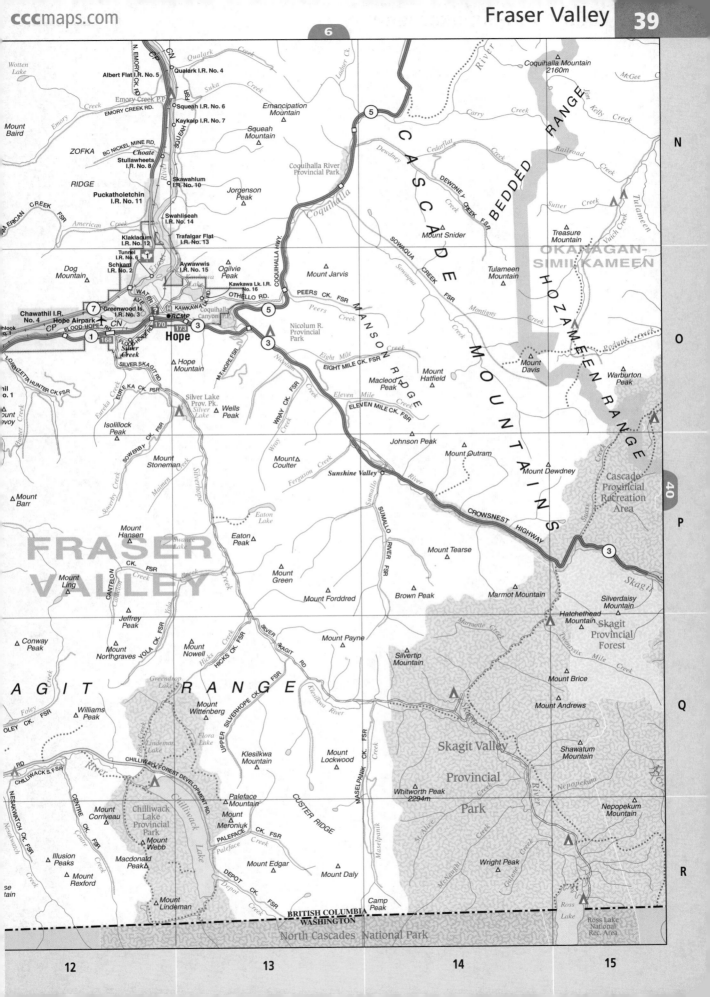

1:250 000

N

0 2.5 5
km

Coalmont

Princeton

Princeton Airport

Vermilion F
I.R. No. 1

RCMP

5A

BELFORT · SUMMERLAND
RD.

PRINCETON · SUMMERLAND
RD.

CARA CREEK RD.
QUINE RD.
W. CHINA CK. RD.

COALMONT RD.
COMBY CK.

RICE RD.

BLAKEBURN RD.

Mount Britton

Olivine Mountain

Mount Jackson

Hamilton Hill

Tanglewood Hill

Lodestone Mountain

Dear Mountain

N

O

P

39

Q

R

McGee Creek

Illal Creek

Jim Kelly Creek

Champion Creek

Vuich Creek

Podunk Creek

Warburton Peak

PARADISE VALLEY

Snass Mountain

FRASER VALLEY

OKANAGAN RANGE

Silverdaisy Mountain

Skagit Provincial Forest

Porcupine Peak

Nepopekum Mountain

Red Mountain

Lone Goat Mountain

Lone Mountain

Bojo Mountain

Manning Park Resort

Memaloose Creek

Thunder Lake

Frosty Mountain

Lightning Lake

Lightning Creek

Windy Joe Mountain

Castle Creek

Chuwanten Mountain

Blackwall Peak

Buckhorn Creek

Three Brothers Mountain 2272m

Big Buck Mountain

Fourth Brother Mountain

E C Manning Provincial Park

CROWSNEST HIGHWAY

Skagit River

NICOMEN RIDGE

Grainger Creek

Granite Mountain

Cascade Provincial Recreation Area

Kettle Mountain

Skaist Mountain

Skaist River

Copper Creek

OKANAGAN

Friday Mountain

Sunday Creek

Garrison Lakes

Goodfellow Creek

BONNEVIER RIDGE

Bonnevier Creek

Eastgate

Similkameen Falls

Simifkameen River

PASAYTEN VALLEY RD.

PLACER MTN. FOREST SERVICE RD.

3

Belgie Creek

Placer Creek

Pasayten River

Flat Top Mo

Trapper Lake

Peeve Creek

Newton Creek

Badger Creek

Arrastra Creek

Granite Creek

Frembly Creek

Twelve Mile Creek

Lamont Creek

WHIPSAW CREEK FSR

Whipsaw Creek

Friday Creek

Robie Creek

Bromley Creek

Mount Kennedy

Smelter Lakes

Wolfe Creek

COAL MONT RD.
BLACK MINE RD.

WRIGHT'S RANCH RD.
WRIGHT'S RD.

CROWSNEST HIGHWAY

COPPER MTN. RD.
ALLENBY RD.

WILLIE'S R

IRON MTN. R

McNAMARA RD.

Me

BRITISH COLUMBIA
WASHINGTON

15   16   17   18

N

O

P

42

Q

R

Okanagan-Similkameen

SIMILKAMEEN

CANADA
U.S.A.

19   20   21

1:250 000

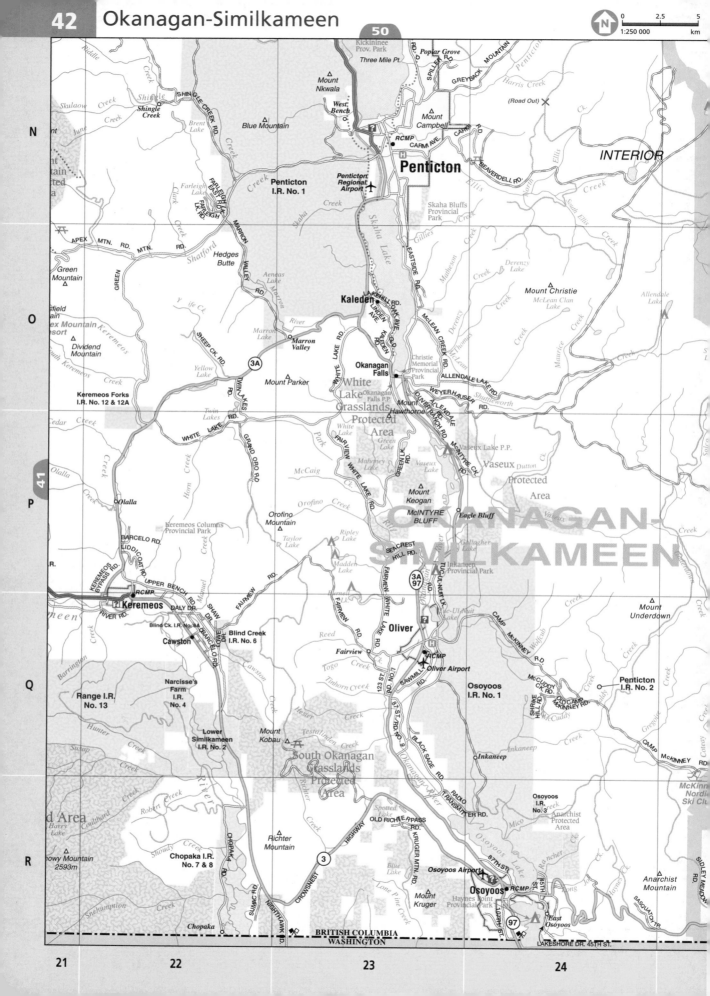

INTERIOR

Penticton

Penticton I.R. No. 1

Penticton Regional Airport

Skaha Bluffs Provincial Park

Blue Mountain

Shingle Creek

Mount Nkwala

West Bench

RCMP

CARMI AVE.

Mount Campbell

Mount Christie

McLean Clan Lake

Allendale Lake

Kaleden

Okanagan Falls

Okanagan Falls P.P.

Christie Memorial Provincial Park

ALLENDALE LAKE RD.

WEYERHAUSER

Mount Hawthorne

Mount Keogan

McINTYRE BLUFF

Eagle Bluff

Vaseux Lake P.P.

Vaseux

Vaseux Protected Area

OKANAGAN-SIMILKAMEEN

White Lake Grasslands Protected Area

Green Lake

Mahoney Lake

Mount Parker

Keremeos Forks I.R. No. 12 & 12A

3A

Marron Valley

Apex Mountain Resort

Green Mountain

Dividend Mountain

Olalla

Keremeos Columns Provincial Park

Orofino Mountain

Taylor Lake

Ripley Lake

Madden Lake

Seacrest Hill Rd.

Inkaneep Provincial Park

3A 97

Mount Underdown

Keremeos

RCMP

Cawston

Blind Ck. I.R. No. 6A

Blind Creek I.R. No. 6

Oliver

Fairview

RCMP

Oliver Airport

Camp McKinney

Range I.R. No. 13

Narcisse's Farm I.R. No. 4

Lower Similkameen I.R. No. 2

Mount Kobau

South Okanagan Grasslands Protected Area

Osoyoos I.R. No. 1

Inkaneep

Penticton I.R. No. 2

Osoyoos I.R. No. 1A

Anarchist Protected Area

McKinney Nordic Ski Area

Chopaka I.R. No. 7 & 8

Richter Mountain

3

Blue Lake

Mount Kruger

Osoyoos Airport

Haynes Point Provincial Park

Osoyoos

RCMP

Anarchist Mountain

Snowy Mountain 2593m

Harry Lake

Chopaka

BRITISH COLUMBIA
WASHINGTON

East Osoyoos

97

LAKESHORE DR. 45TH ST.

21   22   23   24

N   O   P   41   Q   R

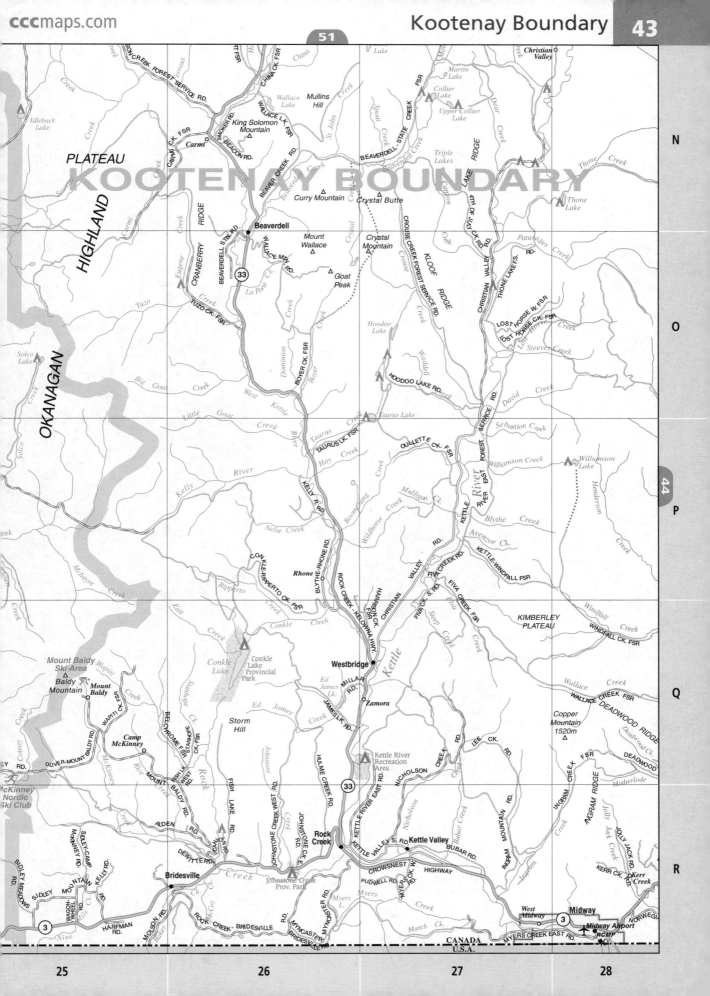

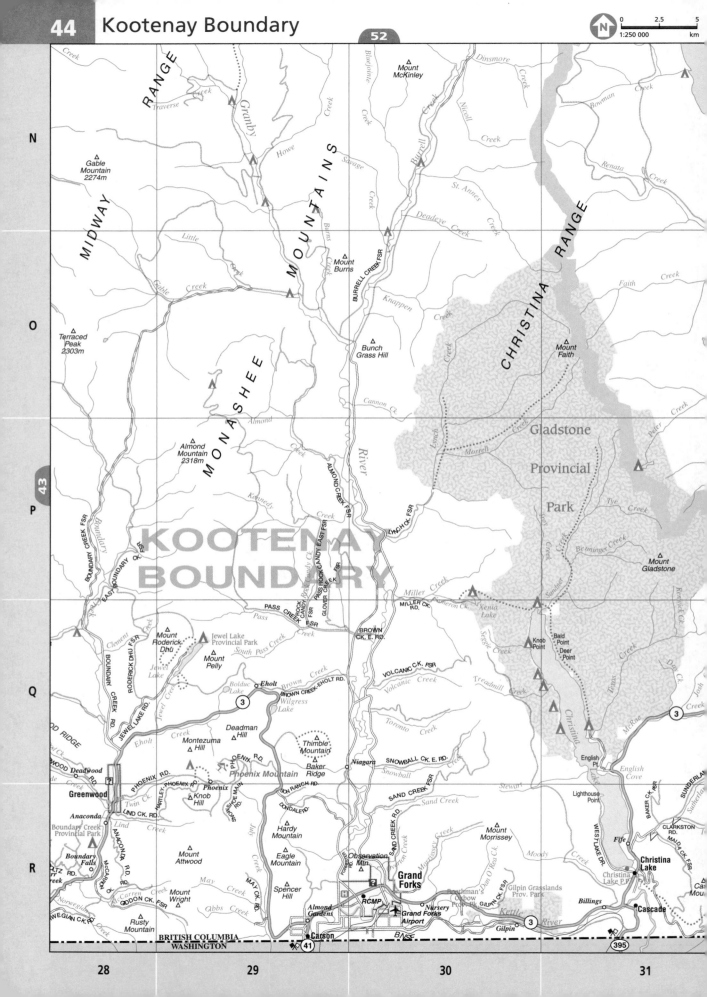

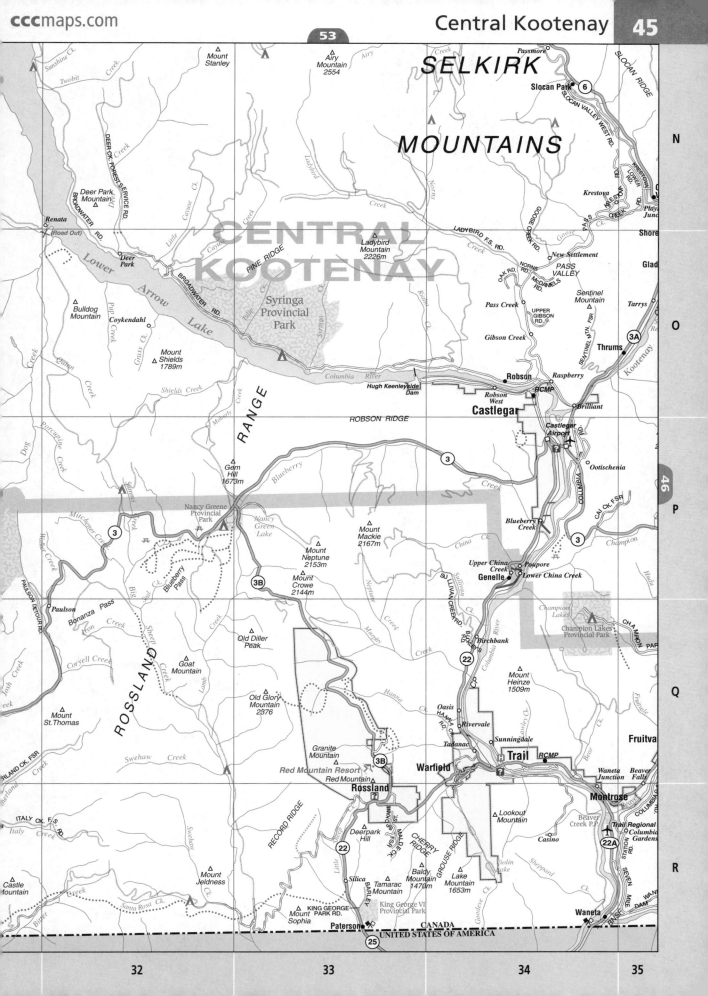

53

SELKIRK

MOUNTAINS

CENTRAL
KOOTENAY

N

O

P

46

Q

R

Passmore

Slocan Park

6

SLOCAN RIDGE

SLOCAN VALLEY WEST RD.

Krestova

Krestova

Playm Junc

Shore

Glad

Mount
Stanley

Airy
Mountain
2554

Ladybird

Norns

Creek

Deer Park
Mountain

DEER CK. FOREST SERVICE RD.

BROADWATER RD.

Twobit

Sunshine Ck.

Creek

Cayuse Ck.

Little

Creek

Creek

PINE RIDGE

Ladybird
Mountain
2226m

LADYBIRD F.S. RD.

GOOSE CREEK RD.

Goose

OAK RD.

NORNS
RD.

McDANIELS
RD.

New Settlement

PASS
VALLEY

PASS
VALLEY

Sentinel
Mountain

SEYTINEL MTN. FSR

Tarrys

3A

Renata
(Road Out)

BROADWATER RD.

Deer
Park

Bulldog
Mountain

Coykendahl

Pup Creek

Grass Ck.

Lower

Arrow

Lake

Mount
Shields
1789m

Syringa
Provincial
Park

Tulip Ck.

Syringa

Creek

Rubb

Creek

Pass Creek

UPPER
GIBSON
RD.

Gibson Creek

Thrums

O

Columbia   River

Robson

Raspberry

RCMP

Kootenay

R

Qmun

Creek

Shields Creek

Moberly

Hugh Keenleyside
Dam

ROBSON RIDGE

Robson
West

Castlegar

Brilliant

Castlegar
Airport

?

Ootischenia

Porcupine Creek

Dog

Creek

RANGE

Gem
Hill
1673m

Blueberry

Creek

3

Creek

COLUMBIA RD.

CAI CK. FSR

Blueberry
Creek

3

Champion

Mitchener Creek

Simms

Paulson Creek

Nancy Greene
Provincial
Park

Nancy
Green
Lake

Mount
Mackie
2167m

China Ck.

Upper China
Creek

Poupore

Genelle

Lower China Creek

P

Paulson

Bonanza Pass

3

Big Sheep Ck.

Blueberry
Pass

3B

Mount
Neptune
2153m

Mount
Crowe
2144m

SULLIVAN CREEK RD.

Sullivan

Ck.

Champion
Lakes

CHAMPION PARK

Champion Lakes
Provincial Park

PAULSON DETOUR RD.

Iron Creek

Coryell Creek

Sheep

Goat
Mountain

Old Diller
Peak

Creek

Lamb

Neptune

Murphy

Creek

Columbia River

22

BC REL'S

Birchbank

CP

Mount
Heinze
1509m

Josh Creek

Mount
St. Thomas

ROSSLAND

Swehaw   Creek

Old Glory
Mountain
2376

Hanna

Creek

Oasis

HANNA
RD.

Rivervale

Sunningdale

Tadanac

Mount
Violin Ck.

Q

Fruitva

RANGE

ITALY CK. F.S. RD.

Italy

Creek

Granite
Mountain

3B

Red Mountain Resort

Red Mountain

RECORD RIDGE

Deerpark
Hill

MALDE FSR RD.

Little Sheep Ck.

Rossland

?

CHERRY
RIDGE

Warfield

Trail

RCMP

?

Lookout
Mountain

GROUSE RIDGE

Casino

Beaver
Creek P.P.

Waneta
Junction

Montrose

Beaver
Falls

Trail Regional
Columbia
Gardens

22A

COLUMBIA

Castle
Mountain

Mount
Jeldness

Swehaw

Creek

Biver

Santa Rosa Ck.

22

Silica

Tamarac
Mountain

Baldy
Mountain
1470m

Lake
Mountain
1653m

Gooderve Ck.

Sherpard

SEVEN MILE RD.

STATION RD.

WANETA

DAM

BNSF

Waneta

INLAND CK. FSR

KING GEORGE
PARK RD.

Mount
Sophia

King George VI
Provincial Park

Paterson

25

CANADA

UNITED STATES OF AMERICA

32   **33**   **34**   **35**

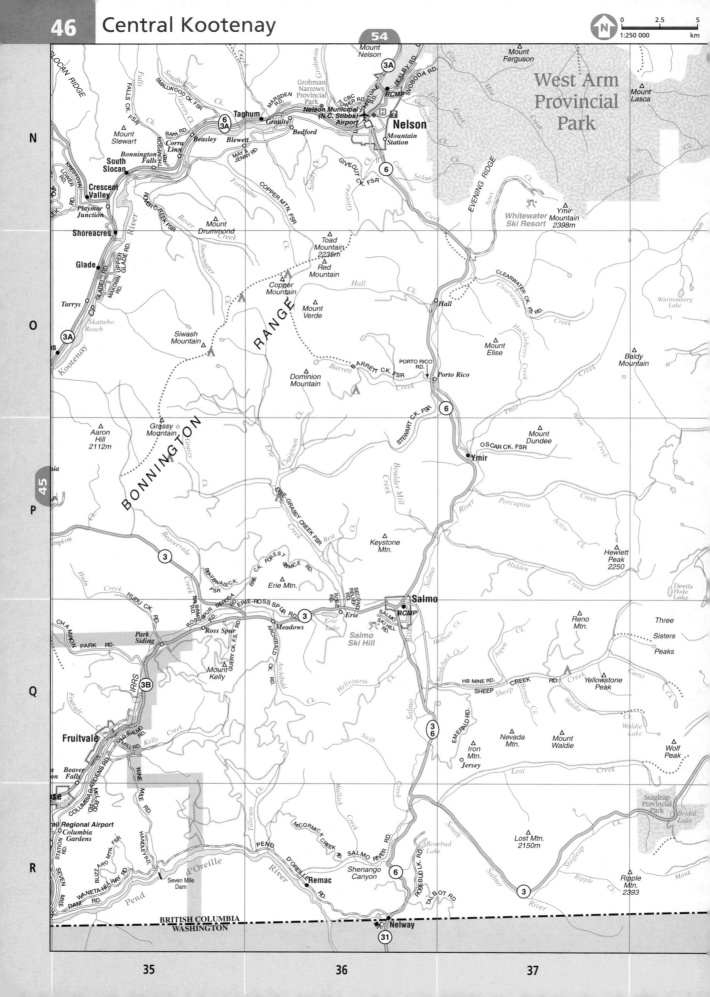

1:250 000

54

West Arm
Provincial
Park

Mount Nelson
Mount Ferguson
Mount Lasca

N

BONNINGTON RANGE

Slocan Ridge

Mount Stewart
Bonnington Falls
South Slocan
Crescent Valley
Playmor Junction
Shoreacres
Glade
Tarrys

Taghum
Beasley
Corra Linn
Blewett
Granite
Bedford

Nelson Municipal (N.C. Stibbs) Airport
Nelson
Mountain Station
RCMP
Grohman Narrows Provincial Park

Whitewater Ski Resort
Ymir Mountain 2398m

O

Mount Drummond
Toad Mountain 2235m
Red Mountain
Copper Mountain
Mount Verde
Siwash Mountain
Dominion Mountain
Hall
Mount Elise
Baldy Mountain
Württemberg Lake
Porto Rico
Porto Rico RD.
BARRETT CK. FSR

Skattebo Reach
Kootenay

P

45

Aaron Hill 2112m
Grassy Mountain
Keystone Mtn.
Ymir
Mount Dundee
OSCAR CK. FSR
Hewlett Peak 2250
Hidden
Devils Hole Lake

STEWART CK. FSR

3

Beavervale
Erie Mtn.
Erie-Ross Spur RD.
Salmo
Reno Mtn.
Three Sisters Peaks

Q

Park Siding
Ross Spur
Meadows
Mount Kelly
Archibald
Erie
Erie Lake
Salmo Ski Hill
RCMP
HB MINE RD.
SHEEP CREEK RD.
Yellowstone Peak
Waldie Lake

3B

Fruitvale
Beaver Falls
Nevada Mtn.
Mount Waldie
Wolf Peak
Iron Mtn.
Jersey
Lost Mtn. 2150m
EMERALD RD.
Staqleap Provincial Park
Bridal Lake

R

Trail Regional Airport
Columbia Gardens
Seven Mile Dam
Remac
Shenango Canyon
Rosebud Lake
Ripple Mtn. 2393

3
6

Nelway
31

BRITISH COLUMBIA
WASHINGTON

35   36   37

N

Blake
Lake

Heather
Lockhart
Creek
Squaw Creek
Lockhart
Creek
Provincial
Park
Mount
Davie
Akokli
Mountain

Mount
Drewry

Lockhart
Beach
Provincial
Park
Rhinoceros
Point

Midge

Conway
Creek

Creek

Akokli
Creek
Haystack
Mountain
2682m

Gillis
Peak
Mountain

Boswell
3A
AKOKLI CK. FSR
HALL RD. TUNGSTEN FSR
Val Creek
Akokli

Kianuko
Provincial
Park

Hughes
Ck.
Creek

Drewry Point
Drewry
Point
Provincial
Park
Columbia
Point

Martel Creek
Creek

Jackson
Peak

Kianuko Creek

O

Sanca
SANCA
CREEK FSR
Sanca
Creek

Laib

Kootenay Lake
Provincial Park–
Midge Creek

CP

Mount
McGregor
Tye
Redman
Point

Twin Bays Creek

Mount
Skelly
2304m

Skelly Creek

Boulder Creek

Mount
Bohan

Bohan Creek

Creek

Kuskonook

Hall Creek

Arrow

P 8

NELSON

Mount
Burnett

CENTRAL
KOOTENAY

Steeple
Mountain

Kootenay
Landing

Creek

Sirdar
3A

Jock Creek
Cory Creek

East Br. to Kootenay River

Duck
Lake

Creek

Elmo
Ck.

Kootenay
Mountain

Creston

CHANNEL RD.

Duck Ck.

Next Creek

Shaw Creek

Valley

Newington

Wall
Mountain

Arkansas
Lake

RANGE

Blazed

Mount
Midgeley

Jersey Creek

Wildlife

Management

Midgeley Creek

Leach
Lake

ROBSON

Wynndel

Q

John Bull
Mountain

Bayonne Creek

Creek

3
TOPAZ CK. F.SR
Area

Nicks Island

No. 5

Lower
Kootenay
I.R.
No. 4

NICKS ISLAND N. RD.

No. 3

No. 2

CP

Alice
Siding

ARROW Ck. E. RD.
WENGER RD.
GOAT R. N. RD.

Arrow
Creek

GOAT MTN. F.S. RD.

Arrow
Mountain

BEAM RD.

3

Creston
Mountain

Teetzel Ck.

Summit

Buckworth Creek

Moreland Ck.

Creek

CORN CK. RD.
SIMMONS RD.

Lower
Kootenay
I.R.
No. 1C

Creek

Lower
Kootenay
I.R. No. 1B

Creston

RCMP H ?

Erickson
Canyon

North Star
Mountain

Corn

Ezakiel Creek

Mount
Huscroft

Mount
Rykert

French Slough

Kootenay River

Creston
I.R. No. 1
Creston Valley
Airport

Lister

Lower
Kootenay
I.R. No.

Huscroft

R

Mount
Irene

Upper

Price River

Ck.

DODGE CK. F.S. RD.

21

CANADA
UNITED STATES OF AMERICA

Rykerts

Boundary
Boundary Creek

1

38   39   40   41

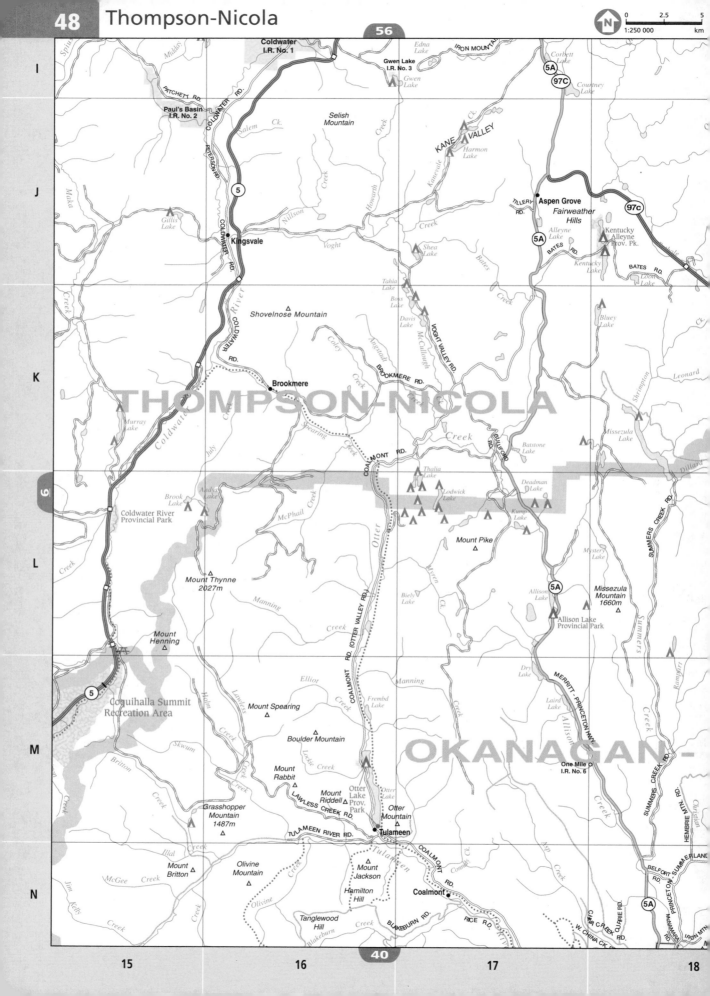

N
0   2.5   5
1:250 000   km

I

Coldwater
I.R. No. 1

Edna
Lake

IRON MOUNTAIN

Corbett
Lake

5A

97C

Courtney
Lake

Gwen Lake
I.R. No. 3

Gwen
Lake

PATCHETT RD.

Paul's Basin
I.R. No. 2

Salem

Ck.

Selish
Mountain

Creek

KANE

VALLEY

Harmon
Lake

Kanevile

Creek

Ck.

J

5

COLDWATER RD.

PETERSON RD.

Nillson

Creek

Howarth

Creek

Creek

TILLERY
RD.

Aspen Grove
Fairweather
Hills

97c

Gillis
Lake

Kingsvale

COLDWATER RD.

Voght

Creek

Shea
Lake

5A

Alleyne
Lake

Kentucky
Alleyne
Prov. Pk.

BATES RD.

Kentucky
Lake

BATES RD.

Loon
Lake

Tahla
Lake

Boss
Lake

River

Shovelnose Mountain

Coley

Creek

Argstadt

BROOKMERE RD.

Creek

McCullough

Davis
Lake

Creek

VOGHT VALLEY RD.

Bluey
Lake

Ck.

K

THOMPSON-NICOLA

COLDWATER
RD.

Brookmere

Spearing

Creek

Creek

COALMONT RD.

GUILFORD RD.

Batstone
Lake

Missezula
Lake

Leonard

Shrimpton Ck.

Murray
Lake

July

Brook
Lake

Andy's
Lake

McPhail

Creek

Thalia
Lake

Lodwick
Lake

Deadman
Lake

Dillard

6

Coldwater River
Provincial Park

Creek

Otter

Creek

Kump
Lake

SUMMERS CREEK RD.

L

Creek

Mount Thynne
2027m

Manning

Myren

Mount Pike

Biely
Lake

Ck.

Mount Henning

Allison
Lake

5A

Missezula
Mountain
1660m

Mystery
Lake

Allison Lake
Provincial Park

Summers

Creek

5

Coquihalla Summit
Recreation Area

Skwum

Helm

Lawless

Mount Spearing

Elliot

Creek

Frembd
Lake

Manning

Dry
Lake

MERRITT - PRINCETON HWY.

Laird
Lake

OKANAGAN -

M

Britton

Creek

Locke Creek

Boulder Mountain

Mount
Rabbit

COALMONT RD. (OTTER VALLEY RD.)

Allison

Creek

One Mile
I.R. No. 6

SUMMERS CREEK RD.

Grasshopper
Mountain
1487m

LAWLESS CREEK RD.

Mount
Riddell

Otter
Lake Prov.
Park

Otter
Lake

Otter
Mountain

BELFORT - SUMMERLAND
RD.

HEMBRIE MTN. RD.

Mount
Britton

Olivine
Mountain

TULAMEEN RIVER RD.

Tulameen

COALMONT

RD.

Connly Ck.

Asp

Creek

PRINCETON - SUMMERLAND
RD.

N

Jim Kelly

McGee
Creek

Creek

Illal

Creek

Olivine

Creek

Mount
Jackson

Hamilton
Hill

Tulameen

RICE RD.

Coalmont

River

CLAPPERTON
RD.

5A

Tanglewood
Hill

Blakeburn

Creek

BLAKEBURN RD.

W. CHINA CK. RD.

CHINA CK. RD.

IRON MTN. RD.

MANAMA RD.

15   16   17   18

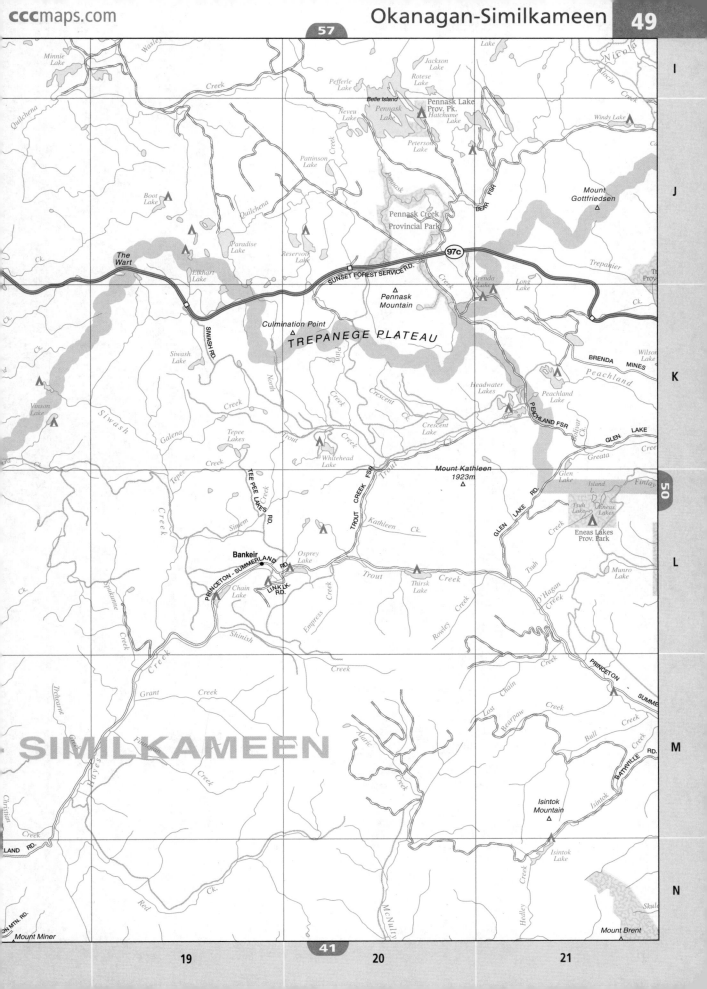

I

Minnie Lake

Wasley Creek

Quilchena

Nicola

J

Jackson Lake

Pefferle Lake

Rotese Lake

Belle Island

Pennask Lake Prov. Pk.

Hatchume Lake

Pennask Lake

Neveu Lake

Peterson Lake

Windy Lake

Mount Gottfriedsen

Boot Lake

Pattinson Lake

Quilchena

Paradise Lake

Reservoir Lake

Pennask Creek Provincial Park

BEAR FSR

Trepanier

The Wart

Elkhart Lake

SUNSET FOREST SERVICE RD.

97c

Brenda Lake

Long Lake

Pro...

Pennask Mountain

Pennask

SIWASH RD.

Culmination Point

TREPANEGE PLATEAU

BRENDA MINES

Wilson Lake

K

Siwash Lake

North

Crescent

Headwater Lakes

Peachland Lake

PEACHLAND FSR

Peachland

Vinson Lake

Siwash

Galena

Creek

Creek

Trout

Crescent Lake

Bolivar Ck.

GLEN LAKE

Tepee Lakes

Whitehead Lake

Mount Kathleen 1923m

Greata

Glen Lake

50

Creek

TEE PEE LAKES RD.

TROUT CREEK FSR

GLEN LAKE RD.

Tsuh Lake

Island L.

Eneas Lakes

Finlay

L

Sinem

Kathleen Ck.

Eneas Lakes Prov. Park

Munro Lake

Bankeir

PRINCETON - SUMMERLAND RD.

Osprey Lake

LINK LK. RD.

Trout

Thirsk Lake

Rowley

O'Hagan

Chain Lake

Empress

Creek

Spukunne

Shinish

Creek

PRINCETON - SUMME...

M

Trehearne

Grant

Creek

Lost

Chain

Bearpaw

Creek

Bull

Creek

BATHVILLE RD.

SIMILKAMEEN

Finnegan

Creek

Alaric

Creek

Isintok

Isintok Mountain

Christian

Creek

LAND RD.

Red

Ck.

McNulty

Hedley Creek

Isintok Lake

Skul...

N

Mount Miner

Mount Brent

1:250 000
N
0 2.5 5
km

I

Eileen Lake
Raymer Lake
Cameron Lake
Porcupine Lake
Islaht Lake
Whiterocks Mountain △
North Lambly Creek
Lambly Creek
Bald Range
Winfield
BEAVER LK. RD.
Duck Lake I.R. No. 7
Vermont
Lake
DEE LAKE RD.
POSTILL

J

Paynter Lake
Powers
BEAR FOREST SERVICE RD.
Lambly Lake
△ Mount Swite
Mount Hayman △
McDougall Creek
Hayman Lake
BEAR CREEK RD.
BEAR FOREST SERVICE RD.
Wilson Landing
Blue Grouse Mountain △
WESTSIDE RD.
CENTRAL
Traders Cove
△ Mount Knox
McKinley Landing
Kelowna International Airport ✈
CLIFTON RD.
GLENMORE RD.
OLD VERNON RD.
97
Postill
SCOTTY CK. RD.
Scotty
Ellison
POSTILL
Ellison Lake
FARMERS RD.
BATTA
Rockface
RA

Lacoma Lake
Trepanier Provincial Park
△ Mount Clements
△ Mount Miller
Jackpine Lake
LAST MOUNTAIN RD.
Crystal Mountain
Carrot Mountain △
Rose Valley Lake
Bear Creek Prov. Park
Manhattan Point
Kelowna
RCMP
?
Benvoulin
Rutland
Black Knight M
△

K

Wilson Lake
Silver Lake
Spring Lake
97c
△ Mount Wilson
Telemark Cross-Country Ski Club
TREPANIER RD.
△ Mount Law
△ Mount Drought
SHANNON LK. RD.
SMITH CK. RD.
GLENROSA
Glenrosa
Westside
RD.
Westbank
97
?
Gellatly
Tsinstikeptum I.R. No. 9
△ Mount Baucherie
BOUCHERIE RD.
WESTLAKE RD.
Westside
Tsinstikeptum I.R. No. 10
Lakeview Heights
PANDOSY ST.
CASORSO RD.
KLO
GORDON DR.
BENVOULIN RD.
Mission Ck. I.R. No. 8
Okanagan Mission
Braeloch
East Kelowna
McCULLOCH RD.
JUNE SPRINGS RD.
Medicine Creek I.R. No. 12
33

L

KNES
LAKE RD.
△ Lookout Mountain
△ Mount Coldham
△ Mount Acland
△ Mount Eneas
Peachland
?
Punchbowl Bay
PRINCETON AVE.
Trepanier
97
Okanagan
Lake
Okanagan Lake Prov. Park
Rattlesnake I.
WILD HORSE CANYON
Squally Pt.
Commando Bay
Goods Creek
Okanagan Mountain Provincial Park
Baker Lake
Okanagan Mountain △
Chute Creek
Chute Lake
LITTLE WHITE FSR
Myra
Myra-Bellevue Provincial Park
K.V.R. MYF
CANYON
(Road Out)
Nuttall Lake
Little White Mountain △

49

Darke Lake Provincial Park
Darke Lake
MEADOW VALLEY
Garnet Lake
FISH LAKE RD.
MEADOW VALLEY RD.
SKYRNE RD.
VALLEY
Greata
Okanagan Mountain
Wild Horse Mountain
Fredrick Creek
Koo Creek
Chute Creek
Chute Lake
CHUTE LAKE RD.
Elinor Lake
NORTH NARAMATA RD.
Naramata Creek
Big Meadow Lake
Ratnip Creek
Gillard Creek
Belleview Creek
Pooley Creek

M

SUMMERLAND RD.
Trout Creek
Darke Creek
Eneas Creek
BATHVILLE RD.
Faulder
Summerland
?
RCMP
Prairie Valley
GIANT'S HEAD RD.
VICTORIA RD.
97
Mount Conkle △
Trout Creek
Crescent Beach
Gartrell Pt.
Naramata
Sun-Oka Beach Prov. Park
NARAMATA RD.
AA-AWANA
Turnbull
OKANAGAN-SIMILKAMEEN
SPILLER RD.
NARAMATA FORESTRY RD.
Greyback Lake
Greyback Mountain △
Mount Atkinson △
△
Reed Creek
Reed Lake
Howard Lake
INTERIOR
Mount Randolph △
Municipal

N

Penticton I.R. No. 3A
SHINGLE CREEK RD.
SHINGLE CREEK
Shingle Creek
Skulaow Creek
Brent Lake
Blue Mountain △
△ Mount Nkwala
West Bench
Three Mile Pt.
Poplar Grove
Kickininee Prov. Park
△ Mount Campbell
97
?
RCMP
GREYBACK RD.
Harris Creek
(Road Out) ✕
June

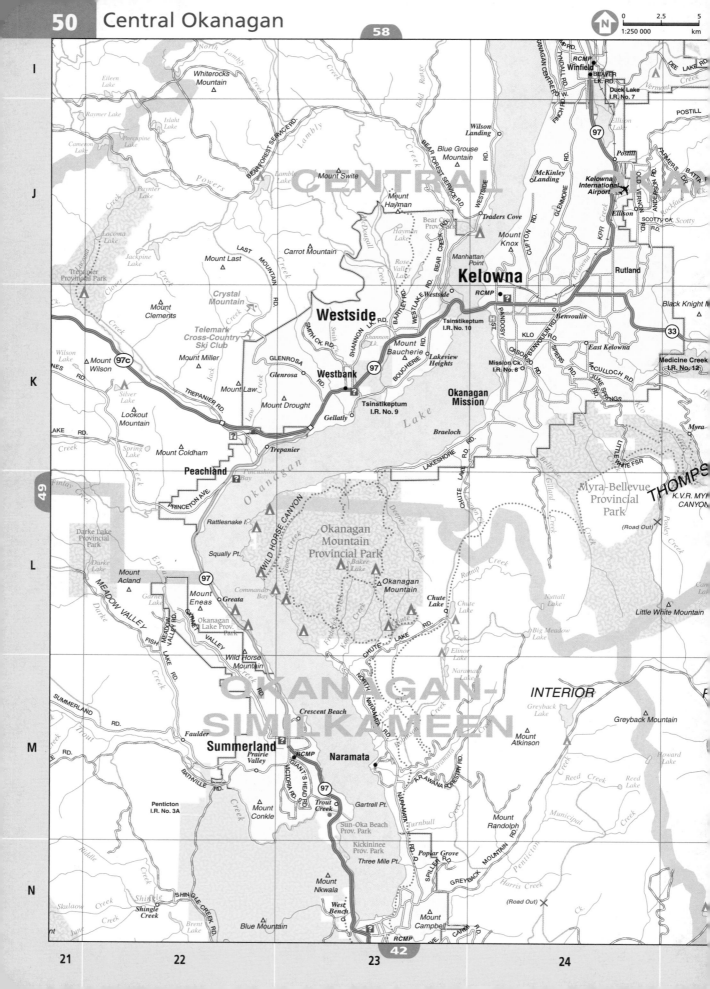

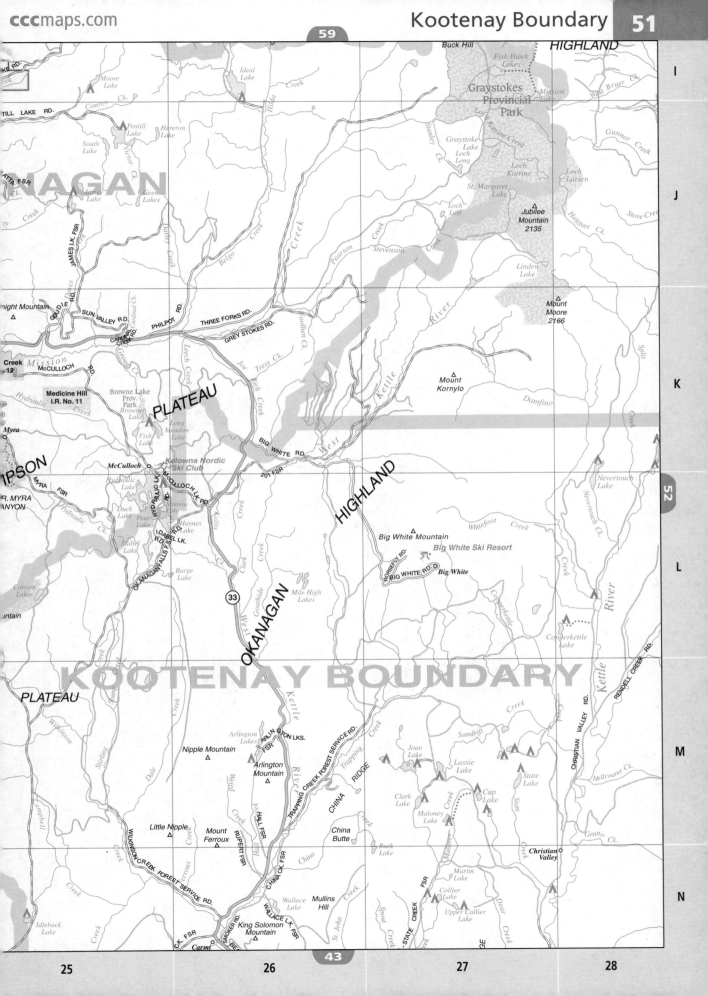

I

J

K

L

52

M

N

HIGHLAND

Buck Hill

Fish Hawk Lakes

Graystokes Provincial Park

Mission Lake

Ideal Lake

Moore Lake

Hareron Lake

Postill Lake

South Lake

Victor Ck.

Green Lakes

James Lake

Conroy Ck.

Hilda Creek

Stanley Ck.

Graystoke Lake

Loch Long

Loch Katrine

Loch Larsen

Gunnar Creek

Stove Creek

St. Margaret Lake

Jubilee Mountain 2135

Haggart Ck.

Loch Lost

Linden Lake

Belgo Creek

Creek

Pearson Creek

Stevenson Creek

Kettle River

Mount Moore 2166

Split

night Mountain

GROUDLE RD.

SUN VALLEY RD.

JAMES LK. FSR

PHILPOT RD.

CARDINAL CREEK RD.

Cardinal Ck.

Darley Creek

Groud Ck.

THREE FORKS RD.

GREY STOKES RD.

Toolhen Ck.

Ice Creek

Tress Ck.

Leech Creek

Rich Creek

Mount Kornylo

Damfino

Creek

Creek

McCULLOCH RD.

Mission Creek

12

Medicine Hill I.R. No. 11

Browne Lake Prov. Park

Browne Lake

PLATEAU

Fish Lake

Long Meadow Lake

Kelowna Nordic Ski Club

BIG WHITE RD.

West Kettle

201 FSR

HIGHLAND

Big White Mountain

Whitefoot Creek

Nevertouch Lake

Nevertouch Ck.

Myra

IPSON

MYRA FSR

R. MYRA CANYON

Hydraulic Ck.

Hydraulic

Creek

McCulloch

Hydraulic Lake

HYDRAULIC LK. RD.

McCULLOCH LK. RD.

IDABEL LK. RD.

Minnow Lake

Duck Lake

Pear Lake

Haynes Lake

Killis Creek

Clark Creek

Goathide Creek

Big White Ski Resort

HORSEFLY RD.

BIG WHITE RD.

Big White

Copperkettle Creek

River

Canyon Lakes

Hydraulic

Isabel Lake

OKANAGAN FALLS FSR

Barge Lake

33

OKANAGAN

West Kettle River

Mile High Lakes

Copperkettle Lake

RENDELL CREEK RD.

Kettle River

CHRISTIAN VALLEY RD.

KOOTENAY BOUNDARY

PLATEAU

Wilkinson Creek

Shirting Creek

Dale Creek

Weird Creek

Sunny Creek

Kettle River

Arlington Lakes

ARLINGTON LKS. FSR

TRAPPING CREEK FOREST SERVICE RD.

Trapping Creek

CHINA RIDGE

Sandrift Creek

Joan Lake

Lassie Lake

State Lake

Hellroarer Ck.

Nipple Mountain

Arlington Mountain

HALL FSR

RUPERT FSR

CHINA CK. FSR

Clark Lake

Maloney Lake

Cup Lake

State Creek

Martin Creek

Grano Ck.

Little Nipple

Mount Ferroux

China Butte

Buck Lake

China Creek

Wolfe Creek

Christian Valley

Ferroux Creek

Campbell Creek

WILKINSON CREEK FOREST SERVICE RD.

Wallace Lake

WALLACE LK. FSR

Mullins Hill

St. John Creek

Spout Creek

STATE CREEK FSR

Martin Lake

Collier Lake

Upper Collier Lake

Deer Creek

RIDGE

Idleback Lake

CK. FSR

SMOKER RD.

Carmi

King Solomon Mountain

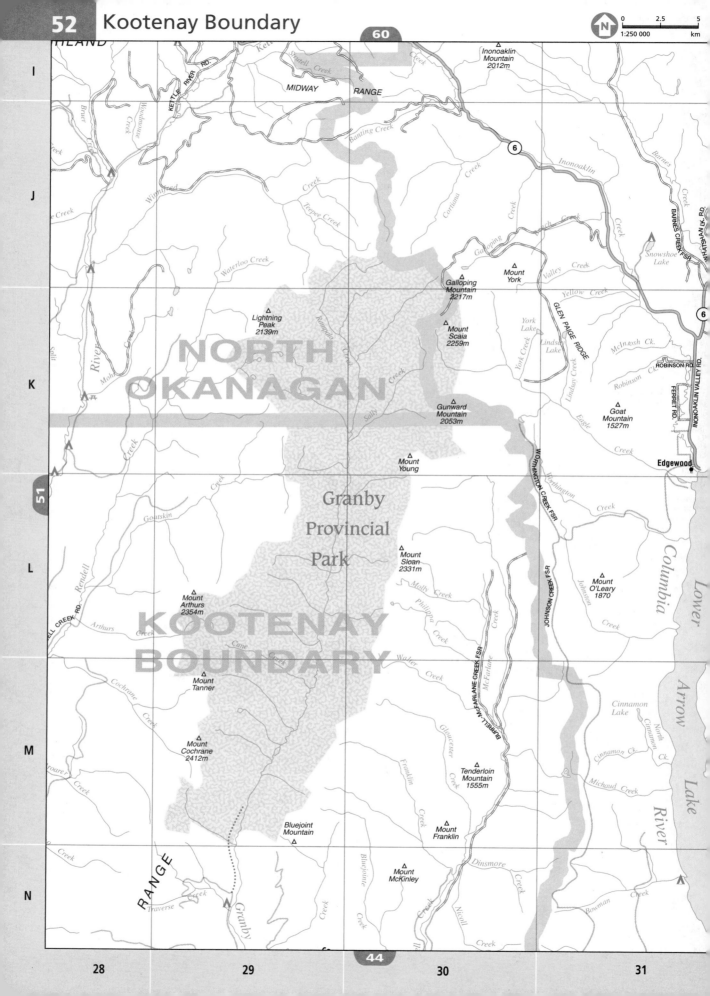

NORTH OKANAGAN

KOOTENAY BOUNDARY

Granby Provincial Park

MIDWAY RANGE

Inonoaklin Mountain 2012m

Galloping Mountain 2217m

Mount York

Mount Scaia 2259m

Lightning Peak 2139m

Gunward Mountain 2053m

Goat Mountain 1527m

Mount Young

Edgewood

Snowshoe Lake

York Lake

Mount Sloan 2331m

Mount Arthurs 2354m

Mount O'Leary 1870

Mount Tanner

Cinnamon Lake

Mount Cochrane 2412m

Tenderloin Mountain 1555m

Bluejoint Mountain

Mount Franklin

Mount McKinley

RANGE

Columbia

Lower Arrow Lake

River

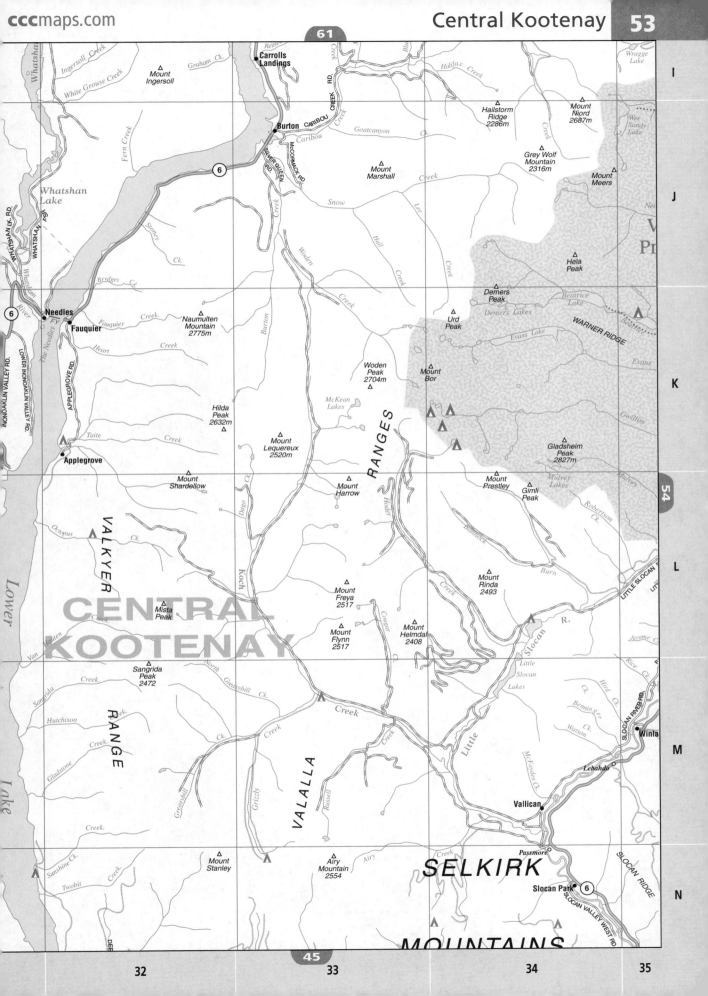

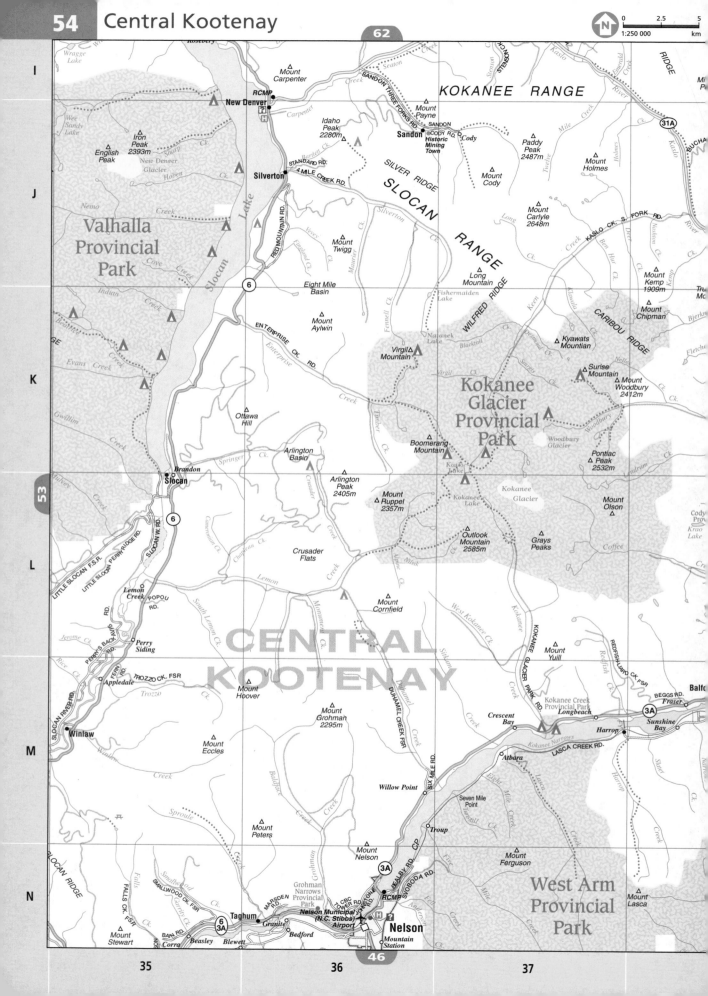

1:250 000

62

35   36   46   37

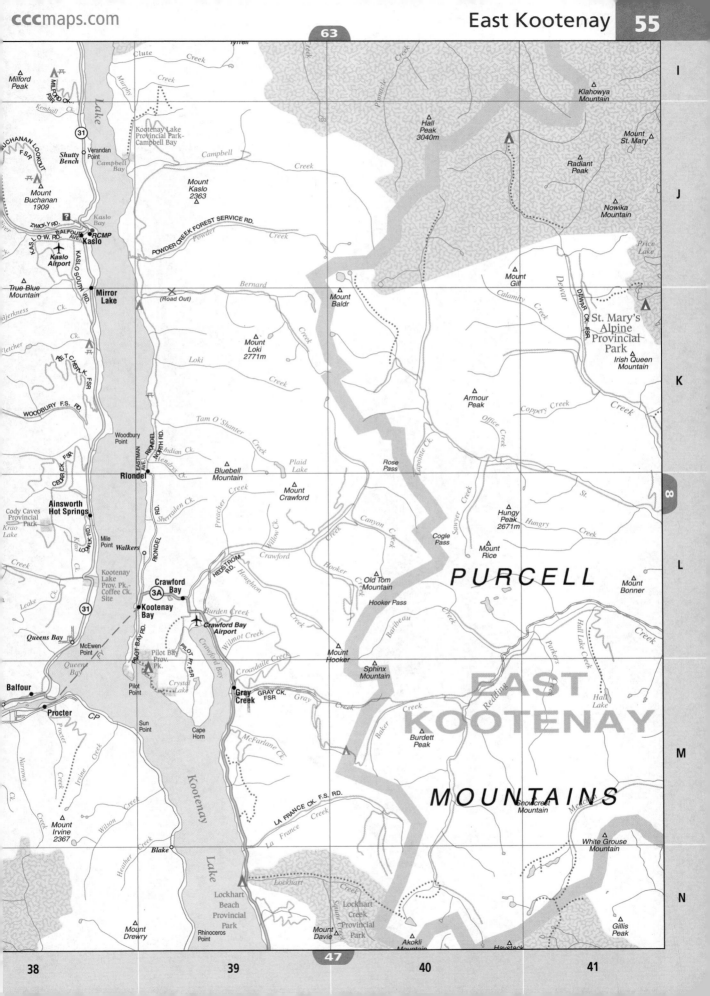

East Kootenay

PURCELL

EAST KOOTENAY

MOUNTAINS

Milford Peak

Klahowya Mountain

Hall Peak 3040m

Mount St. Mary

Radiant Peak

Mount Kaslo 2363

Nowika Mountain

Price Lake

Buchanan Lookout FSR

Shutty Bench

Verandan Point

Campbell Bay

Kootenay Lake Provincial Park-Campbell Bay

Campbell Creek

Mount Gill

Dewar

St. Mary's Alpine Provincial Park

Mount Buchanan 1909

Kaslo Bay

RCMP

Kaslo

Kaslo Airport

POWDER CREEK FOREST SERVICE RD.

Powder Creek

Calamity Creek

DEWAR CK. FSR

True Blue Mountain

Mirror Lake

(Road Out)

Bernard Creek

Mount Baldr

Irish Queen Mountain

Mount Loki 2771m

Loki Creek

Armour Peak

Coppery Creek

Creek

Woodbury Point

WOODBURY F.S. RD.

Tam O'Shanter Creek

Indian Ck.

Plaid Lake

Rose Pass

Office Creek

Lapointe Ck.

Sawyer Creek

St.

Hungry Creek

Riondel

Bluebell Mountain

Mount Crawford

Hungy Peak 2671m

Ainsworth Hot Springs

Cody Caves Provincial Park

Krao Lake

Mile Point

Walkers

Preacher Creek

Willow Ck.

Canyon Creek

Cogle Pass

Mount Rice

Mount Bonner

Kootenay Lake Prov. Pk.-Coffee Ck. Site

Crawford Bay

Kootenay Bay

HEDSTROM RD.

Houghton Creek

Crawford Creek

Hooker Creek

Old Tom Mountain

Hooker Pass

Queens Bay

McEwen Point

Burden Creek

Crawford Bay Airport

Wilmot Creek

Baribeau Creek

Redding Creek

Parkers Creek

Hall Lake Creek

Balfour

Procter

Pilot Bay Prov. Pk.

Pilot Point

Sun Point

Crystal Lake

Cape Horn

Croasdaile Creek

Gray Creek

GRAY CK. FSR

Gray Creek

Baker Creek

Sphinx Mountain

Mount Hooker

Hall Lake

Narrows Creek

Procter Creek

Irvine Creek

Mount Irvine 2367

Wilson Creek

Blake

McFarlane Ck.

Burdett Peak

Snowcrest Mountain

Meachen

White Grouse Mountain

Kootenay Lake

LA FRANCE CK. F.S. RD.

La France Creek

Lockhart Beach Provincial Park

Mount Drewry

Rhinoceros Point

Lockhart Creek

Mount Davie

Lockhart Creek Provincial Park

Squaw Creek

Akokli Mountain

Haystack Mountain

Gillis Peak

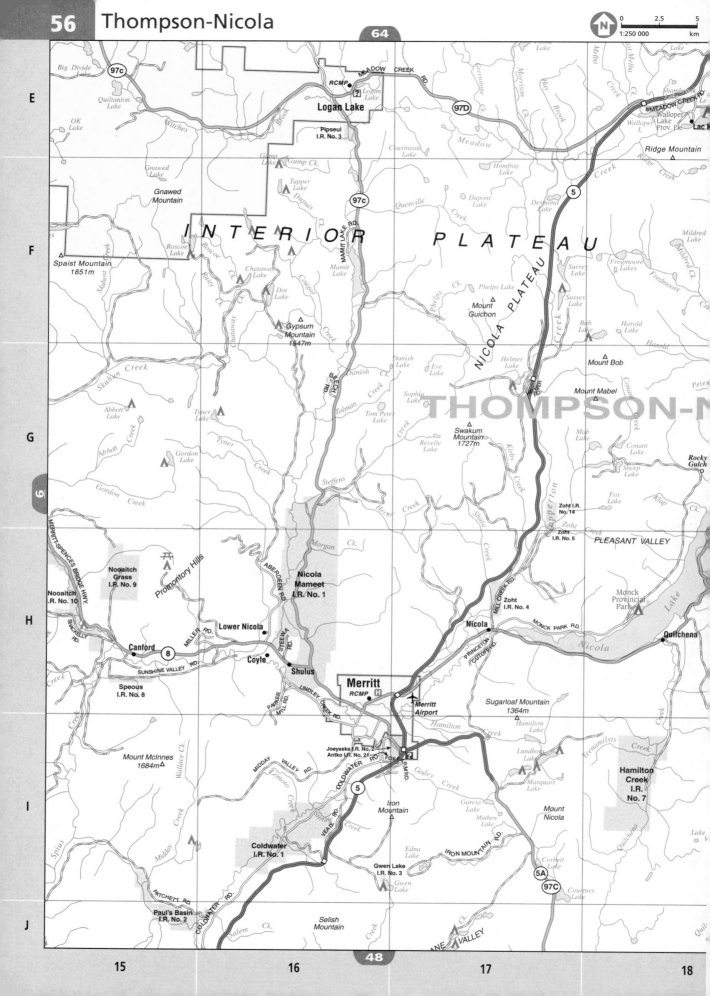

1:250 000

64

E

97c
Big Divide Lake
Quiltanton Lake
OK Lake
Witches Brook
MEADOW CREEK RD.
RCMP
Logan Lake
Pipseul I.R. No. 3
97D
Meadow Creek
Meadow Creek
MEADOW CREEK
Walloper Lake
Walloper Lake Prov. Pk.
Lac
Ridge Mountain

Gnawed Lake
Gnawed Mountain
Roscoe Lake
Gump Lake
Gump Ck.
Tupper Lake
Dupuis
MAMIT LAKE RD.
Mamit Lake
97c
Quenville Creek
Cousineau Lake
Homfray Lake
Dupont Lake
Desmond Lake
5
Ridge Creek
Mildred Lake

F

Spaist Mountain 1851m
Skuhost Creek
Chataway Lake
Roscoe Ck.
Rusty Ck.
Dot Lake
Chataway Ck.
Gypsum Mountain 1547m
Cougar Creek
BRECHA RD.
Danish Ck.
Danish Lake
Eve Lake
Sophia Lake
Phelps Ck.
Mount Guichon
Helmer Lake
NICOLA PLATEAU
Surre Lake
Frogmoore Lakes
Mildred Ck.
Fredmoore
Bob Lake
Harold Lake
Harold
Mount Bob

INTERIOR PLATEAU

G

Abbott Lake
Skuhun Creek
Tyner Lake
Gordon Lake
Abbott Creek
Tyner Creek
Gordon Lake
Gordon Creek
Steffens Creek
Tolman Creek
Tom Peter Lake
Hero Creek
Revelle Lake
Swakum Mountain 1727m
Kirby Creek
Shula Creek
RIVER RD.
Mount Mabel
Mob Lake
Conant Lake
Sheep Lake
Fox Lake
Klup Ck.
Rocky Gulch

THOMPSON-N

6

Merritt-Spences Bridge Hwy.
Nooaitch I.R. No. 10
Nooaitch Grass I.R. No. 9
Promontory Hills
ABERDEEN RD.
Morgan Ck.
Nicola Mameet I.R. No. 1
Zoht I.R. No. 14
Zoht I.R. No. 5
PLEASANT VALLEY
Monck Provincial Park
Nicola Lake

H

Shackelly Creek
Canford
8
SUNSHINE VALLEY RD.
Lower Nicola
MILLER RD.
STEEWA RD.
Coyle
Shulus
LINDLEY CREEK RD.
Spences Creek
Speous I.R. No. 8
PACKER MILL RD.
Merritt
RCMP
MILL CREEK RD.
Zoht I.R. No. 4
Nicola
PRINCETON CUTOFF RD.
MONCK PARK RD.
Nicola
Quilchena

Merritt Airport
Joeyaska I.R. No. 2
Antko I.R. No. 21
FOX FARM RD.
COLDWATER RD.
5
MIDDAY VALLEY RD.
Mount McInnes 1684m
Wallace Ck.
Lemoto Creek
Hamilton Lake
Hamilton Creek
Sugarloaf Mountain 1364m
Godey Creek
Lundbom Lake
Marquart Lake
Hamilton Creek I.R. No. 7
Keenamilsts Creek

I

Spius Creek
Midday Ck.
VEALE RD.
Stirling Creek
Coldwater I.R. No. 1
Iron Mountain
Gwen Lake I.R. No. 3
Edna Lake
Garcia Lake
Mathew Lake
IRON MOUNTAIN RD.
Mount Nicola
Corbett Lake
5A
97C
Courtney Lake
Quilchena

Patchett Rd.
Paul's Basin I.R. No. 2
COLDWATER RD.
Salem Ck.
Gwen Lake
Selish Mountain
Kane Ck.
VALLEY

J

15

16

48

17

18

N
0   2.5   5
km

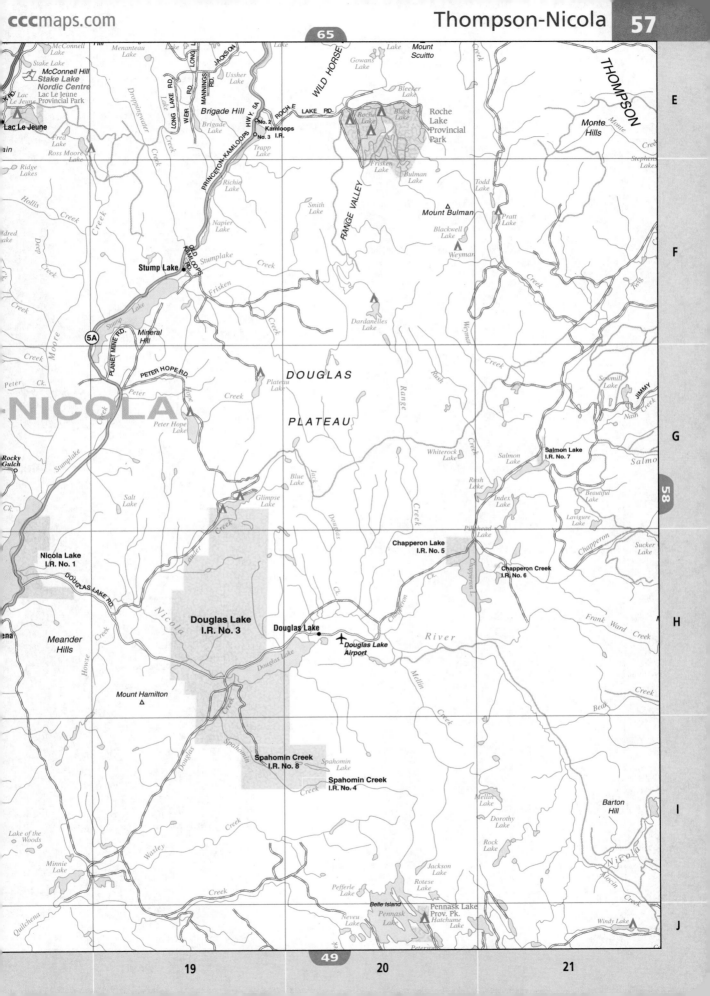

THOMPSON

McConnell Lake
McConnell Hill
Stake Lake
Stake Lake Nordic Centre
Lac Le Jeune Provincial Park
Lac Le Jeune

Menanteau Lake
Droppingwater Creek

LONG LAKE RD.
WER RD.
MANNINGS RD.
JACKSON

Lake

WILD HORSE
Gowans Lake
Mount Scuitto

Bleeker Lake
Roche Lake RD.
Roche Lake
Black Lake
Roche Lake Provincial Park

Monte Hills
Monte

Stephens Lakes

Fred Lake
Ross Moore Lake

Ridge Lakes

Brigade Hill
Brigade Lake

PRINCETON-KAMLOOPS HWY. 5A

No. 2
Kamloops No. 3 I.R.
Trapp Lake

Richie Lake

Napier Lake

Smith Lake

RANGE VALLEY

Frisken Lake
Bulman Lake

Mount Bulman

Blackwell Lake
Weyman

Todd Lake
Pratt Lake

Hollis Creek
Deep Creek
Idred ake

OLD KAMLOOPS KAMLOOPS RD.
Stump Lake

Stumplake

Frisken Creek

Creek

Creek

Dardanelles Lake

Weyman Creek

F

5A
PLANET MINE RD.
Mineral Hill

Stump Lake

Moore Creek

Peter Ck.

PETER HOPE RD.
Peter Hope Lake
Hope

Creek

Plateau Lake

DOUGLAS

PLATEAU

Range

Rush Creek

Rush Lake

Sowmill Lake
JIMMY
Nash Creek

-NICOLA

Stumplake

Rocky Gulch

Salt Lake

Glimpse Lake

Blue Lake

Jack Creek

Whiterock Lake

Salmon Lake

Salmon Lake I.R. No. 7

Salmo

Index Lake

Beautiful Lake

Lavigure Lake

Sucker Lake

G

Ck.

Nicola Lake I.R. No. 1

Lauder Creek

Douglas Ck.

Chapperon Lake I.R. No. 5

Pillhead Lake

Chapperon Creek I.R. No. 6

Chapperon Creek

DOUGLAS LAKE RD.

Douglas Lake I.R. No. 3

Douglas Lake

Douglas Lake Airport

Chapperon Ck.

River

Frank Ward Creek

H

ena

Meander Hills

Howse Creek

Douglas lake

Mellin Creek

Mellin

Beak Creek

Mount Hamilton

Spahomin Creek

Spahomin Creek I.R. No. 8
Spahomin Lake

Mellin Lake

Barton Hill

I

Douglas Creek

Spahomin Creek
Spahomin Creek I.R. No. 4

Dorothy Lake

Rock Lake

Nicola

Lake of the Woods

Minnie Lake

Wasley Creek

Creek

Jackson Lake
Rotese Lake

Atocin Creek

Windy Lake

Pefferle Lake

Belle Island
Pennask Lake Prov. Pk.
Hatchume Lake

Neveu Lake
Pennask Lake

J

Quilchena Creek

58

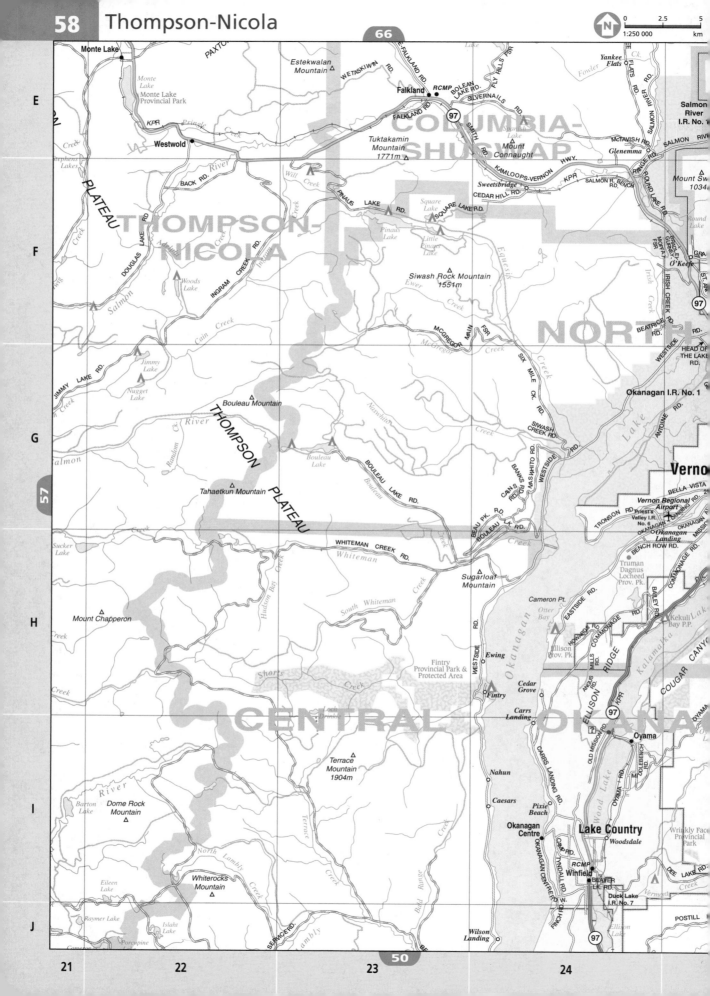

1:250 000

0   2.5   5
km

66

E

Monte Lake

Monte Lake
Provincial Park

Monte
Lake

Falkland

RCMP

Estekwalan
Mountain

WETASKIWIN RD.

COLUMBIA-

PAXTON

PRE-FALKLAND RD.

FALKLAND RD.

BOLEAN
LAKE RD.

SILVERNAILS RD.

FLY HILLS FSR

Fowler Ck.

Yankee
Flats

SALMON RIVER RD.

Salmon
River
I.R. No. 1

KPR

Pringle

Westwold

SHUSWAP

97

Mount
Connaught

KAMLOOPS-VERNON HWY.

McTAVISH RD.

RANGE RD.

Glenemma

Mount Sw
1034

BACK RD.

Witt Creek

Tuktakamin
Mountain
1771m

SMITH RD.

Spanish
Lake

Sweetsbridge

CEDAR HILL RD.

KPR

SALMON R. BENCH RD.

ROUND LAKE RD.

Round
Lake

PLATEAU

Stephens
Lakes

Creek

DOUGLAS LAKE RD.

Adrian

PINAUS LAKE RD.

Square
Lake

SQUARE LAKE RD.

Equesis

MOFFAT FSR

BRADLEY
CURRIE RD.

O'Keefe

IRISH CREEK RD.

GRA

ST AN

THOMPSON-

Woods
Lake

INGRAM CREEK RD.

Inkum

Creek

Pinaus
Lake

Little
Pinaus
Lake

Creek

F

NICOLA

Cain Creek

Siwash Rock Mountain
1551m

Ewer

Creek

McGREGOR MAIN FSR

Creek

97

Irish Creek

Salmon

Jimmy LAKE RD.

Jimmy
Lake

Nugget
Lake

River

Random Ck.

THOMPSON

Bouleau Mountain

Naswhito

Creek

SIX MILE CK. RD.

Siwash
Creek

SIWASH
CREEK RD.

NORTH

BEATRICE RD.

WESTSIDE RD.

HEAD OF
THE LAKE
RD.

Okanagan I.R. No. 1

ANTOINE RD.

G

57

Salmon

Creek

Bouleau
Lake

Tahaetkun Mountain

PLATEAU

BOULEAU LAKE RD.

Bouleau

BANKS RD.

NASWHITO RD.

CAN S RD.

WESTSIDE RD.

Lake

Vernon

BELLA VISTA RD.

Vernon Regional
Airport

TRONSON RD.

Trieste
Valley I.R.
No. 6

OKANAGAN

Okanagan
Landing

Sucker
Lake

Creek

BEAU PK. RD.

BOULEAU L.K. RD.

Creek

BENCH ROW RD.

Truman
Dagnus
Locheed
Prov. Pk.

WHITEMAN CREEK RD.

Whiteman

Creek

H

Mount Chapperon

Hudson Bay Creek

South Whiteman

Creek

Sugarloaf
Mountain

Cameron Pt.

Otter
Bay

EASTSIDE RD.

Ellison
Prov. Pk.

HOWARD RD.

ANGUS
MILLS
RD.

COMMONAGE RD.

Okanagan

RIDGE

Kalamalka

COUGAR CANYO

Creek

Shorts

Creek

Loch
Drinkie

WESTSIDE RD.

Ewing

Fintry
Provincial Park &
Protected Area

Fintry

Cedar
Grove

Carrs
Landing

97

ELLISON

KPR

CENTRAL

OKANA

Terrace
Mountain
1904m

OLD MISSION RD.

Oyama

DOLEBENCH RD.

OYAMA RD.

I

Barton
Lake

Dome Rock
Mountain

River

North Lambly Creek

Terrace

Creek

Nahun

Caesars

Pixie
Beach

CARRS LANDING RD.

Okanagan
Centre

Lake Country

Woodsdale

Wrinkly Face
Provincial
Park

Wood Lake

Eileen
Lake

Whiterocks
Mountain

Lambly Creek

Bald Range

OKANAGAN CENTRE RD.

CAMP RD.

TYNDALL RD.

RCMP

Winfield

BEAVER
LK. RD.

Duck Lake
I.R. No. 7

DEE LAKE RD.

Vermont

J

Raymer Lake

Islaht
Lake

Porcupine

SERVICE RD.

Lambly

Wilson
Landing

97

Ellison
Lake

POSTILL

Cameron

50

21   22   23   24

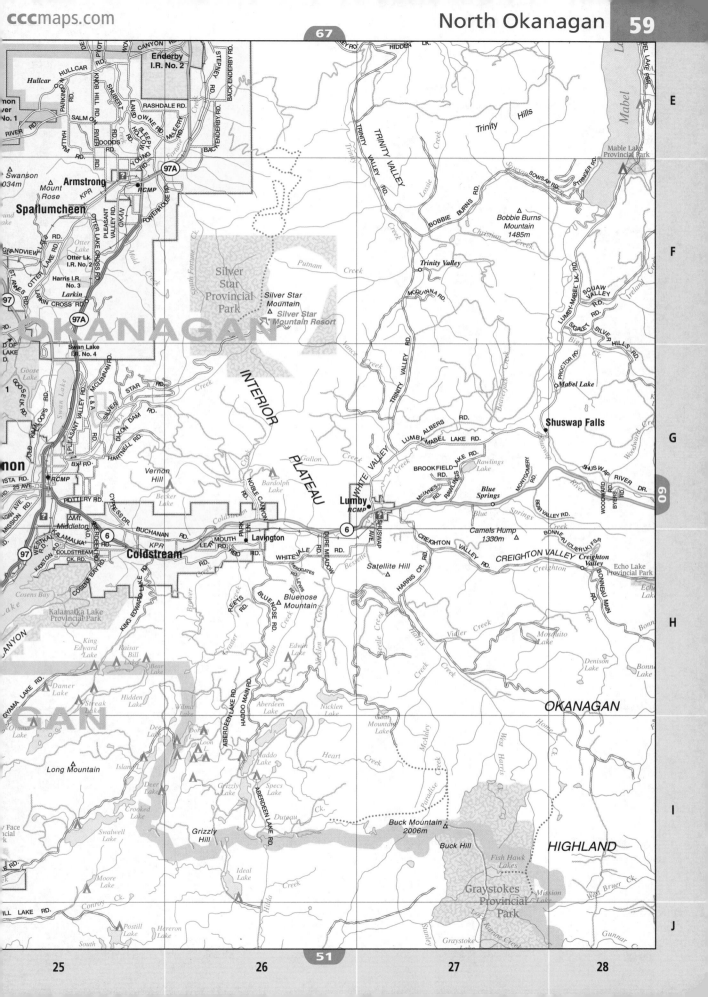

1:250 000

Park

Cariboo
Mountain

RANGE

Peters
Lake

E

Apeles Ck.

Latewhos

Spectrum
Lake

Mount
Fosthall
2680

Margie
Lake

Mo
Sym

Mabel Lake
Provincial Park

PARK

Park
Mountain
2057m

Monashee
Prov. Pk. Spectrum
(Site 2)

Rainbow Falls

Kate
Lake

Sugar
Mountain

Pillar Pass

Twin Peaks
Lake

South Cariboo
Pass

RANGE

Kate
Lake

Sugar
Mountain

Goat
Mountain

Sitkum
Plateau

Mount
Baldur

MOUNTAINS

F

Ireland

Creek

Sugar

Lake

KATE-SITKUM FSR

Sitkum

VIDLER RIDGE

Creek

Rottacker
Lake

MOUNTAINS

Haggkvist
Lake

Sigalet
Lake

SUGAR LAKE RD.

KATE CREEK FSR

Fosthall

South

Plant

Creek

Brenda
Falls

Onlet

Creek

Kathy
Lake

Holstein
Lake

Holstein Creek

CHERRY

RIDGE

NORTH

OKANAGAN

Severide

Creek

Cusson

Creek

Cre

G

Creek

River

SUGAR LAKE RD.

Shuswap

WHATSHAN

59

DR.

Cherryville

NORTH FORK RD.

Currie

Creek

Mount
Beaven
2150m

Rioux

RICHLANDS RD.

Cherry

Creek

THE PINACLES

Fife

H

Echo Lake
Provincial Park

CREIGHTON VALLEY RD.

Monashee

Creek

Yeoward
Mountain
2130m

Kettle

Creek

Echo
Lake

Bonneau Ck.

HECKMAN CREEK FSR

Yeoward

Creek

RANGE

Bonneau
Lake

Creek

Inches Ck.

Big Goat C.

Heckman

Monashee
Mountain

Keefer
Lake

Holmes
Lake

Whatshan
Peak
2256m

ANAGAN

Ferry

Monashee
Pass

KEEFER LAKE RD.

River

Barnes

Creek

I

HLAND

Coalboa

Creek

Eureka
Mountain

Inonoaklin

Creek

6

Bisson
Lake

Kettle

Inonoaklin
Mountain
2012m

KETTLE RIVER RD.

Sindell

Creek

J

Bracr

Woodmouse

Creek

MIDWAY

RANGE

Banting Creek

6

28   29   30   31

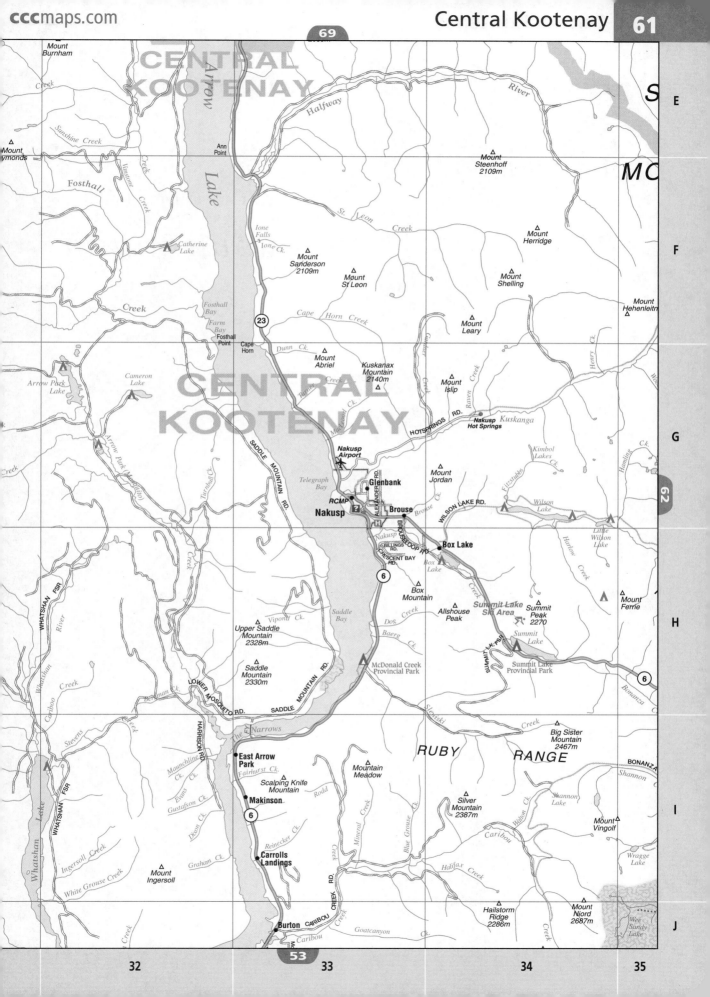

69

E

S

MO

Mount
Burnham

CENTRAL
KOOTENAY

Creek

Sunshine Creek

Mount
ymonds

Fosthall

Creek

Vanstone Creek

Catherine
Lake

Ann
Point

Halfway

River

St. Leon

Creek

Mount
Steenhoff
2109m

Mount
Herridge

F

Ione
Falls
Ione Ck.

Fosthall
Bay

Farm
Bay

Fosthall
Point

23

Cape
Horn

Mount
Sanderson
2109m

Mount
St Leon

Cape Horn Creek

Mount
Shelling

Mount
Hehenleitn

Creek

Arrow Park
Lake

Cameron
Lake

CENTRAL
KOOTENAY

Arrow Park (Needles)

Turnbull Ck.

SADDLE MOUNTAIN RD.

Telegraph
Bay

Dunn Ck.

Mount
Abriel

Kuskanax
Mountain
2140m

Macdonald Ck.

Turner Ck.

HOTSPRINGS RD.

Gardner Creek

Mount
Islip

Mount
Leary

Raven Creek

Nakusp
Hot Springs

Kuskanga

Mount
Jordan

Kimbol
Lakes

Fitzstubbs Ck.

Henry Ck.

Humling Ck.

G

62

Nakusp
Airport

Glenbank

RCMP

?

Nakusp

H

ALEXANDER RD.

Brouse

Brouse

Nakusp

BROUSE LOOP RD.

BILLINGS RD.

CRESCENT BAY RD.

6

WILSON LAKE RD.

Box Lake

Box Lake

Box
Mountain

Wilson
Lake

Little
Wilson
Lake

Harlow Creek

Mount
Ferrie

Upper Saddle
Mountain
2328m

Vipond Ck.

Saddle
Bay

Saddle
Mountain
2330m

SADDLE MOUNTAIN RD.

Dog

Creek

Baerg Ck.

Allshouse
Peak

Summit Lake
Ski Area

Summit
Peak
2270

Summit
Lake

Summit Lake
Provincial Park

SUMMIT LK. FSR

6

H

WHATSHAN FSR

Whatshan
River

Whatshan Creek

LOWER MOSQUITO RD.

HARRISON RD.

Bergman Ck.

SADDLE

The Narrows

McDonald Creek
Provincial Park

Slewiski Creek

Bonanza Ck.

Stevens Creek

Cariboo Creek

East Arrow
Park

Fairhurst Ck.

Scalping Knife
Mountain

Mountain
Meadow

Rodd

RUBY

RANGE

Big Sister
Mountain
2467m

BONANZA

Shannon

I

Whatshan
Lake

Ingersoll Creek

White Grouse Creek

Mount
Ingersoll

Dixon Ck.

Graham Ck.

Gustafson Ck.

Evans Ck.

Maunchline Ck.

Makinson

6

Reinecker Ck.

Carrolls
Landings

CREEK RD.

Mineral Creek

Blue Grouse Creek

Halifax Creek

Silver
Mountain
2387m

Caribou Creek

Wigton Ck.

Shannon
Lake

Shannon Ck.

Mount
Vingolf

Wragge
Lake

Burton

CARIBOU CREEK RD.

Caribou Creek

Goatcanyon Ck.

Hailstorm
Ridge
2286m

Creek

Mount
Niord
2687m

Creek

Wee
Sandy
Lake

J

53

32 | 33 | 34 | 35

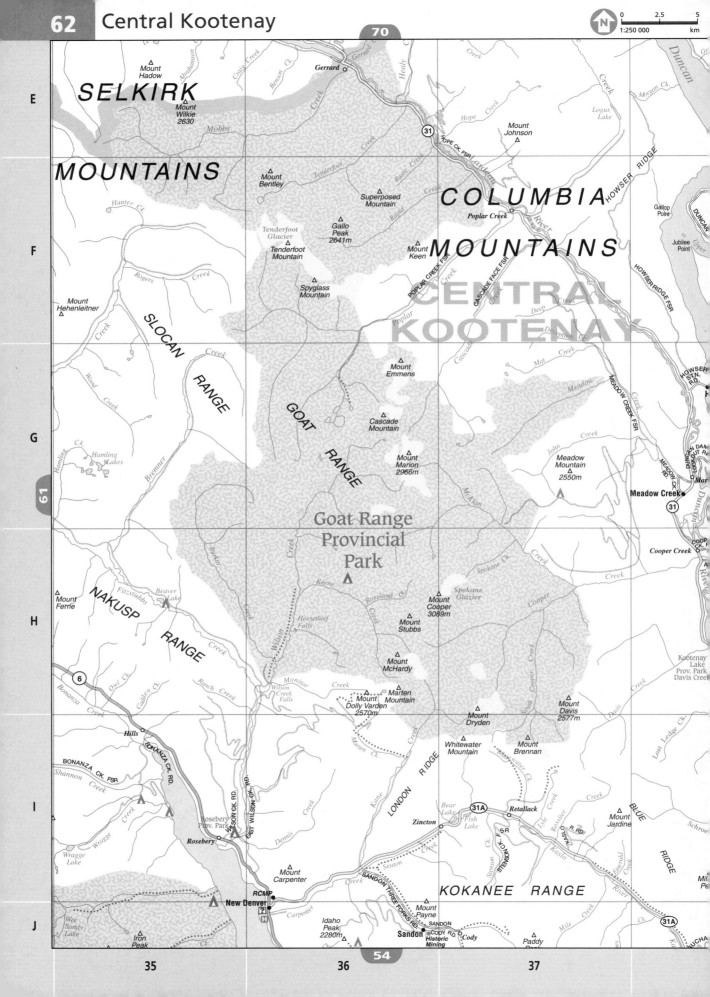

1:250 000

N

0   2.5   5
km

SELKIRK

MOUNTAINS

△ Mount Hadow

△ Mount Wilkie 2630

Mobbs

Craig Creek

Benson Ck.

Gerrard Creek

Gerrard

Healy

Creek

70

Hope Creek

31

Mount Johnson △

Logus Lake

Morgan Ck.

HOWSER RIDGE

Duncan Creek

Hunter Ck.

Mount Bentley △

Tenderfoot Creek

Superposed Mountain △

Rusty Creek

Rapid Creek

COLUMBIA

Poplar Creek ●

River

HOWSER RIDGE FSR

Gallop Point

Jubilee Point

Upper Duncan

Rogers Creek

Tenderfoot Glacier

Gallo Peak 2641m △

Tenderfoot Mountain △

Mount Keen △

MOUNTAINS

Poplar Creek FSR

Mount Hehenleitner △

Spyglass Mountain △

Poplar

Cascade

Cascade Face FSR

CENTRAL

Deep Creek

Deception Ck.

SLOCAN

Creek

Mat Creek

Meadow Creek

Mount Emmens △

Meadow Creek FSR

Meadow Creek FSR

HOWSER STN. RD.

Wood Creek

RANGE

GOAT

Cascade Mountain △

KOOTENAY

John Creek

Meadow Mountain 2550m △

DUNCAN DAM LOOKOUT Re.

Howser Ck. Rd.

Meadow Ck. Rd.

Mar

Hamling Ck.

Hamling Lakes

Brenner Creek

RANGE

Mount Marion 2966m △

McKian Creek

△

Meadow Creek ●

31

Duncan

Cooper Creek ●

Coop. Ck.

Mount Ferrie △

Fitzstubbs △

Beaver Lake △

NAKUSP

Goat Range Provincial Park

Keene Creek

Rossland Ck.

△

Spokane Ck.

Spokane Glacier

Cooper Creek

River

RANGE

Wilson Creek

Horsethief Falls

Mount Stubbs △

Mount Cooper 3089m △

South Cooper Creek

Kootenay Lake Prov. Park Davis Creek

6

Bonanza Creek

Owl Ck.

Cadden Ck.

Ranch Creek

Wilson Creek Falls

Monitor Creek

Mount McHardy △

Creek

Marten Mountain △

Mount Dolly Varden 2570m △

Mount Dryden △

Mount Davis 2577m △

Davis Creek

Lost Ledge Ck.

Shannon Creek

BONANZA CK. FSR

Hills ●

BONANZA CK. RD.

Wragge Creek

Rosebery Prov. Park

Marten Ck.

Kane Creek

LONDON RIDGE

Whitewater Mountain △

Mount Brennan △

Whitewater Ck.

BLUE

△

△

Rosebery ●

WILSON CK. RD.

EAST WILSON CK. RD.

Dennis Creek

Bear Lake

Zincton ●

31A

Fish Lake

Retallack ●

Lyle Creek

Rossiter Creek

Kaslo

R. RD.

Mount Jardine △

RIDGE

Wragge Lake

Iron Peak △

Wee Sandy Lake

Mount Carpenter △

New Denver ▲

RCMP

?

H

Carpenter Creek

Idaho Peak 2280m △

Sandon ●

△

SANDON THREE FORKS RD.

Seaton Creek

Mount Payne △

SANDON

CODY RD.

Cody ●

Historic Mining

KOKANEE RANGE

STENSON CK. FSR

Kaslo River

Emerald Ck.

Mill Pe

Paddy

31A

uchan

35   36   37

61

G

E

F

H

I

J

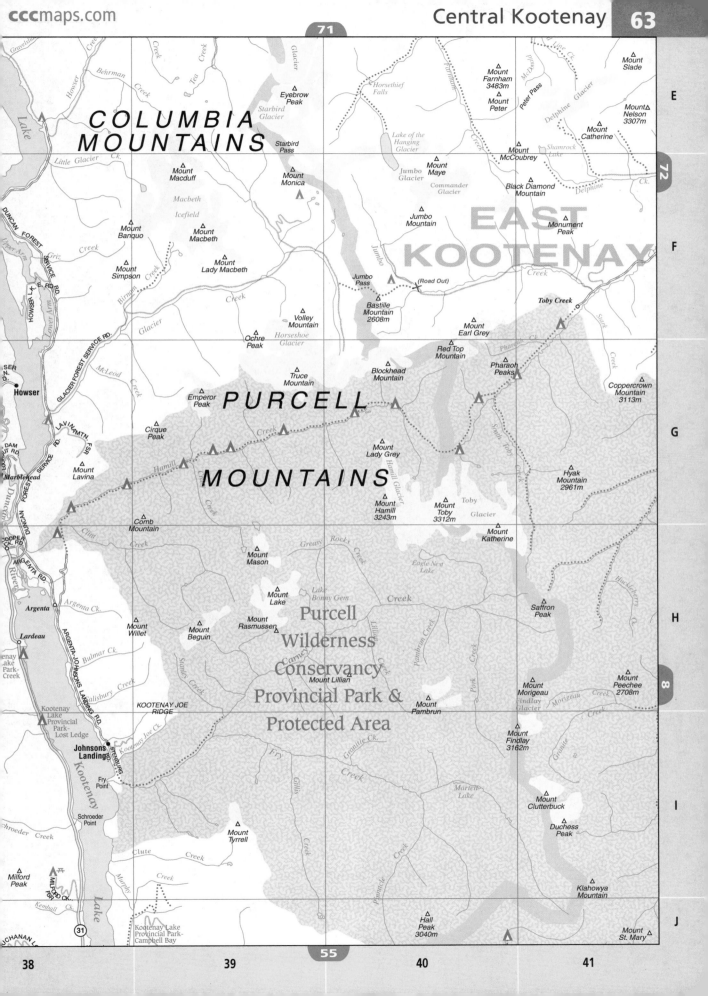

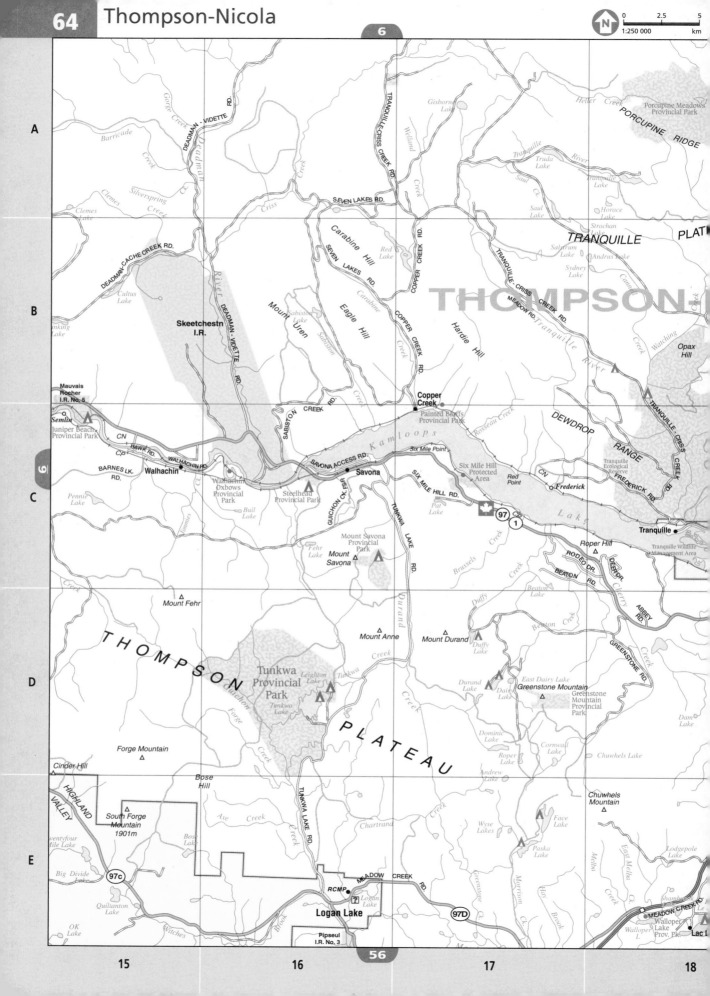

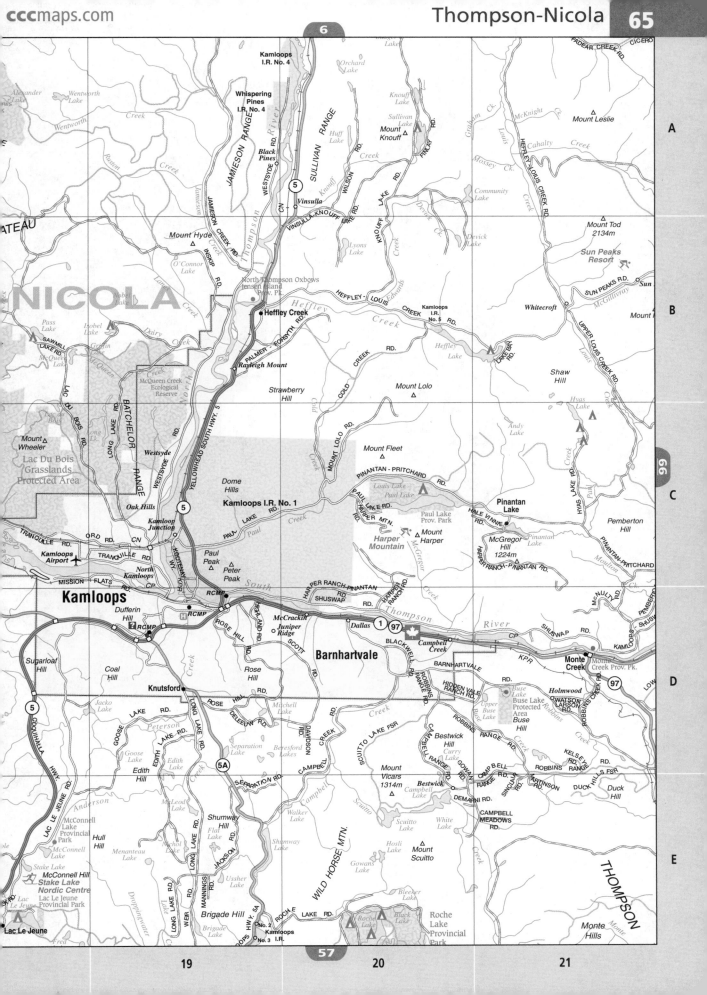

NICOLA

Kamloops

Kamloops Airport

Barnhartvale

Monte Creek

Knutsford

THOMPSON

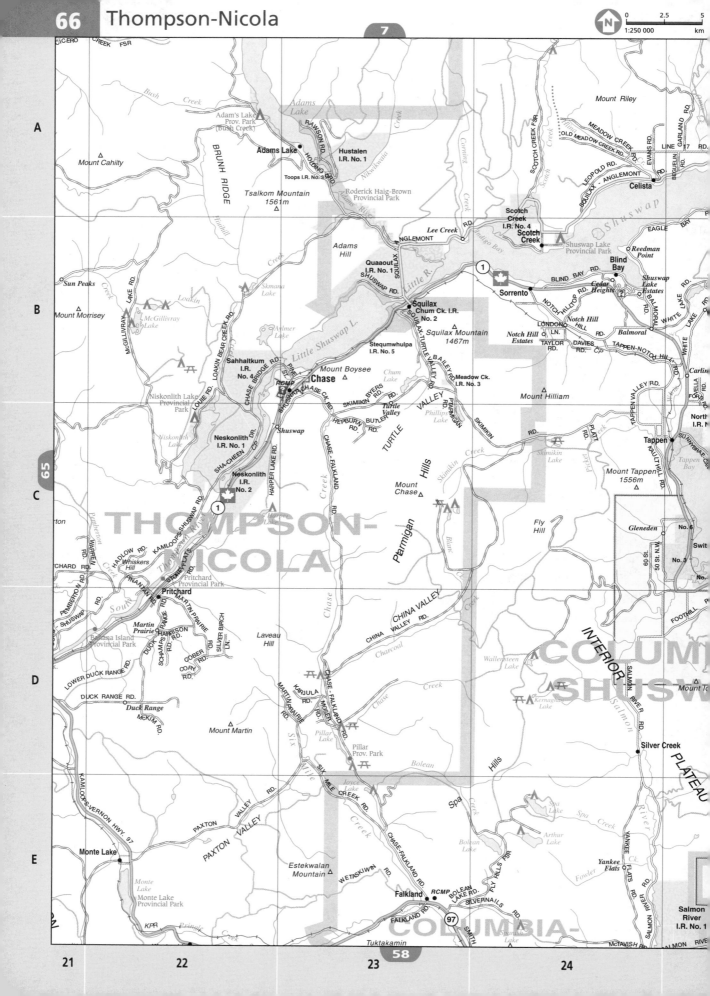

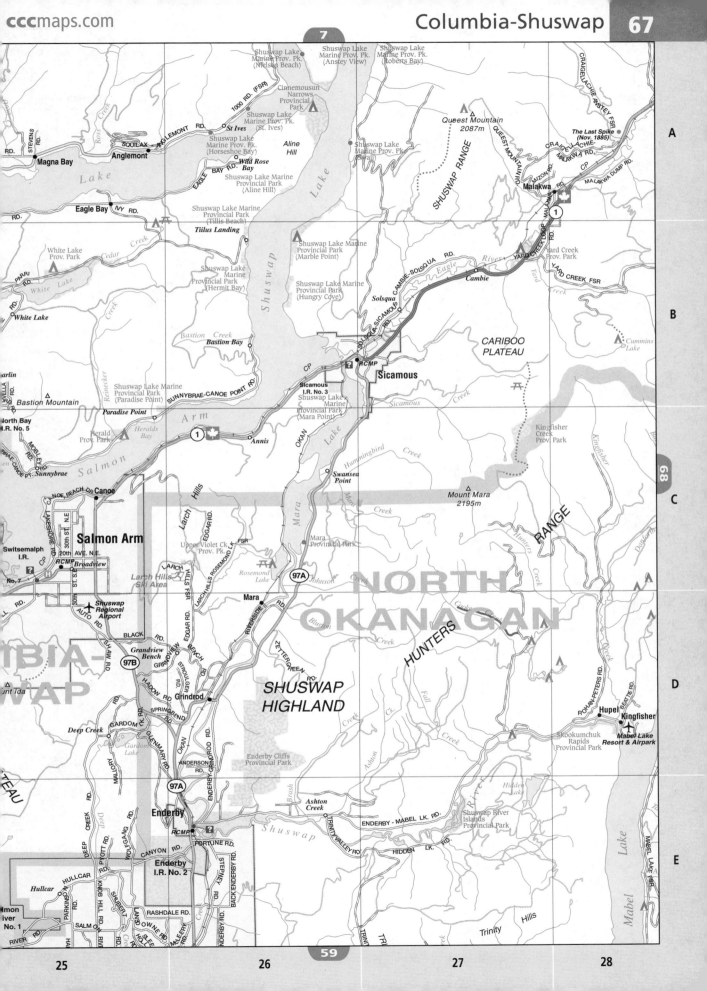

7

A

B

68

C

D

E

25   26   27   28

Shuswap Lake Marine Prov. Pk. (Nielsen Beach)

Shuswap Lake Marine Prov. Pk. (Anstey View)

Shuswap Lake Marine Prov. Pk. (Roberts Bay)

CRAIGELLACHIE ANSTEY FSR

Quest Mountain 2087m

The Last Spike (Nov. 1885)

QUEST MOUNTAIN RD.

CRAIGELLACHIE-

7000 RD. (FSR)

Cinnemousun Narrows Provincial Park

Shuswap Lake Marine Prov. Pk. (St. Ives)

St Ives

ANGLEMONT RD.

SHUSWAP RANGE

MIZON RD.

CRAIGELLACHIE-MALAKWA RD.

CP

MALAKWA DUMP RD.

Malakwa

1

Shuswap Lake Marine Prov. Pk. (Horseshoe Bay)

Wild Rose Bay

EAGLE BAY RD.

Shuswap Lake Marine Provincial Park (Aline Hill)

Aline Hill

Shuswap Lake Marine Prov. Pk. (Swall)

MALAKWA RD.

SQUILAX

Anglemont

Magna Bay

STEVENS RD.

ROSS

Creek

ANGLEMONT RD.

Lake

Eagle Bay

IVY RD.

Shuswap Lake Marine Provincial Park (Tillis Beach)

Tülus Landing

Lake

Eagle

River

Yard Creek Prov. Pk.

YARD CREEK LOOP RD.

Cambie

YARD CREEK FSR

Yard

Creek

White Lake Prov. Park

PARRI RD.

Cedar

Creek

CAMBIE-SOLSQUA RD.

White Lake

White Lake

Shuswap Lake Marine Provincial Park (Hermit Bay)

Shuswap Lake Marine Provincial Park (Marble Point)

Shuswap Lake Marine Provincial Park (Hungry Cove)

Solsqua

SOLSQUA-SICAMOUS RD.

CARIBOO PLATEAU

Cummins Lake

Bastion Creek

Bastion Bay

RENECKER RD.

Shuswap

Arm

CP

RCMP

Sicamous

1

Sicamous I.R. No. 3

Shuswap Lake Marine Provincial Park (Mara Point)

Sicamous

Creek

Kingfisher Creek Prov. Park

Kingfisher

Shuswap Lake Marine Prov. Park (Paradise Point)

SUNNYBRAE-CANOE POINT RD.

Paradise Point

Bastion Mountain

North Bay I.R. No. 5

Herald Prov. Park

Heralds Bay

1

Annis

OKAN

Mara

Lake

Hummingbird Creek

Mount Mara 2195m

RANGE

Duteau

Sunnybrae

Salmon

Arm

Larch Hills

NOE BEACH DR.

Canoe

20th ST. N.E.

Salmon Arm

RCMP

Broadview

20th AVE. N.E.

Swansea Point

Mara

Creek

NORTH

Switsemalph I.R. No. 7

LAKESHORE RD.

CP

Larch Hills

LARCH HILLS RD.

Upper Violet Ck. Prov. Park

LARCH HILLS ROSEMOND RD.

Rosemond Lake

Mara Provincial Park

97A

Johnson

OKANAGAN

HUNTERS

ROJAHN-PETERS RD.

Shuswap Regional Airport

Larch Hills Ski Area

LARCH HILLS FSR

EDGAR RD.

Mara

97A

Bluffon Creek

Cooke Creek

Fall Creek

BEATTIE RD.

Hupel

Kingfisher

BLACK RD.

SHAW RD.

97B

Grandview Bench

GRANDVIEW BENCH RD.

STOULGER RD.

Grindrod

ZETTERGREEN RD.

RIVERSIDE RD.

SHUSWAP HIGHLAND

Ashton Creek

Skookumchuk Rapids Provincial Park

Mabel Lake Resort & Airpark

Mabel Lake

unt Tda

MBIA-

WAP

Deep Creek

GARDOM RD.

GLENMARY RD.

OKAN

Gardom Lake

SPRINGBEND RD.

ANDERSON RD.

ENDERBY-GRINDROD RD.

Enderby Cliffs Provincial Park

Ashton Ck.

Hidden Lake

TEAU

MALLORY RD.

97A

Enderby

RCMP

FORTUNE RD.

Shuswap

ENDERBY-MABEL LK. RD.

Shuswap River Islands Provincial Park

River

Mabel Lake

DEEP CREEK RD.

WOLFGANG RD.

CANYON RD.

STEPNEY RD.

BACK ENDERBY RD.

TRINITY VALLEY RD.

HIDDEN LK. RD.

MABEL LAKE FSR

Salmon River No. 1

Hullcar

PARKINSON RD.

HULLCAR RD.

KNOB HILL RD.

SHUBER RD.

LANSDOWNE RD.

McLEERY RD.

RASHDALE RD.

Enderby I.R. No. 2

Trinity Hills

Trinity

Columbia-Shuswap

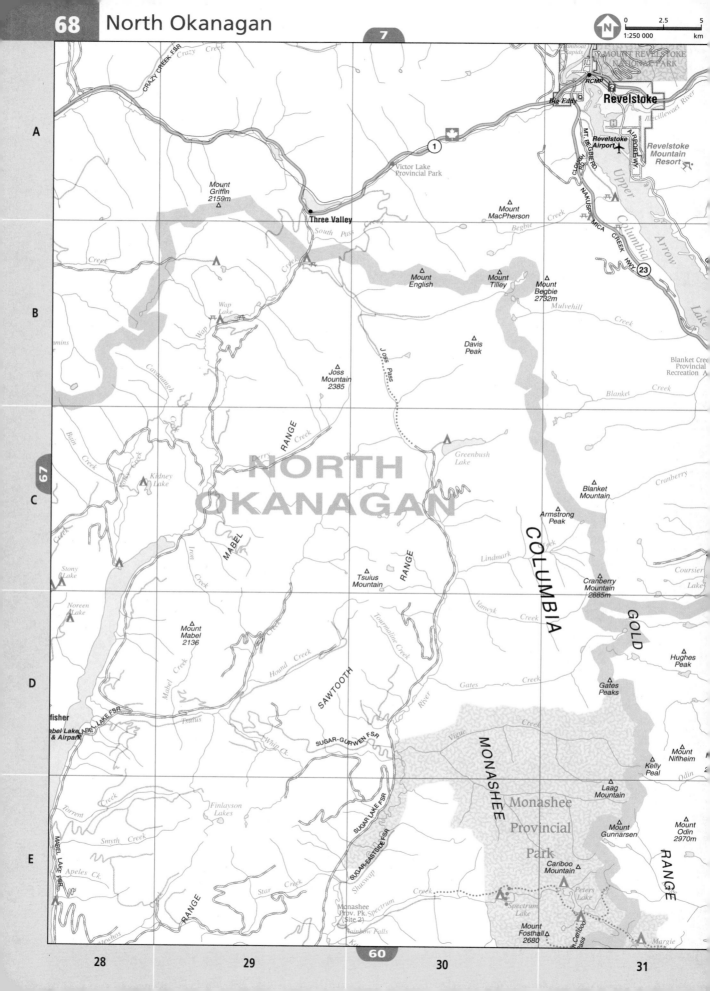

N
1:250 000
0   2.5   5
km

A

MOUNT REVELSTOKE
NATIONAL PARK

RCMP

Big Eddy

Revelstoke

Revelstoke
Airport

Revelstoke
Mountain
Resort

Illecillewaet River

Mount
Griffin
2159m

Victor Lake
Provincial Park

Three Valley

South Pass

Mount
MacPherson

Begbie   Creek

Mulvehill

Upper Columbia

Arrow Lake

23

B

Wap
Lake

Mount
English

Mount
Tilley

Mount
Begbie
2732m

Davis
Peak

Joss Pass

Blanket Creek
Provincial
Recreation A

Blanket   Creek

Joss
Mountain
2385

RANGE

Greenbush
Lake

Cranberry

67

C

NORTH
OKANAGAN

Kidney
Lake

Stony
Lake

Noreen
Lake

MABEL

Tsuius
Mountain

RANGE

Lindmark

COLUMBIA

Blanket
Mountain

Armstrong
Peak

Cranberry
Mountain
2885m

Coursier
Lake

GOLD

Hughes
Peak

D

Mount
Mabel
2136

SAWTOOTH

Tourmaline Creek

Hound Creek

Vanwyk   Creek

Gates   Creek

River

Gates
Peaks

fisher

bel Lake
& Airpark

MABEL LAKE FSR

Mabel   Creek

Tsuius

Whip Ck.

SUGAR-GURWEN F.S.R

Vigue   Creek

MONASHEE

Mount
Niflheim

Kelly
Peal

E

MABEL LAKE FSR

Torrent   Creek

Smyth   Creek

Apeles Ck.

RANGE

Finlayson
Lakes

Star   Creek

SUGAR LAKE FSR

SUGAR-EASTSIDE F.S.R

Shuswap

Creek

Monashee
Prov. Pk. Spectrum
(Site 2)

Rainbow Falls

Monashee

Provincial

Park

Cariboo
Mountain

Spectrum
Lake

Mount
Fosthall
2680

Cariboo Pass

Laag
Mountain

Mount
Gunnarsen

Mount
Odin
2970m

Peters
Lake

Margie

RANGE

28   29   30   31

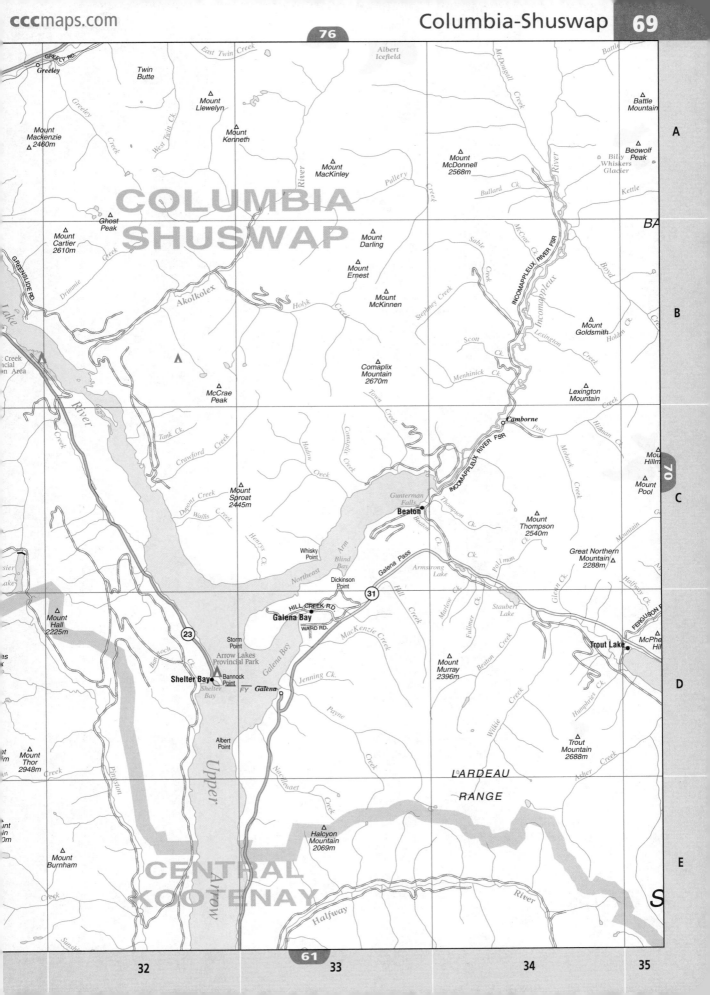

COLUMBIA
SHUSWAP

Greeley

Twin Butte

Mount Llewelyn

Mount Kenneth

Mount MacKinley

Albert Icefield

Mount McDonnell 2568m

Battle Mountain

Beowolf Peak

Billy Whiskers Glacier

Mount Mackenzie 2460m

Mount Cartier 2610m

Ghost Peak

Mount Darling

Mount Ernest

Mount McKinnen

Mount Goldsmith

GREENSLIDE RD.

Akolkolex

Comaplix Mountain 2670m

Lexington Mountain

McCrae Peak

Camborne

Mount Hillm

Mount Pool

Mount Sproat 2445m

Gunterman Falls

Beaton

Mount Thompson 2540m

Great Northern Mountain 2288m

Whisky Point

Blind Bay

Dickinson Point

Galena Pass

Armstrong Lake

Mount Hall 2225m

31

HILL CREEK RD.
Galena Bay
WARD RD.

MacKenzie Creek

Staubert Lake

Trout Lake

McPhe Hil

23

Storm Point

Arrow Lakes Provincial Park

Mount Murray 2396m

FERGUSON

Shelter Bay
Bannock Point
Shelter Bay

FY *Galena*

Jenning Ck.

Albert Point

Mount Thor 2948m

Payne

LARDEAU

RANGE

Trout Mountain 2688m

Mount Burnham

CENTRAL KOOTENAY

Halcyon Mountain 2069m

Upper

Arrow

Halfway

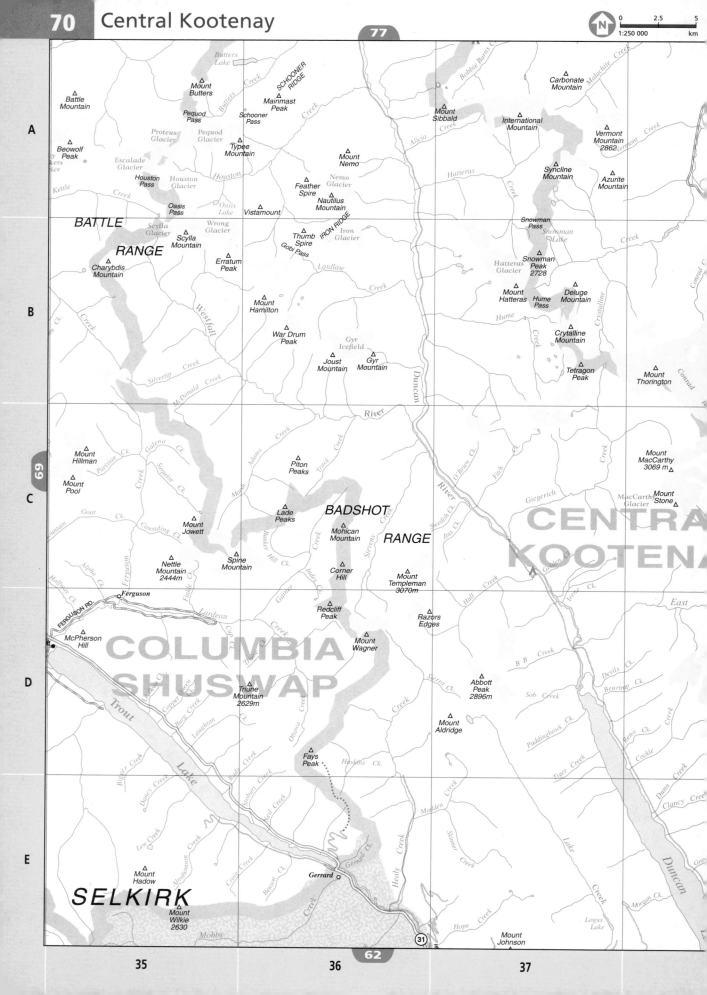

N 1:250 000

0   2.5   5 km

Butters Lake

Mount Butters

Battle Mountain

Beowolf Peak

SCHOONER RIDGE

Mainmast Peak

Pequod Pass

Schooner Pass

Proteus Glacier

Pequod Glacier

Escalade Glacier

Houston Pass

Houston Glacier

Typee Mountain

Mount Nemo

Carbonate Mountain

Mount Sibbald

International Mountain

Vermont Mountain 2862

Syncline Mountain

Azurite Mountain

Feather Spire

Nemo Glacier

Nautilus Mountain

A

Kettle

BATTLE

RANGE

Oasis Pass

Oasis Lake

Vistamount

Scylla Glacier

Scylla Mountain

Wrong Glacier

Thumb Spire

Gobi Pass

Iron Glacier

IRON RIDGE

Snowman Pass

Snowman Lake

Snowman Peak 2728

Charybdis Mountain

Erratum Peak

Hatteras Glacier

Mount Hatteras

Hume Pass

Deluge Mountain

B

Westfall

Mount Hamilton

War Drum Peak

Gyr Icefield

Joust Mountain

Gyr Mountain

Laidlaw

Creek

Hume

Crytalline Mountain

Tetragon Peak

Mount Thorington

Silvertip

McDonald Creek

River

Duncan

Conrad

69

Mount Hillman

Galena Ck.

Purtsian Ck.

Surprise Ck.

Adams

Piton Peaks

Track Creek

O'Brien Ck.

Fitch

Giegerich

Mount MacCarthy 3069 m

C

Mount Pool

Goat Ck.

Cascading Ck.

Myoff

Lade Peaks

BADSHOT

Mohican Mountain

RANGE

Swedish Ck.

Jim Ck.

River

MacCarthy Glacier

Mount Stone

CENTRA

KOOTENA

Mount Jowett

Nettle Mountain 2444m

Spine Mountain

Bunker Hill Ck.

Corner Hill

Stevens

Mount Templeman 3070m

Hall

Creek

Irene

Godur

East

Halfway Ck.

Alpha Ck.

Ferguson

Ferguson

FERGUSON RD.

Finkle Ck.

Lardeau

Creek

Cup

Thumb Ck.

Gainer

Inder Ck.

Redcliff Peak

Razors Edges

D

McPherson Hill

COLUMBIA

SHUSWAP

Blue Cliff

Copper Creek

Bugs Creek

Triune Mountain 2629m

Ottawa

Creek

Mount Wagner

Serra Ck.

Abbott Peak 2896m

Sob Creek

B B Creek

Puddingbowl Ck.

Reno Ck.

Devils Ck.

Beartrap Ck.

Trout

Lake

Laughton

Ck.

Mount Aldridge

E

Mount Hadow

Abrahamson Creek

Craigs Creek

Lew Creek

Neil Creek

Linhart Creek

Kody Ck.

Fays Peak

Haskins Ck.

Mudden Creek

Skinner Creek

Lake

Tiger Creek

Cockle Ck.

Dann Creek

Clancy Ck.

SELKIRK

Mount Wilkie 2630

Mobbs

Benson Ck.

Gerrard

Gerrard Ck.

Healy Creek

Hope Creek

Mount Johnson

Logus Lake

Duncan

Denny Creek

Bigger Creek

31

35   36   37

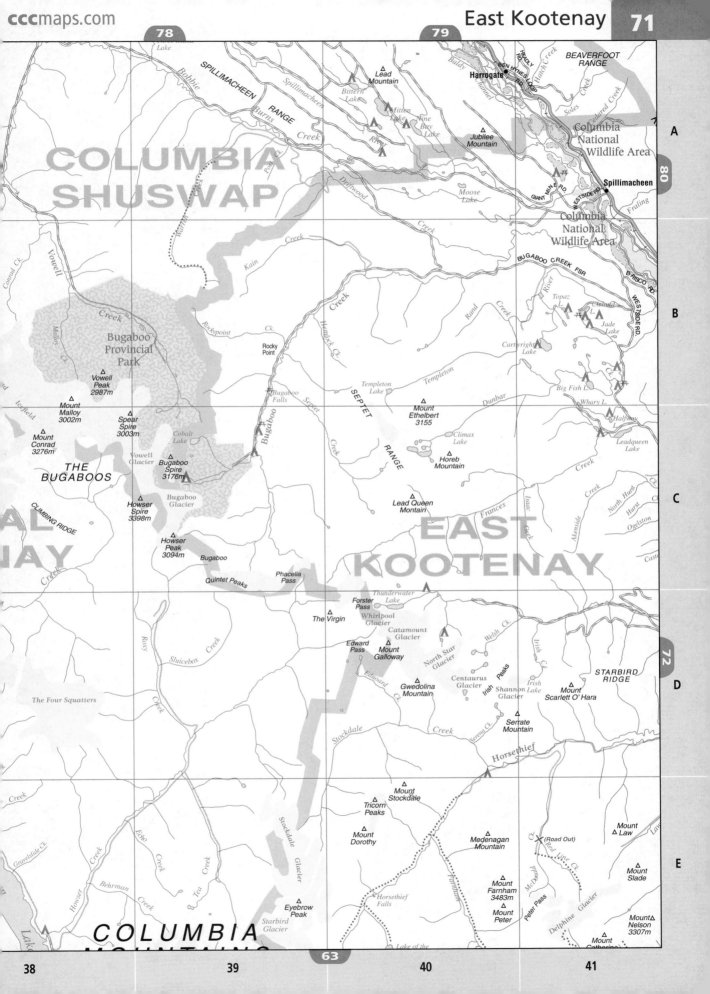

COLUMBIA
SHUSWAP

BEAVERFOOT
RANGE

Harrogate

Columbia
National
Wildlife Area

Spillimacheen

Columbia
National
Wildlife Area

SPILLIMACHEEN RANGE

Lead
Mountain

Bittern
Lake

Mitten
Lake

Nine Bay
Lake

Jubilee
Mountain

Moose
Lake

BUGABOO CREEK FSR

Topaz

Jade
Lake

Cartwright
Lake

Big Fish L.

Bugaboo
Provincial
Park

Rocky
Point

Septet

Templeton
Lake

Templeton

Dunbar

Whary L.

Vowell
Peak
2987m

Mount
Malloy
3002m

Spear
Spire
3003m

Cobalt
Lake

Bugaboo
Falls

SEPTET

Mount
Ethelbert
3155

Climax
Lake

Leadqueen
Lake

Halfway
L.

Mount
Conrad
3276m

THE
BUGABOOS

Vowell
Glacier

Bugaboo
Spire
3176m

Bugaboo
Glacier

RANGE

Horeb
Mountain

Howser
Spire
3398m

Lead Queen
Mountain

EAST

Frances

Isaac

Akenside

North Hurst

Hurst

Ogelston

Howser
Peak
3094m

Bugaboo

KOOTENAY

Quintet Peaks

Phacelia
Pass

Thunderwater
Lake

STARBIRD
RIDGE

The Four Squatters

Forster
Pass

Whirlpool
Glacier

Catamount
Glacier

Welsh Ck.

Irish

The Virgin

Edward
Pass

Mount
Galloway

North Star
Glacier

Centaurus
Glacier

Irish
Peaks

Shannon
Glacier

Mount
Scarlett O'Hara

Gwedolina
Mountain

Irish
Lake

Serrate
Mountain

Horsethief

Mount
Stockdale

Mount
Law

Tricorn
Peaks

Medenagan
Mountain

(Road Out)

Red Line Ck

Mount
Slade

Mount
Dorothy

Mount
Farnham
3483m

Peter Pass

COLUMBIA

Eyebrow
Peak

Starbird
Glacier

Horsethief
Falls

Mount
Peter

Delphine Glacier

Mount
Nelson
3307m

Mount
Catherine

Lake of the

MOUNTAINS

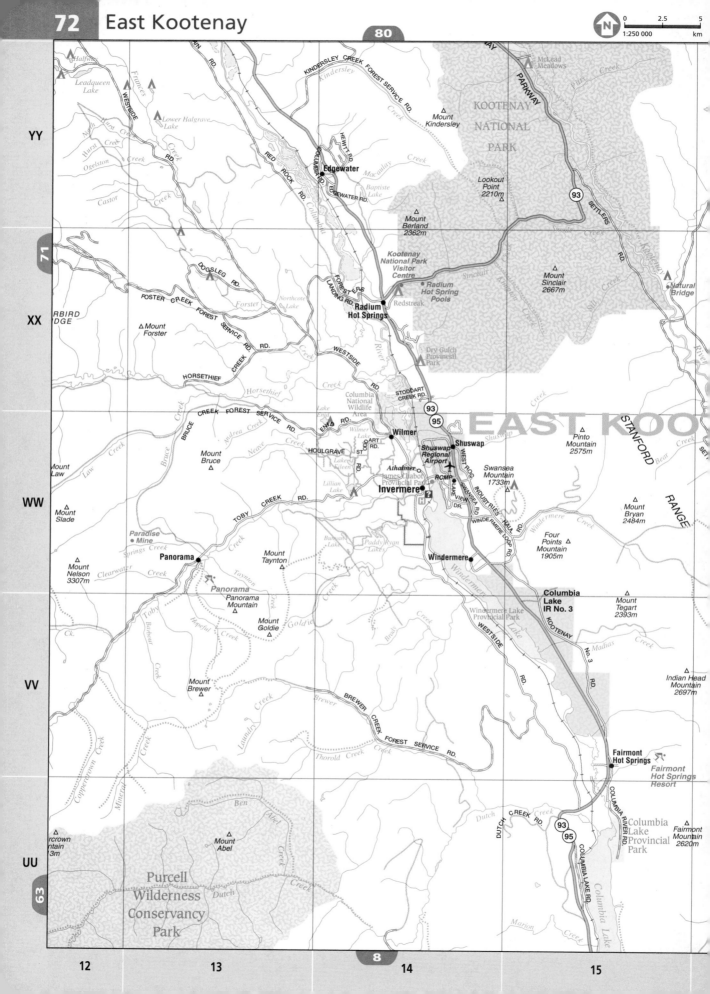

1:250 000

0   2.5   5
km

YY

71

XX

WW

VV

UU

63

12   13   8   14   15

Halfway

Leadqueen
Lake

Frances Creek

WESTSIDE RD.

Lower Halgrave
Lake

North Hurst Creek

Ogelston Creek

Hurst Creek

Castor Creek

Columbia River

RED ROCK RD.

COLUMBIA RD.

Edgewater

HEWITT RD.

EDGEWATER RD.

Macaulay Creek

Baptiste Lake

KINDERSLEY CREEK FOREST SERVICE RD.

Kindersley Creek

Mount Kindersley

KOOTENAY NATIONAL PARK

PARKWAY

McLead Meadows

Pitts Creek

Lookout Point 2210m

93

SETTLERS RD.

Mount Berland 2362m

DOGSLEG RD.

FOSTER CREEK FOREST SERVICE RD.

Forster Creek

Northcote Lake

FORSTERS LANDING RD.

Kootenay National Park Visitor Centre

Sinclair Creek

Radium Hot Spring Pools

Redstreak

Mount Sinclair 2667m

Kindian Creek

Kootenay River

Natural Bridge

RBIRD IDGE

Mount Forster

WESTSIDE RD.

HORSETHIEF CREEK RD.

Horsethief Creek

Silk Creek

River

Dry Gulch Provincial Park

BRUCE CREEK FOREST SERVICE RD.

Lake Enid

Columbia National Wildlife Area

STODDART CREEK RD.

93 95

EAST KOO

STANFORD

Bear Creek

Andrea Creek

Neave Creek

HOULGRAVE

ENID RD.

Wilmer Lake

ART RD.

Wilmer

Shuswap Regional Airport

Shuswap

Shuswap Creek

Pinto Mountain 2575m

RANGE

Mount Law

Bruce Creek

Mount Bruce

Lake Eileen

COOL ST RD.

Athalmer

James Chabot Provincial Park

Invermere

RCMP

WEST ROG

Swansea Mountain 1733m

Swansea Creek

INDUSTRIES RD.

Mount Bryan 2484m

Mount Law

Lillian Lake

Mount Slade

Paradise Mine

Toby Creek

Springs Creek

Clearwater Creek

Mount Nelson 3307m

Panorama

Bunkar Lakes

Paddy Ryan Lakes

LANE VIEW DR.

WINDERMERE LOOP RD.

Windermere Creek

Four Points Mountain 1905m

Panorama Mountain

Mount Taynton

Taynton Creek

Windermere

Columbia Lake IR No. 3

Mount Tegart 2393m

Toby Creek

Buchnut Creek

Hopeful Creek

Mount Goldie

Goldie Creek

Windermere Lake

Windermere Lake Provincial Park

WESTSIDE RD.

KOOTENAY No. 3 RD.

Madias Creek

Indian Head Mountain 2697m

Mount Brewer

BREWER CREEK FOREST SERVICE RD.

Brewer Creek

Laundry Creek

Thorold Creek

Fairmont Hot Springs

Fairmont Hot Springs Resort

Coppercrown Creek

Mineral Creek

Ben Abel Creek

DUTCH CREEK RD.

Dutch Creek

93 95

COLUMBIA RIVER RD.

Columbia Lake Provincial Park

Fairmont Mountain 2620m

rcrown ntain 3m

Mount Abel

Creek

COLUMBIA LAKE RD.

Columbia Lake

UU

63

Purcell Wilderness Conservancy Park

Dutch Creek

Marion Creek

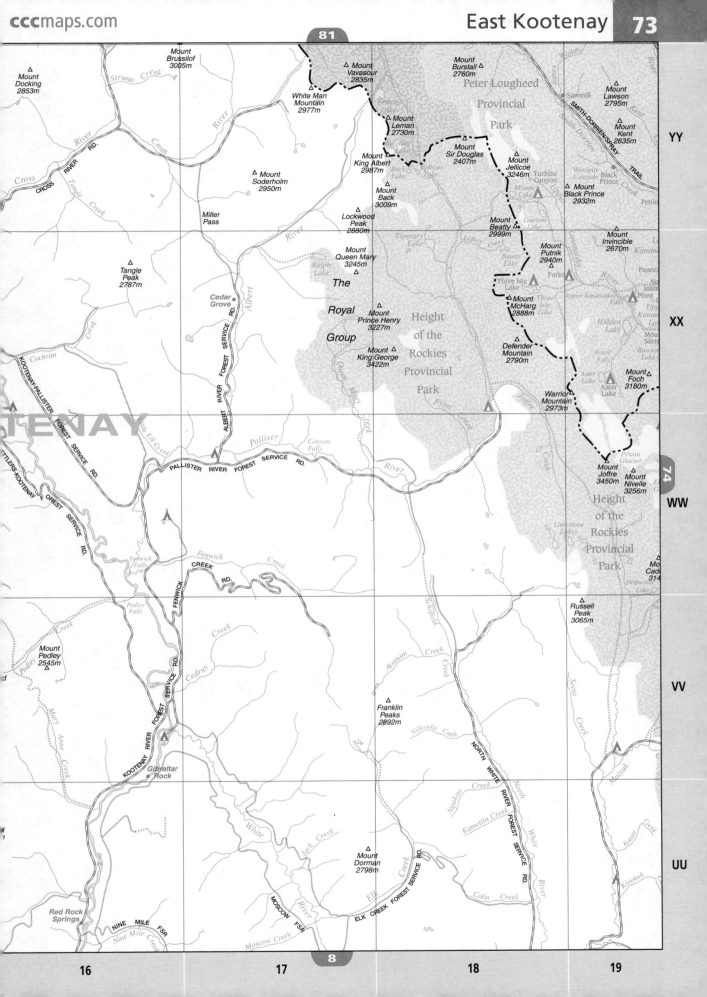

Mount Docking 2853m

Mount Brussilof 3005m

White Man Mountain 2977m

Mount Vavasour 2835m

Mount Burstall 2760m

Peter Lougheed Provincial Park

Mount Lawson 2795m

Mount Kent 2635m

YY

Mount Leman 2730m

Mount Soderholm 2950m

Mount King Albert 2987m

Mount Sir Douglas 2407m

Mount Jellicoe 3246m

Turbine Canyon

Mount Black Prince 2932m

Warspite Cascade

Black Prince

Cross River

CROSS RIVER RD.

Tangle Creek

Miller Pass

Mount Back 3009m

Lockwood Peak 2880m

Mount Queen Mary 3245m

Ralph Lake

Mount Beatty 2999m

Tiperary Lake

LeRoy Creek

Beatty Lake

Lawson Lake

Mount Putnik 2940m

Mount Invincible 2670m

XX

Tangle Peak 2787m

Cedar Grove

The Royal Group

Mount Prince Henry 3227m

Three Isle Lake

Mount McHarg 2888m

Forks

Upper Kananaskis Falls

Point

Hidden Lake

Mount Sarra

Cochran Creek

ALBERT RIVER FOREST SERVICE RD.

Mount King George 3422m

Queen Mary Creek

Height of the Rockies Provincial Park

Defender Mountain 2790m

Aster Lake

Aster Lake

Mount Foch 3180m

KOOTENAY-PALLISER FOREST SERVICE RD.

TENAY

Little Elk Creek

Palliser River

Canyon Falls

Fynn Creek

Warrior Mountain 2973m

Jolifee Creek

Pétain Glacier

74

TTLERS-KOOTENAY FOREST SERVICE RD.

PALLISTER RIVER FOREST SERVICE RD.

Palliser River

Mount Joffre 3450m

Mount Nivelle 3256m

WW

Height of the Rockies Provincial Park

Fenwick Falls

Fenwick Creek

FENWICK CREEK RD.

Fenwick Creek

Cedrus Creek

Limestone Lakes

Mo Cad 314

Driftwood Lake

Pedley Falls

Mount Pedley 2545m

Pedley Creek

KOOTENAY RIVER FOREST SERVICE RD.

Creek

Russell Peak 3065m

VV

Mary Anne Creek

Gibraltar Rock

Franklin Peaks 2892m

Akamam Creek

Scholfield Creek

Seela Creek

Nilksuka Creek

NORTH WHITE RIVER FOREST SERVICE RD.

Majuuk Creek

UU

Red Rock Springs

NINE MILE FSR

MOSCOW FSR

White River

Jack Creek

Elk Creek

ELK CREEK FOREST SERVICE RD.

Mount Dorman 2798m

Napkoo Creek

Kametlin Creek

North White River

Colin Creek

Keaus Creek

Klookuh Creek

Nine Mile Creek

Moscow Creek

16   17   18   19

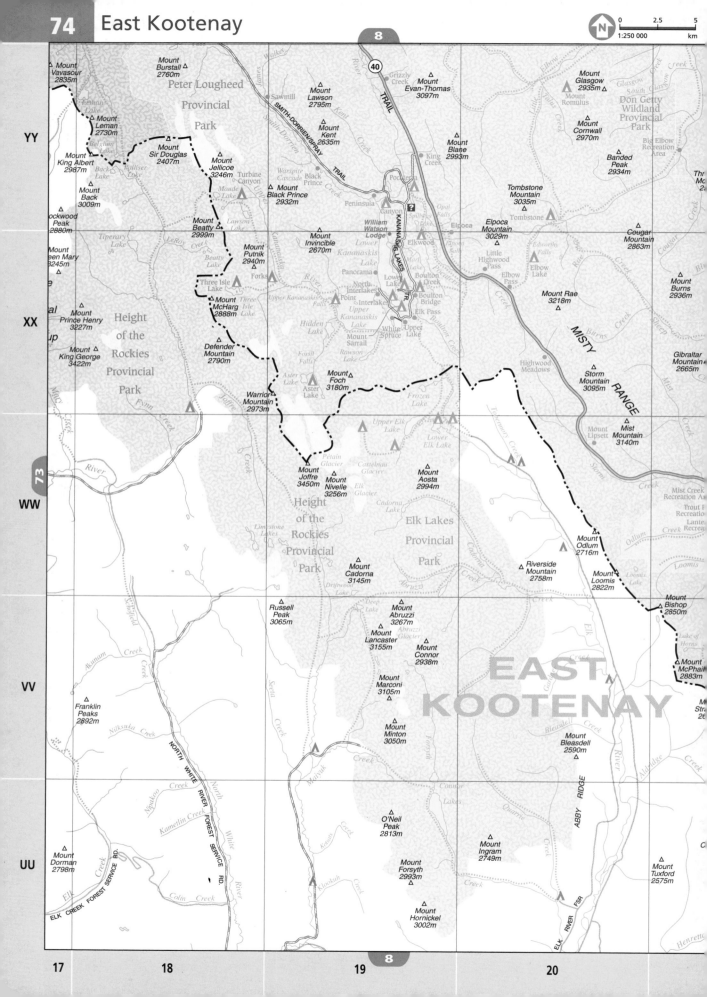

N 1:250 000
0   2.5   5
km

8

Mount Vavasour 2835m
Mount Burstall 2760m
Peter Lougheed Provincial Park
Mount Lawson 2795m
Grizzly Creek
Mount Evan-Thomas 3097m
Mount Glasgow 2935m
Mount Romulus
Glasgow South
Don Getty Wildland Provincial Park

Mount Leman 2730m
Behnan Lake
Sawmill
Mount Kent 2635m
King Creek
Mount Cornwall 2970m
Big Elbow Recreation Area

YY

Mount King Albert 2987m
Mount Sir Douglas 2407m
Mount Jellicoe 3246m
Turbine Canyon
Warspite Cascade
Black Prince
Pocaterra
Mount Blane 2993m
King Creek
Banded Peak 2934m
Thr Mo 2

Mount Back 3009m
Maude Lake
Mount Black Prince 2932m
Peninsula
William Watson Lodge
Spillway
Tombstone Mountain 3035m
Elpoca
Tombstone

ockwood Peak 2880m
Mount Beatty 2999m
Lawson Lake
Mount Invincible 2670m
Elkwood
Mount Putnik 2940m
Lower Kananaskis Lake
Panorama
Elpoca Mountain 3029m
Little Highwood Pass
Elbow Pass
Elbow Lake
Cougar Mountain 2863m

een Mary 3245m
Tiperary Lake
LeRoy Creek
Beatty Lake
Three Isle Lake
Forks
North Interlakes Point
Boulton Creek
Boulton Bridge
Mount Rae 3218m
Mount Burns 2936m

XX

Mount Prince Henry 3227m
Height of the Rockies Provincial Park
Mount McHarg 2888m
Three Isle Lake
Upper Kananaskis Falls
Interlakes
Upper Kananaskis Lake
White Spruce
Upper Lake
Elk Pass
MISTY

Mount King George 3422m
Defender Mountain 2790m
Hidden Lake
Mount Sarrail
Rawson Lake
Fossil Falls
Highwood Meadows
Storm Mountain 3095m
Gibraltar Mountain 2665m

Fynn Creek
Warrior Mountain 2973m
Aster Lake
Aster Lake
Mount Foch 3180m
Frozen Lake
RANGE
Burns

73

River
Joffre Creek
Petain Glacier
Upper Elk Lake
Lower Elk Lake
Mount Lipsett
Mist Mountain 3140m

WW

Mount Joffre 3450m
Mount Nivelle 3256m
Castelnau Glacier
Elk Glacier
Mount Aosta 2994m
Tokumm Creek
Mount Odlum 2716m
Mist Creek Recreation Ar
Trout Recreation
Lante Recrea

Height of the Rockies Provincial Park
Limestone Lakes
Cadorna Lake
Elk Lakes Provincial Park
Storm Creek

Schofield Creek
Mount Cadorna 3145m
Driftwood Lake
Riverside Mountain 2758m
Mount Loomis 2822m
Loomis
Loomis Lake

Russell Peak 3065m
Deep Lake
Mount Abruzzi 3267m
Mount Bishop 2850m

VV

Akanam Creek
North White River Forest Service Rd.
Niliksuka Creek
Franklin Peaks 2892m
Seeta Creek
Mount Lancaster 3155m
Abruzzi Glacier
Mount Connor 2938m
EAST
Lake of Horns
Mount McPhail 2883m

Mount Marconi 3105m
KOOTENAY
Mr Stra 26

Kametlin Creek
North White River Forest Service Rd.
Marnuk Creek
Mount Minton 3050m
Fossyll Creek
Mount Bleasdell 2590m
Abby Ridge

Nyakon Creek
Keasu Creek
Connor Lakes

UU

Mount Dorman 2798m
Elk Creek Forest Service Rd.
Colin Creek
O'Neil Peak 2813m
Mount Ingram 2749m
Quarrie Creek
Mount Tuxford 2575m

Mount Forsyth 2993m
Elk River FSR
Klookuh Creek
Aldridge

Mount Hornickel 3002m
Henrette

17   18   19   20

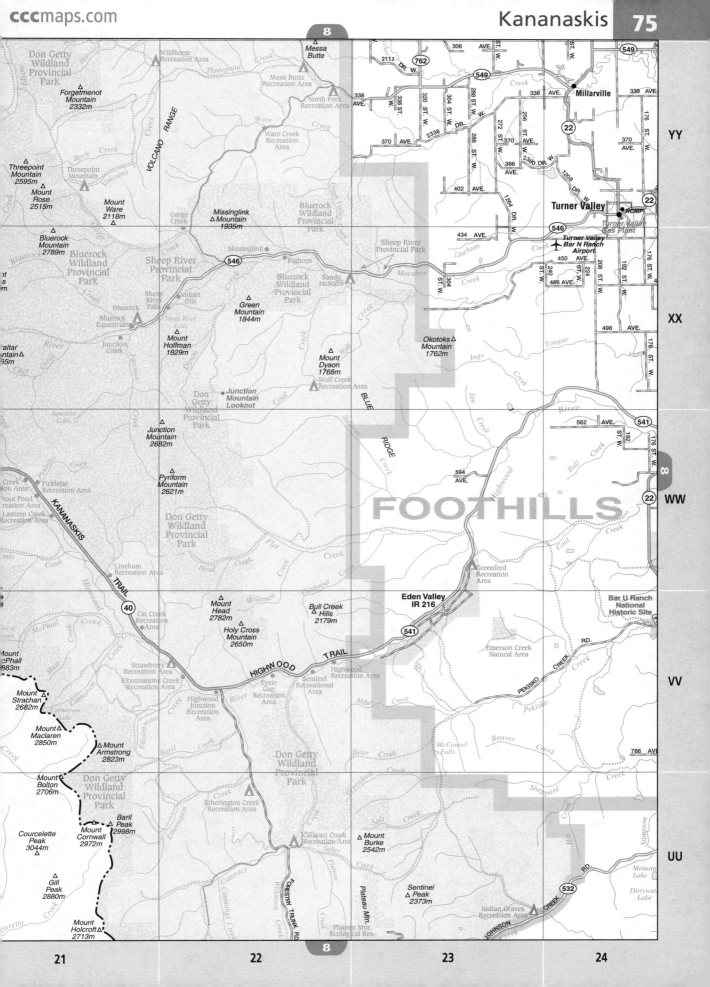

Don Getty
Wildland
Provincial
Park

Wildhorse
Recreation Area

Messa
Butte

Mesa Butte
Recreation Area

North Fork
Recreation Area

Forgetmenot
Mountain
2332m

VOLCANO RANGE

Ware Creek
Recreation
Area

Bluerock
Wildland
Provincial
Park

306 AVE.
2111
DR. W.
762
549
549
Creek
Millarville
338 AVE.
336 ST. W.
320 ST. W.
304 ST. W.
288 ST. W.
272 ST. W.
256 ST. W.
338 AVE.
338 AVE.
176 ST. W.
22
370 AVE.
2338 DR.
288 ST. W.
370 ST. W.
370 AVE.
370 AVE.
386 AVE.
2360 DR. W.
1208 DR. W.
402 AVE.
1264 DR. W.
Turner Valley
22
RCMP
Turner Valley
Gas Plant

Threepoint
Mountain
2595m

Threepoint
Mountain

Mount
Rose
2515m

Mount
Ware
2118m

Gorge
Creek

Missinglink
Mountain
1935m

Missinglink

546

Bighorn

Sheep River
Provincial Park

Turner Valley
Bar N Ranch
Airport
434 AVE.
450 AVE.
304 ST. W.
240 ST. W.
466 AVE.
224 ST. W.
208 ST. W.
192 ST. W.
176 ST. W.

Bluerock
Mountain
2789m

Bluerock
Wildland
Provincial
Park

Sheep
River
Falls

Indian
Oils

Green
Mountain
1844m

Bluerock
Wildland
Provincial
Park

Sandy
McNabb

Sheep River
Provincial
Park

498 AVE.

Bluerock
Equestrian

Bluerock

Mount
Hoffman
1829m

Sheep River
Falls

Junction
Creek

Mount
Dyson
1768m

Wolf Creek
Recreation Area

Okotoks
Mountain
1762m

Tongue
Creek

Junction
Lake

Don Getty
Wildland
Provincial
Park

Junction
Mountain
Lookout

BLUE

RIDGE

562 AVE.
192 ST. W.
541
176 ST. W.
8
22
WW

Junction
Mountain
2682m

Pyriform
Mountain
2621m

594
AVE.

FOOTHILLS

KANANASKIS

Picklejar
Recreation Area

Trout Pond
Recreation Area

Lantern Creek
Recreation Area

TRAIL

Lineham
Recreation Area

Greenford
Recreation
Area

Bar U Ranch
National
Historic Site

40

Cat Creek
Recreation
Area

Mount
Head
2782m

Holy Cross
Mountain
2650m

Bull Creek
Hills
2179m

Sentinel
Recreational
Area

Eden Valley
IR 216

541

Highwood
Recreation
Area

Emerson Creek
Natural Area

PEKISKO CREEK RD.

Mount
McPhail
2883m

Mount
Strachan
2682m

Strawberry
Recreation Area

Fitzsimmons Creek
Recreation Area

HIGHWOOD

Highwood
Junction
Recreation
Area

Eyrie
Gap
Recreation
Area

TRAIL

McConnel
Falls

Pekisko

786 AVE.
VV

Mount
Maclaren
2850m

Mount
Armstrong
2823m

Don Getty
Wildland
Provincial
Park

Mount
Bolton
2706m

Don Getty
Wildland
Provincial
Park

Etherington Creek
Recreation Area

Courcelette
Peak
3044m

Baril
Peak
2998m

Mount
Cornwall
2972m

Cataract Creek
Recreation Area

Mount
Burke
2542m

Indian Graves
Recreation Area

UU

Gill
Peak
2880m

FORESTRY TRUNK RD.

Plateau Mtn.
Ecological Res.

Sentinel
Peak
2373m

532

JOHNSON CREEK

Meinsin
Lake

Dirtywater
Lake

Mount
Holcroft
2713m

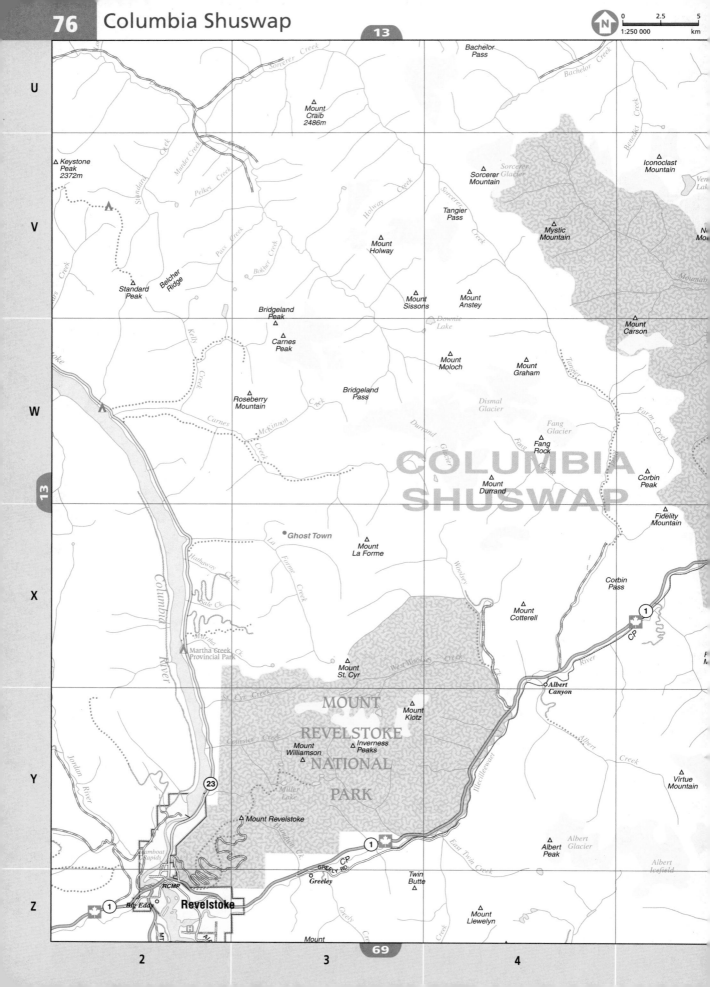

1:250 000

U

V

W

X

Y

Z

2   **3**   **4**

13

Bachelor
Pass

△ Mount
Craib
2486m

△ Keystone
Peak
2372m

Sorcerer
Glacier

△ Iconoclast
Mountain

△ Sorcerer
Mountain

Tangier
Pass

△ Mystic
Mountain

△ Standard
Peak

Belcher
Ridge

△ Mount
Holway

△ Bridgeland
Peak

△ Carnes
Peak

△ Mount
Sissons

△ Mount
Anstey

Downie
Lake

△ Mount
Carson

△ Roseberry
Mountain

Bridgeland
Pass

△ Mount
Moloch

△ Mount
Graham

Dismal
Glacier

COLUMBIA
SHUSWAP

Fang
Glacier

△ Fang
Rock

△ Corbin
Peak

△ Mount
Durrand

△ Fidelity
Mountain

• Ghost Town

△ Mount
La Forme

Corbin
Pass

Columbia
River

Martha Creek
Provincial Park

△ Mount
Cotterell

Albert
Canyon ○

1

CP

△ Mount
St. Cyr

MOUNT

△ Mount
Klotz

REVELSTOKE

△ Mount
Williamson

Inverness
Peaks

NATIONAL

△ Virtue
Mountain

PARK

Miller
Lake

Jordan
River

23

△ Mount Revelstoke

1

△ Albert
Peak

Albert
Glacier

Steamboat
Rapids

GREELY RD

CP

Albert
Icefield

RCMP

Greeley ○

Twin
Butte

1

Big Eddy

Revelstoke

△ Mount
Llewelyn

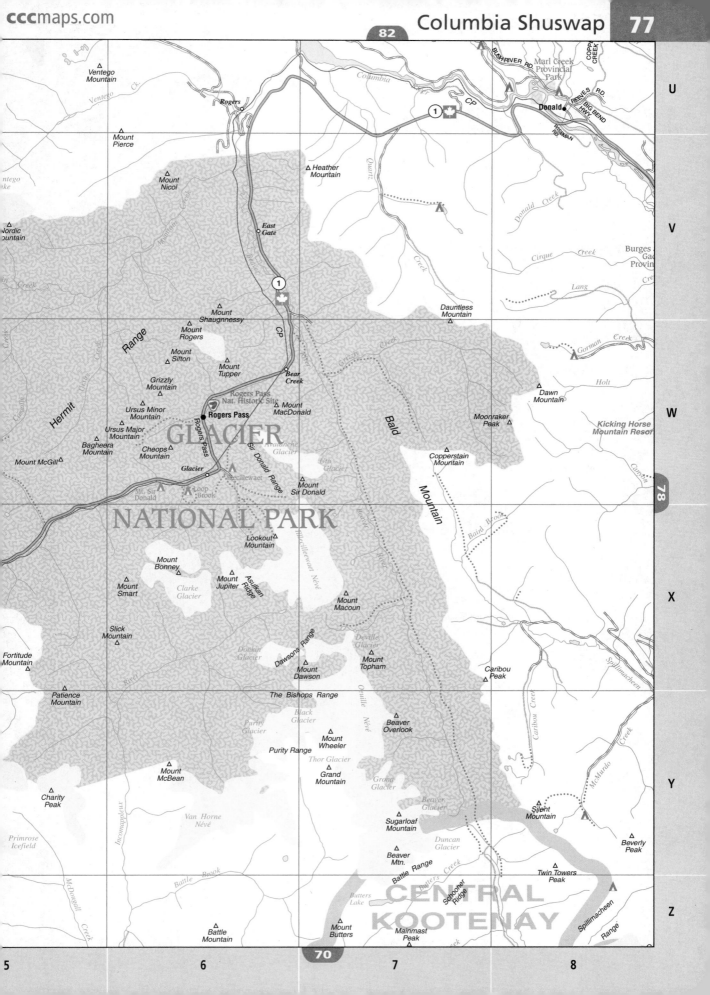

U

V

W

X

Y

Z

5   6   70   7   8

BUSH RIVER RD.
Marl Creek
Provincial
Park
COPPER CREEK
REEVES RD.
Columbia
CP
Donald
BIG BEND HWY.
WISEMAN RD.
Quartz
Ventego Mountain
Ck.
Ventego
Rogers
Mount Pierce
Mount Nicol
Heather Mountain
Creek
Donald Creek
Cirque Creek
Burges Ga Provin
Lang
Creek
Holt
East Gate
Nordic ountain
Creek
Bridge Creek
Mount Shaugnnessy
Mount Rogers
Range
Mount Silton
Mount Tupper
CP
Bear Creek
Creek
Dauntless Mountain
Gorman Creek
Dawn Mountain
Grizzly Mountain
Ursus Minor Mountain
Rogers Pass Nat. Historic Site
Rogers Pass
Mount MacDonald
Moonraker Peak
Kicking Horse Mountain Resor
Hermit
Ursus Major Mountain
Bagheera Mountain
Cheops Mountain
GLACIER
Rogers Pass
Sir Donald Range
Avalanche Glacier
Illecillewaet Glacier
Bald
Copperstain Mountain
Mount McGill
Glacier
Illecillewaet
Mount Sir Donald
Mountain
Mt. Sir Donald
Loop Brook
Baird Brook
NATIONAL PARK
Lookout Mountain
Illecillewaet Névé
Beaver River
Canyon
Spillimacheen
Mount Bonney
Mount Jupiter
Asulkan Ridge
Mount Macoun
Mount Smart
Clarke Glacier
Deville Glacier
Mount Topham
Caribou Peak
Slick Mountain
Dawsons Range
Donkin Glacier
Dawsons Range
Mount Dawson
Fortitude Mountain
River
The Bishops Range
Oraille Névé
Caribou Creek
McMurdo
Patience Mountain
Purity Glacier
Black Glacier
Beaver Overlook
Purity Range
Mount Wheeler
Thor Glacier
Grand Mountain
Grand Glacier
Beaver Glacier
Silent Mountain
Mount McBean
Charity Peak
Incomappleux River
Van Horne Névé
Sugarloaf Mountain
Duncan Glacier
Beverly Peak
Primrose Icefield
Beaver Mtn.
Battle Range
Butters Creek
Twin Towers Peak
Spillimacheen Range
McDougall Creek
Battle Brook
Butters Lake
CENTRAL
Schooner Ridge
Battle Mountain
Mount Butters
Mainmast Peak
KOOTENAY

78
70

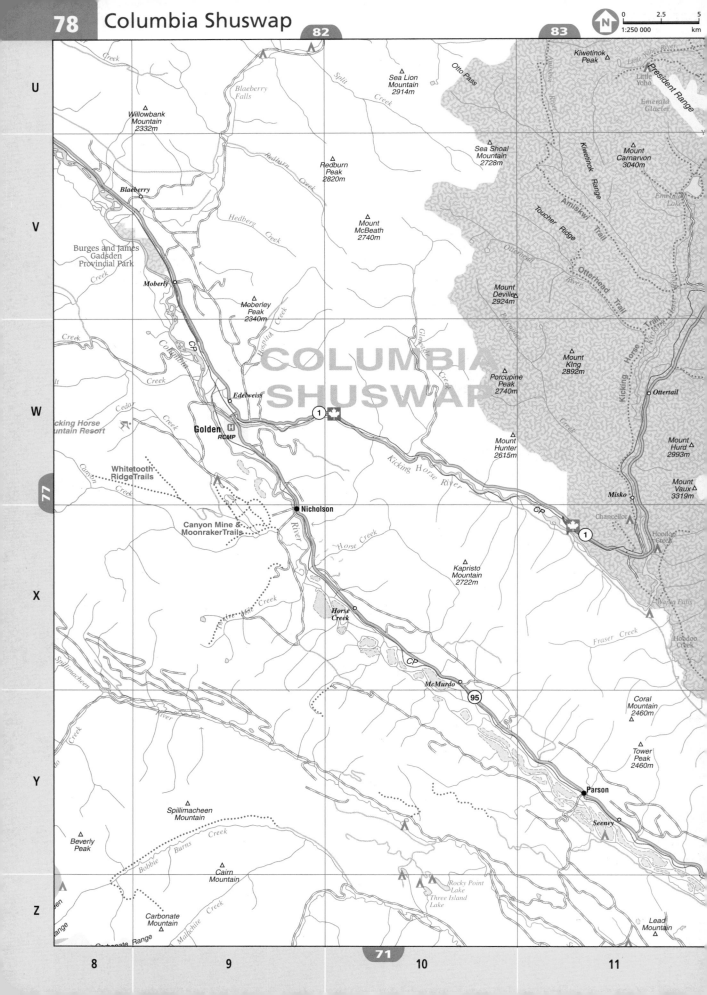

1:250 000

82
83

U

Willowbank
Mountain
2332m

Creek

Split
Creek

Sea Lion
Mountain
2914m

Otto Pass

Kiwetinok
Peak

Little Yoho

President Range

Blaeberry
Falls

Redburn
Peak
2820m

Kiwetinok Range

Mount
Carnarvon
3040m

Emerald
Glacier

Blaeberry

Hedberg Creek

Redburn Creek

Sea Shoal
Mountain
2728m

Amiskwi River

Amiskwi Trail

Emerald
Lake

V

Burges and James
Gadsden
Provincial Park

Moberly

Mount
McBeath
2740m

Toucher Ridge

Mount
Deville
2924m

Otterhead River

Otterhead Trail

Moberley
Peak
2340m

Hospital Creek

COLUMBIA

Glenogle Creek

Porcupine Creek

Porcupine
Peak
2740m

Mount
King
2892m

Kicking Horse Trail

Ottertail

W

Columbia River

Edelweiss

SHUSWAP

Mount
Hunter
2615m

Mount
Hurd
2993m

Golden
RCMP

Kicking Horse Mountain Resort

Whitetooth
Ridge Trails

Kicking Horse River

Misko

Mount
Vaux
3319m

77

Nicholson

CP

Chancellor

Hoodoo
Creek

Canyon Mine &
Moonraker Trails

Horse Creek

Kapristo
Mountain
2722m

Wapta Falls

X

Columbia River

Thirtreenine Creek

Horse
Creek

Fraser Creek

Hoodoo
Creek

CP

McMurdo

95

Coral
Mountain
2460m

Y

Spillimacheen River

Spillimacheen
Mountain

Burns Creek

Parson

Tower
Peak
2460m

Seeney

Beverly
Peak

Bobbie Burns Creek

Cairn
Mountain

Rocky Point
Lake

Three Island
Lake

Z

Carbonate
Mountain

Mollchite Creek

Carbonate Range

Lead
Mountain

71

8
9
10
11

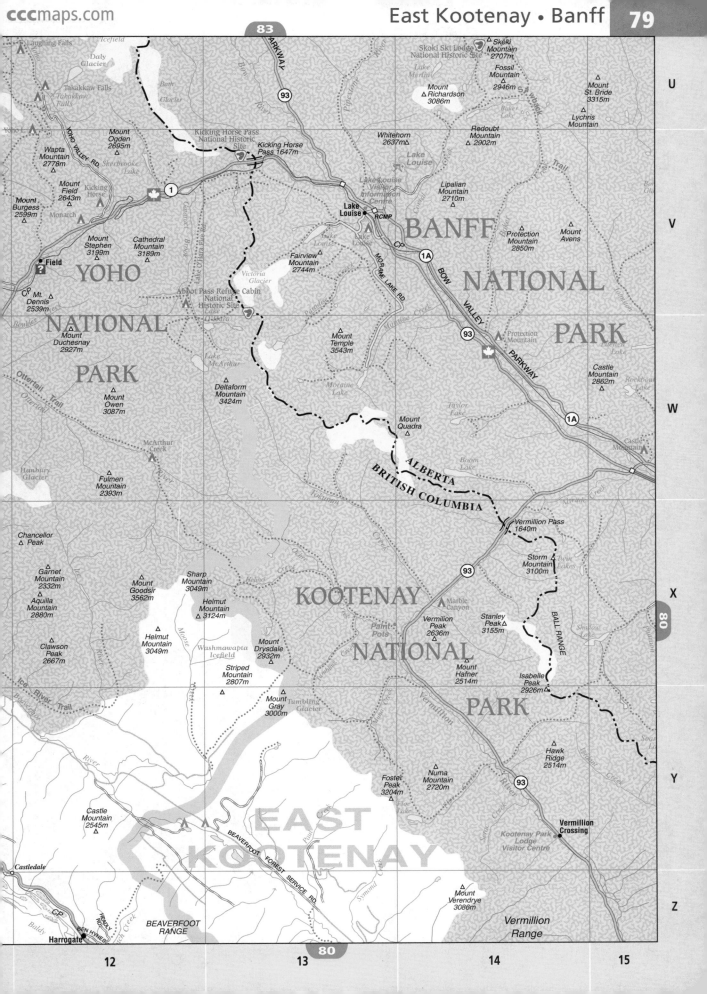

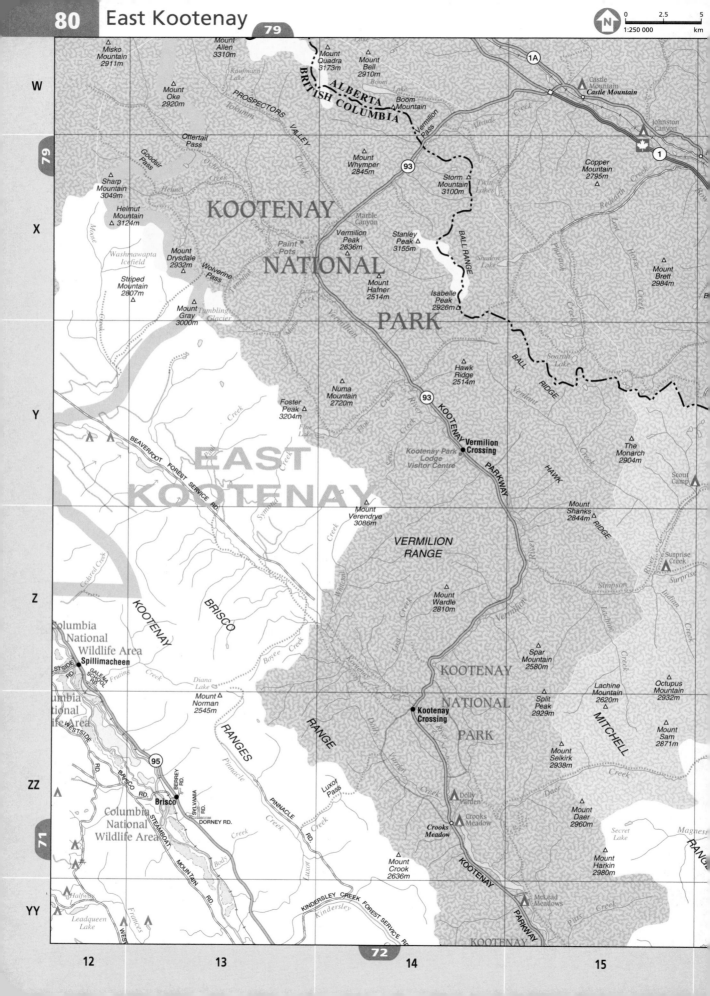

N

1:250 000

0   2.5   5
km

W

X

Y

Z

ZZ

YY

79

71

Misko
Mountain
2911m

Mount
Allen
3310m

Mount
Quadra
3173m

Mount
Bell
2910m

1A

Castle
Mountain
Castle Mountain

Mount
Oke
2920m

PROSPECTORS

BRITISH COLUMBIA

ALBERTA

Boom
Mountain

Vermilion Pass

Johnston
Canyon

1

Ottertail
Pass

VALLEY

Mount
Whymper
2845m

93

Storm
Mountain
3100m

Copper
Mountain
2795m

Goodsir
Pass

Tokumm

Orient

Helmet

Twin
Lakes

Sharp
Mountain
3049m

Helmut
Mountain
3124m

KOOTENAY

Marble
Canyon

Vermilion
Peak
2636m

Stanley
Peak
3155m

BALL RANGE

Shadow
Lake

Mount
Brett
2984m

Washmawapta
Icefield

Mount
Drysdale
2932m

Paint
Pots

NATIONAL

Mount
Hafner
2514m

Isabelle
Peak
2926m

Pharaoh

Striped
Mountain
2807m

Wolverine
Pass

Mount
Gray
3000m

Tumbling
Glacier

PARK

Hawk
Ridge
2514m

BALL

Soaruh
Lake

RIDGE

Moose

Numa
Mountain
2720m

93

Verdant

Scout
Camp

Foster
Peak
3204m

Floe
Lake

Floe

KOOTENAY

Hawk
Ridge
2514m

Vermilion
Crossing

The
Monarch
2904m

EAST

Dainard

Creek

Symond

Vermilion

River

Kootenay Park
Lodge
Visitor Centre

PARKWAY

HAWK

Surprise
Creek

KOOTENAY

Mount
Verendrye
3086m

VERMILION
RANGE

Mount
Shanks
2844m

RIDGE

Simpson

Indian

Surprise

Columbia
National
Wildlife Area

KOOTENAY

BRISCO

Cedared Creek

Boyce

Mount
Wardle
2810m

Vermilion

Spar
Mountain
2580m

Spillimacheen

GALENA
SCHOOL
RD

Fruting

Diana
Lake

KOOTENAY

Daer

Lachine
Mountain
2620m

Octopus
Mountain
2932m

Columbia
National
Wildlife Area

WESTSIDE

Mount
Norman
2545m

RANGES

RANGE

Kootenay
Crossing

NATIONAL

Split
Peak
2929m

MITCHELL

Mount
Sam
2871m

95

BERREY
RD

Pinnacle

PARK

Mount
Selkirk
2938m

Brisco

BRISCO
RD

SYLVANIA
RD

PINNACLE

Luxor
Pass

Dolly
Varden

Crooks
Meadow

Mount
Daer
2960m

Secret
Lake

Magnest

STEAMBOAT

DORNEY RD.

RD

Crooks
Meadow

Columbia
National
Wildlife Area

MOUNTAIN

Luxor

Creek

Bobs

Mount
Crook
2636m

KOOTENAY

Mount
Harkin
2980m

RANGE

Halfway
Lake

KINDERSLEY CREEK FOREST SERVICE RD

Kindersley

McKead
Meadows

Pitts

Leadqueen
Lake

Frances

WEST

YY

PARKWAY

KOOTENAY

72

12   13   14   15

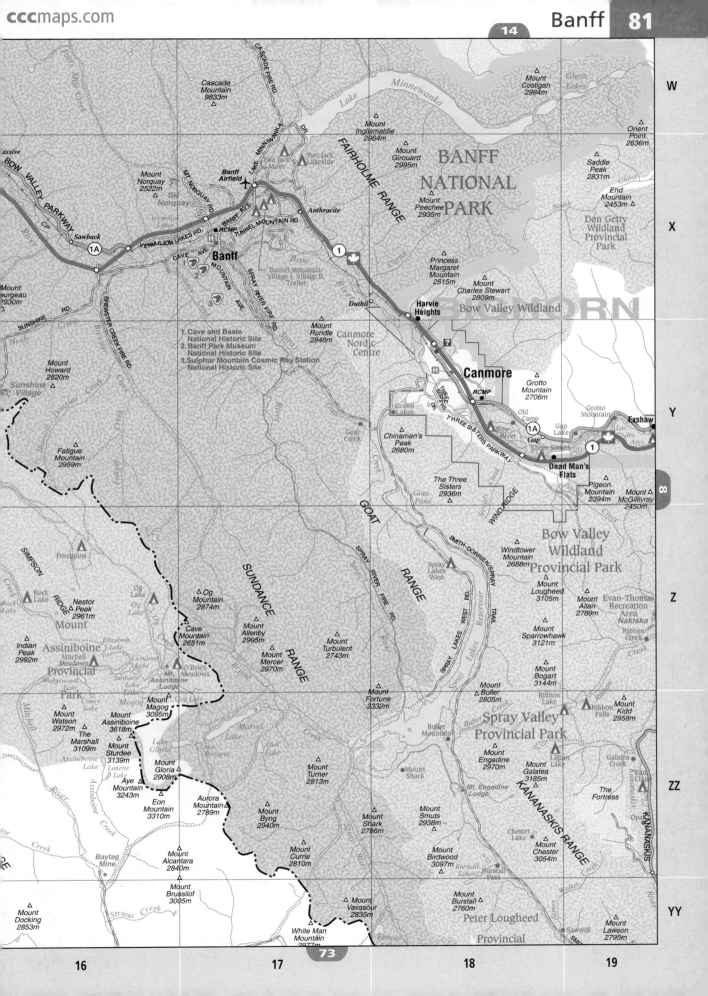

73

W

X

Y

Z

ZZ

YY

8

16   17   18   19

Bow Valley Parkway

Mount Norquay 2522m
Ski Norquay

Cascade Mountain 9833m

Mount Inglismaldie 2964m

Mount Girouard 2995m

Mount Costigan 2984m

Ghost Lakes

Orient Point 2636m

BANFF NATIONAL PARK

Saddle Peak 2831m

End Mountain 2453m

Don Getty Wildland Provincial Park

Mount Peechee 2935m

FAIRHOLME RANGE

Lake Minnewanka

Two Jack Main
Two Jack Lakeside

Banff Airfield
Anthracite

RCMP

Banff

Mount Bourgeau 2930m

Sawback

1A

Sunshine Rd.

Brewster Creek Fire Rd.

Spray River Fire Rd.

Cave Ave.
Mountain Ave.
Banff Ave.

Tunnel Mountain Rd.

Tunnel Mountain-Village I, Village II, Trailer

Bow River

Duthil

Harvie Heights

Princess Margaret Mountain 2515m

Mount Charles Stewart 2809m

Bow Valley Wildland

Mount Rundle 2846m

Canmore Nordic Centre

Canmore

RCMP

Grotto Mountain 2706m

Grotto Mountain

Exshaw

Lac des Arcs

1. Cave and Basin National Historic Site
2. Banff Park Museum National Historic Site
3. Sulphur Mountain Cosmic Ray Station National Historic Site

Mount Howard 2820m

Sunshine Village

Healy Creek

Fatigue Mountain 2959m

Grassi Lakes

Three Sisters Dr.

Chinaman's Peak 2680m

Goat Creek

Old Camp

Bow River

Gap

Gap Lake

Three Sisters

Dead Man's Flats

Pigeon Mountain 2394m

Mount McGillivray 2450m

The Three Sisters 2936m

Bow Valley Wildland Provincial Park

Windtower Mountain 2688m

Mount Lougheed 3105m

Mount Allan 2789m

Evan-Thomas Recreation Area Nakiska

SIMPSON RIDGE

Porcupine

Og Lake

Og Mountain 2874m

SUNDANCE RANGE

GOAT RANGE

SPRAY LAKES WEST RD.

Spray Lakes Reservoir

SMITH-DORRIEN/SPRAY TRAIL

Mount Sparrowhawk 3121m

Ribbon Creek

Z

Rock Lake
Rock Lake

Nestor Peak 2961m

Og Lake

Cave Mountain 2651m

Mount Allenby 2995m

Mount Mercer 2970m

Mount Turbulent 2743m

Mount Bogart 3144m

Mount Assiniboine

Indian Peak 2992m

Provincial

Mitchell Meadows
Elizabeth Lake

Cerulean Lake

Sunburst Lake
Mt. Assiniboine Lodge

O'Brien Meadows

Bryant Creek

Mount Fortune 2332m

Mount Buller 2805m

Ribbon Lake

Ribbon Falls

Mount Kidd 2958m

Park

Wedgewood Lake

Coney Lake

Magog

Mount Magog 3095m

Og Lake
Gog Lake

Butler Mountain

Spray Valley Provincial Park

Mount Watson 2972m

The Marshall 3109m

Mount Assiniboine 3618m

Mount Sturdee 3139m

Marvel Lake

Lake Gloria

Owl Lake

Lake Terrapin

Mitchell River

Assiniboine Lake

Lunette Lake

Mount Gloria 2908m

Aye Mountain 3243m

Eon Mountain 3310m

Aurora Mountain 2789m

Mount Byng 2940m

Mount Turner 2813m

Mount Shark

Mount Engadine 2970m

Mt. Engadine Lodge

Mount Galatea 3185m

Lillian Lake

Galatea Creek

The Fortress

KANANASKIS RANGE

ZZ

Assiniboine Creek

Baytag Mine

Mount Alcantara 2840m

Mount Currie 2810m

Mount Shark 2786m

Mount Smuts 2938m

Chester Lake

Mount Chester 3054m

Kananaskis

Mount Docking 2853m

Mount Brussilof 3005m

Struna Creek

White Man Mountain 2977m

Mount Vavasour 2835m

Mount Burstall 2760m

Mount Birdwood 3097m

Burstall Lakes
Burstall Pass

Peter Lougheed Provincial

Sawmill

Mount Lawson 2795m

YY

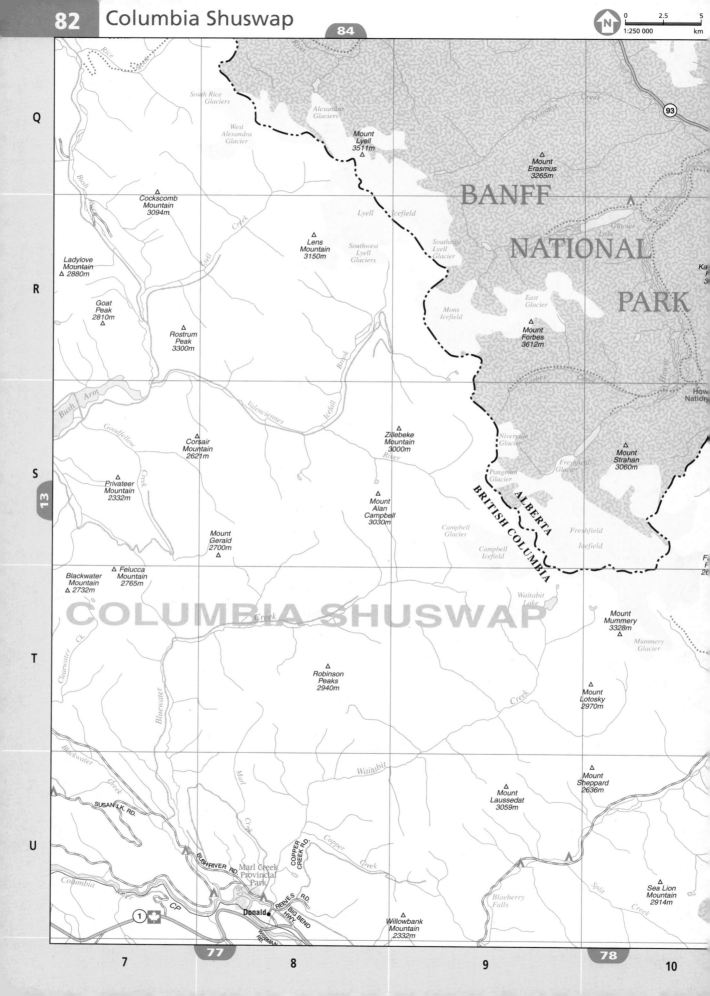

1:250 000

N

0 2.5 5
km

Q

R

S

T

U

BANFF

NATIONAL

PARK

COLUMBIA SHUSWAP

South Rice Glaciers

West Alexandra Glacier

Alexandra Glaciers

△ Mount Lyell 3511m

Lyell Icefield

Southwest Lyell Glaciers

Southeast Lyell Glacier

△ Mount Erasmus 3265m

△

Glacier Lake

Mons Icefield

East Glacier

△ Mount Forbes 3612m

Ka

Howse River

Forbes Creek

Howse Nation

Niverville Glacier

Freshfield Glacier

△ Mount Strahan 3060m

Pangman Glacier

Campbell Glacier

Freshfield Icefield

F P

Campbell Icefield

ALBERTA
BRITISH COLUMBIA

△ Cockscomb Mountain 3094m

△ Lens Mountain 3150m

Ladylove Mountain △ 2880m

△ Goat Peak 2810m

△ Rostrum Peak 3300m

Bush Arm

Goodfellow Creek

△ Corsair Mountain 2621m

△ Privateer Mountain 2332m

△ Mount Gerald 2700m

Blackwater Mountain △ 2732m

△ Felucca Mountain 2765m

Valenciennes

River

Icefall Brook

Iceball

△ Zillebeke Mountain 3000m

△ Mount Alan Campbell 3030m

Waitabit Lake

△ Mount Mummery 3328m

Mummery Glacier

Creek

△ Robinson Peaks 2940m

△ Mount Lotosky 2970m

Clearwater Ck.

Bluewater

Blackwater

Creek

Waitabit

Mari Creek

Mount Laussedat 3059m △

△ Mount Sheppard 2636m

Creek

Split

Creek

SUSAN LK. RD.

BUSH RIVER RD.

Marl Creek Provincial Park

COPPER CREEK RD.

Copper Creek

RENIE'S RD.

BIG BEND HWY

Columbia

CP

Donald ●

1

WISEMAN

77

Willowbank Mountain 2332m △

Blaeberry Falls

Sea Lion Mountain 2914m △

78

84

93

13

7   77   8   9   78   10

Q

R

S

14

T

U

DAVID THOMPSON HIGHWAY
Thompson Creek
Recreation Area

11

Saskatchewan
River Crossing

Falls

Siffleur

Creek

Whiterabbit Creek

CLEARWATER

Kaufmann
Peaks
3094m

93

Caxona Creek

Spreading Creek

Porcupine Creek

Mount
Loudon
3221m

River

Escarpment

River

Ram River

Siffleur

Wilderness

Area

Ram River
Glacier

Mount
Chephren
3266m

Waterfowl
Lake

Waterfowl
Lakes

Chephren Lake

Howse
Peak
3290m

Howse Pass
National Historic
Site

Breaker
Mountain
3058m

Mistaya Lake

Silverhorn Creek

ICEFIELDS PARKWAY

River

Mistaya River

Siffleur River

Mount
Patterson
3197m

Peyto
Lake

BANFF

Mount
Harris
3299m

Mount
Willingdon
3373m

Devon
Lakes

Fisher
Peak
2621m

Wildcat Creek

Caldron
Lake

Bow Pass
2068m

NATIONAL

Pipestone River

Baker
Glacier

Mount
Baker
3172m

Peyto
Glacier

Bow
Lake

PARK

Mosquito Creek

Molar
Glacier

Collie Creek

Stick

ALBERTA

BRITISH COLUMBIA

Wapta
Icefield

Crowfoot
Glacier

Bow Peak
2868m

Mosquito
Creek

Molar Creek

Yoho
Glacier

YOHO

Glacier
des
Poilus

Hector
Lake

Hector
Glacier

Mount
Hector
3394m

NATIONAL

Diableret
Glacier

Mount
Balfour
3272m

Waputik

ICEFIELDS PARKWAY

Blaeberry River

Otto Pass

PARK

Twin Falls Tea House
Nat. Historic Site

Twin Falls

Waputik
Icefield

Bow River

Kiwetinok
Peak

Little Yoho River

Laughing Falls

Daly Glacier

Pipestone River

President Range

Little
Yoho

Takakkaw Falls
Takakkaw
Falls

Bath
Glacier

Emerald
Glacier

Yoho L.

Mount

Kicking Horse Pass

93

White

78

11

12

79

13

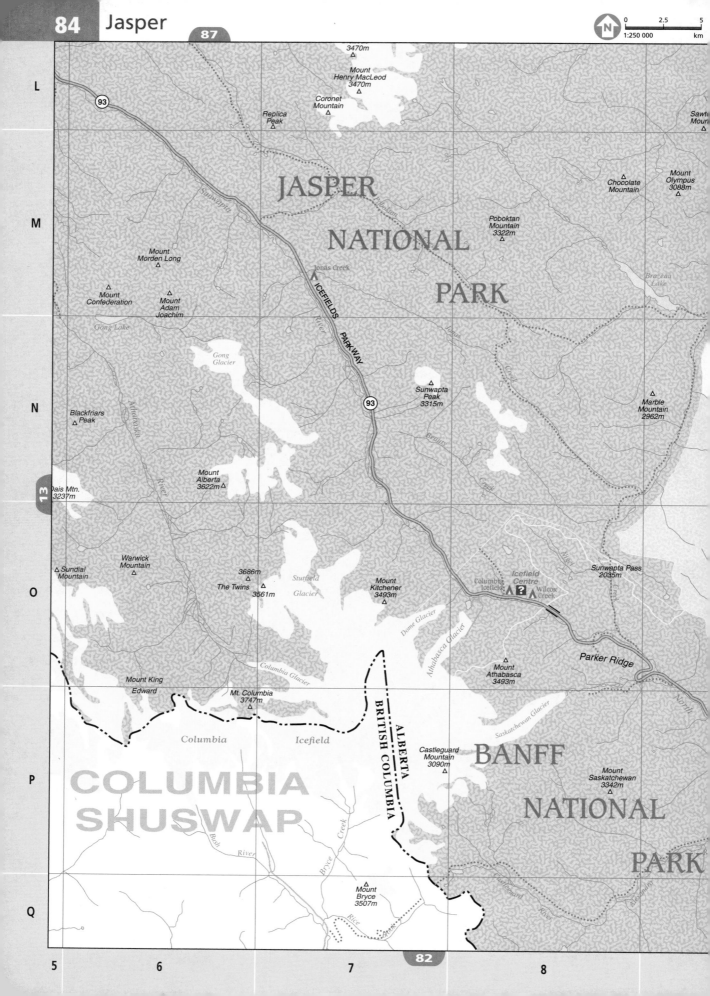

1:250 000

0   2.5   5
km

L

M

N

13

O

P

Q

93

Replica
Peak
△

3470m
△

Mount
Henry MacLeod
3470m
△

Coronet
Mountain
△

Sawte
Moun

JASPER

Chocolate
Mountain
△

Mount
Olympus
3088m
△

Poboktan
Mountain
3322m
△

NATIONAL

Mount
Morden Long
△

Jonas Creek

Brazeau
Lake

PARK

Mount
Confederation
△

Mount
Adam
Joachim
△

Gong Lake

Gong
Glacier

ICEFIELDS PARKWAY

River

Jonas

Blackfriars
Peak
△

Sunwapta
Peak
3315m
△

Marble
Mountain
2962m
△

93

Dais Mtn.
3237m
△

Athabasca

Mount
Alberta
3622m △

Beauty

Creek

River

Warwick
Mountain
△

3686m
△

Stutfield
Glacier

Sundial
Mountain
△

The Twins
3561m
△

Mount
Kitchener
3493m
△

Icefield
Centre
Columbia
Icefield

Sunwapta Pass
2035m
△

Wilcox
Creek

Nigel

Dome Glacier

Columbia Glacier

Athabasca Glacier

Parker Ridge

Mount King
Edward
△

Mt. Columbia
3747m
△

ALBERTA
BRITISH COLUMBIA

Mount
Athabasca
3493m
△

Saskatchewan Glacier

North

Columbia   Icefield

Castleguard
Mountain
3090m
△

BANFF

COLUMBIA

SHUSWAP

Bush

River

Bryce

Creek

Mount
Saskatchewan
3342m
△

NATIONAL

PARK

Mount
Bryce
3507m
△

Rice

River

5   6   7   8

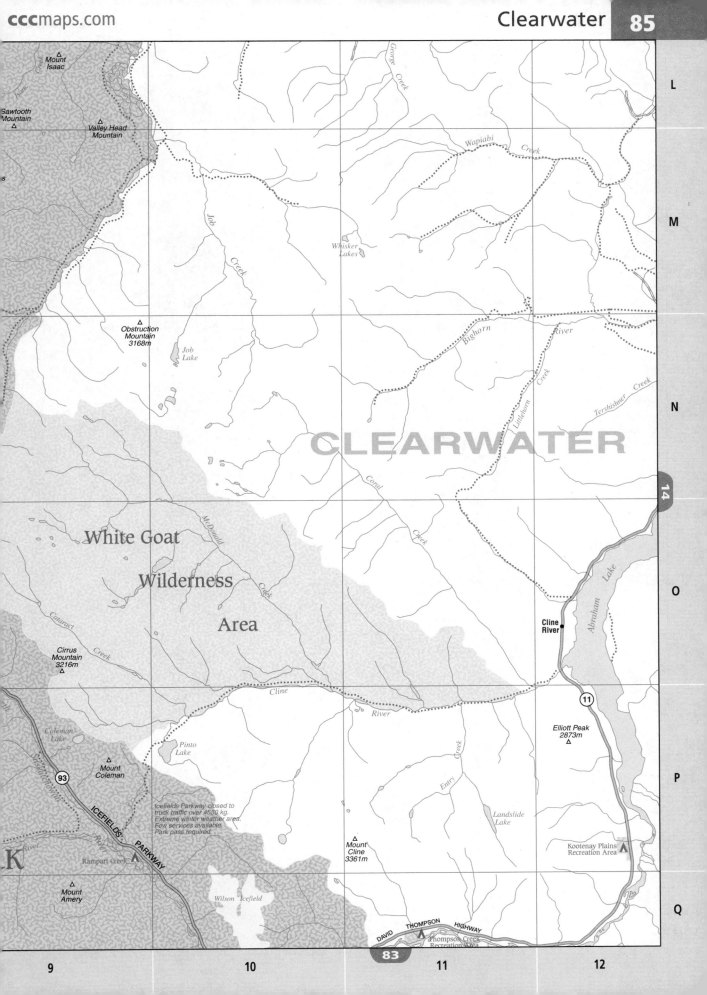

Mount Isaac

Sawtooth Mountain

Valley Head Mountain

George Creek

Wapiabi Creek

Job Creek

Whisker Lakes

Obstruction Mountain 3168m

Job Lake

Bighorn River

Littlehorn Creek

Tershishner Creek

CLEARWATER

Coral Creek

White Goat

McDonald Creek

Wilderness

Area

Cataract Creek

Cirrus Mountain 3216m

Cline River

Abraham Lake

Cline River

11

Cline River

Elliott Peak 2873m

Coleman Lake

Pinto Lake

93

Mount Coleman

Icefields Parkway closed to truck traffic over 4550 kg. Extreme winter weather area. Few services available. Park pass required.

Entry Creek

Landslide Lake

ICEFIELDS PARKWAY

Rampart Creek

Kootenay Plains Recreation Area

Mount Amery

Mount Cline 3361m

Wilson Icefield

K

DAVID THOMPSON HIGHWAY

Thompson Creek Recreation Area

83

9   10   11   12

L   M   N   14   O   P   Q

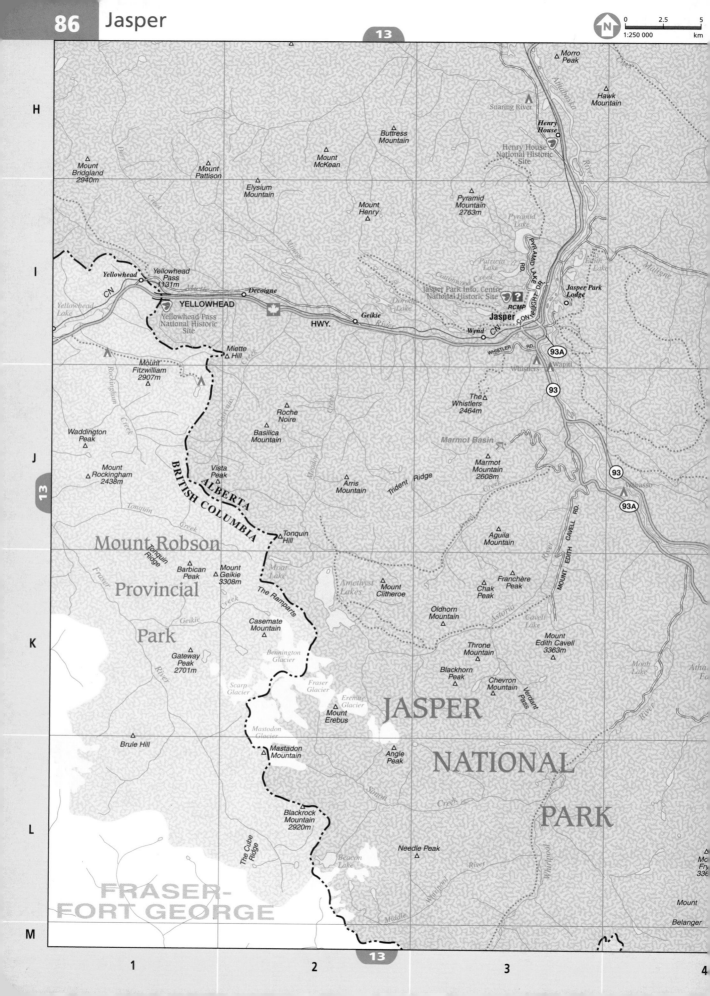

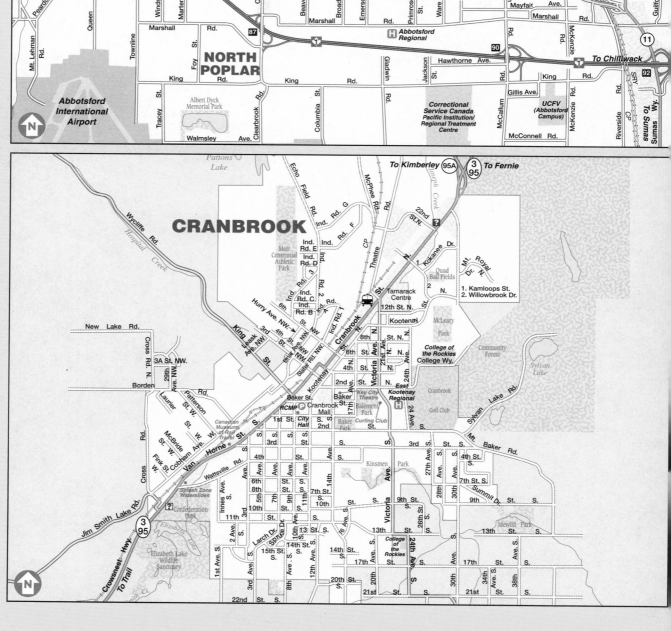

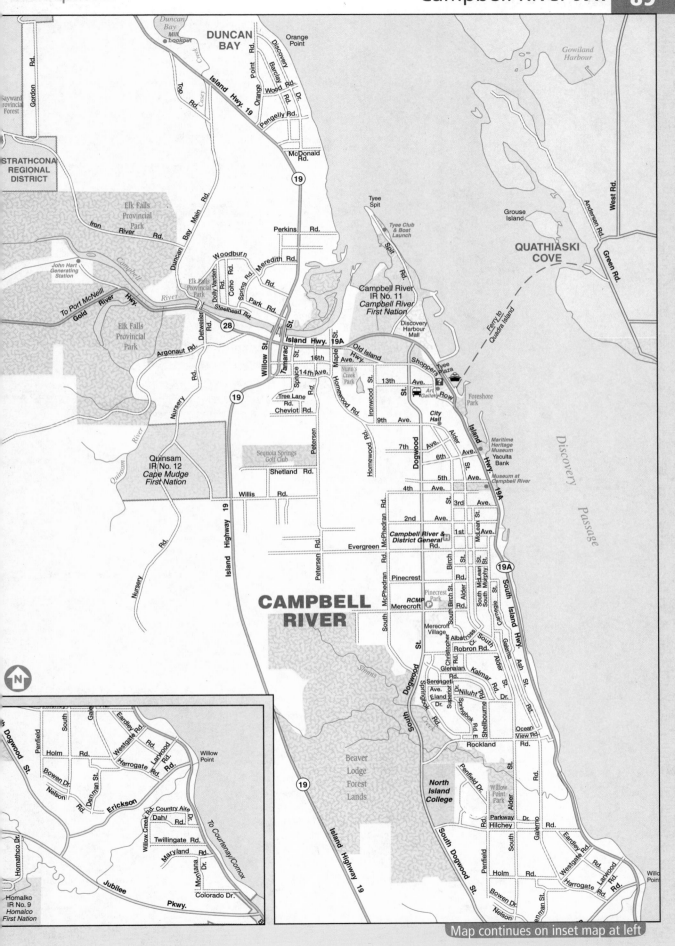

DUNCAN BAY

Duncan Bay Mill Lookout

Orange Point

STRATHCONA REGIONAL DISTRICT

Sayward Provincial Forest

Gordon Rd.

Island Hwy. 19

Top Rd.

Casey Creek

Discovery Dr.

Barclay Rd.

Wood Rd.

Pengelly Rd.

McDonald Rd.

Gowiland Harbour

19

Elk Falls Provincial Park

Iron River Rd.

Duncan Bay Main Rd.

Campbell River

John Hart Generating Station

Elk Falls Provincial Park

Perkins Rd.

Woodburn

Meredith Rd.

Dolly Varden Rd.

Coho Rd.

Spring Rd.

Park Rd.

Grouse Island

QUATHIASKI COVE

Andersen Rd.

West Rd.

Green Rd.

Tyee Spit

Tyee Club & Boat Launch

Spit Rd.

To Port McNeill

Gold River Hwy.

Campbell River

Elk Falls Provincial Park

Detweiler Rd.

Steelhead Rd.

28

Campbell River IR No. 11 Campbell River First Nation

Discovery Harbour Mall

Ferry to Quadra Island

Argonaut Rd.

Willow St.

Tamarac St.

16th Ave.

Maple St.

Old Island Hwy.

Island Hwy. 19A

Shopper's Row

Tyee Plaza

19

14th Ave.

Spruce St.

Tree Lane Rd.

Cheviot Rd.

Nunn's Creek Park

Homewood Rd.

Ironwood St.

13th Ave.

Art Gallery Row

Foreshore Park

Quinsam IR No. 12 Cape Mudge First Nation

Quinsam River

Nursery Rd.

Petersen Rd.

Sequoia Springs Golf Club

Shetland Rd.

9th Ave.

7th Ave.

Dogwood St.

6th St.

Alder St.

City Hall

Maritime Heritage Museum
Yaculta Bank

Discovery Passage

Island Highway 19

Willis Rd.

4th Ave.

St.

5th Ave.

3rd Ave.

McLean St.

19A

Museum at Campbell River

McPhedran Rd.

2nd Ave.

1st Ave.

Campbell River & District General Rd.

Birch St.

Rd.

McLean St.

South McLean St.

South Murphy St.

Evergreen Rd.

Petersen Rd.

Pinecrest

Pinecrest Park

South McPhedran Rd.

RCMP
Merecroft

South Birch St.

Alder Rd.

Carnegie St.

19A

South Island Hwy.

Ash St.

CAMPBELL RIVER

Merecroft Village

Christopher St.

Albatross St.

Robron Rd.

South Galerno Rd.

Glenalan Rd.

Kalmar Rd.

Alder St.

Ocean View Rd.

Simms

Beaver Lodge Forest Lands

Serengeti Ave.
Eland Dr.

Superior Dr.

Niluht Rd.

Shellbourne St.

Springbok Rd.

Rockland Rd.

19

Springbok Creek

North Island College

Penfield Dr.

Willow Point Park

Parkway

Hilchey Rd.

Eardley Rd.

Larwood Rd.

Westgate Rd.

South Alder Dr.

Galerno Rd.

N

Dogwood St.

Penfield Rd.

South Gale Rd.

Eardley Rd.

Larwood Rd.

Westgate Rd.

Harrogate Rd.

Willow Point

Holm Rd.

Bowen Dr.

Nelson Rd.

Denman St.

Erickson Rd.

Willow Creek Rd.

Country Aire Rd.

Dahl Rd.

Twillingate Rd.

Maryland Rd.

Montana Dr.

Colorado Dr.

Jubilee Pkwy.

Homalko IR No. 9 Homalco First Nation

South Dogwood St.

Island Highway 19

Penfield Rd.

South Rd.

Holm Rd.

Bowen Dr.

Nelson Rd.

Denman St.

Harrogate Rd.

Willow Point

Map continues on inset map at left

1:50 000 km
0   0.5   1.0

Skumalasph IR 16

Fraser River

Fairfield Island

Hog Island

Brinx Rd.
Fairfield Rd.
Teton Ave.
McDonald
Brice Rd.
Bell Rd.
McSween
Hope River Rd.

Island 22 Regional Park

Cartmell Rd.

Skwali IR 3

Fairfield Island Pk.
Clare Ave.
Elliott Ave.
Wedgewood Dr.
Chartwell Dr.
Strathcona Rd.
Bonavista St.
Gwynne-Vaughn Park
Killarney
Hope
River
Kent
Menzies Ave.
Skwahla IR 2
Swallow Pl.
Swallow Cr.
Mountain Park Dr.

Teathquathill Rd.
Lower Landing Rd.
Berkeley Ave.
Riverside Dr.
Bonny Ave.
Hazel St.
Portage Ave.
Quarry Rd.
1A

Skway Rd.

Skwah IR 4

Henley Ave.
Lewis Ave.
Reece St.
Portage Ave.
Yale
Rd.
McNaught Rd.
Prest Rd.

Old Dyke Rd.
Ashwell Rd.
Wellington
Corbould St.
Cook St.
College St.
Young
Mellard Ave.
Bole Ave.
Williams
Charles St.
Hazel
Broadway
Coote St.

Skway IR 5

Wolfe Rd.
The Landing
Spadina
Edward St.
May St.
Princess
1st
1st Ave.
Garden St.
1st Ave.

Townsend Park
Hodgins Ave.
2nd Ave.
3rd Ave.

Schweyey Rd.

Westview
Bernard Ave.
Chilliwack General
Cheam Ave.
Museum
Charles
Sweet Briar Ave.
Prest

Chilliwack Mountain Rd.
Kwawkwawapilt IR 6

Crescent Dr.
McIntosh Dr.
Railway Ave.
Chilliwack Central Rd.

Squiaala IR 8

Grandview Dr.
Bracken Dr.

Chilliwack Mountain Rd.

Ashwell Rd.
Deans
Meadowbrook Dr.
Hocking Ave.
Elm Dr.
Brooks
Baker
Broadway

Jimmie
UFV (Chilliwack Campus)
YMCA
City Hall
Cessna Dr.
Airport
123
1

Squiaala IR 7
Yale
Airport Rd.
RCMP
Young
Chilliwack Airport
1A

Aitchelitch IR 9

Progress Rd.
Aitken Rd.
Eagle Landing Pkwy.
Parr Rd.
Olds Dr.
120
Prairie Central Rd.

Industrial Wy.
116
Yale Rd. W.
Creek Rd.
119
Luckakuck Wy.
Chilliwack River Rd.

Yale Rd. W.
Luckakuck Wy.
Cottonwood Mall
Cheam Golf Centre
Chilliwack Heritage Park
Knight Rd.
Chilliwack Mall
Knight Rd.
Skowkale IR 10

CHILLIWACK

Storey Ave.
Skowkale IR 11
Yakweakwioose IR 12

Lickman Rd.
Central Rd.
Wells Rd.
Webb Ave.
McGuire Rd.

Sumas
Richardson Ave.
Rochester Ave.
Spruce Dr.
Britton Ave.

Adams Rd.
Wiltshire St.
Vedder Rd.
Manuel Rd.
School Ln.
Stevenson Rd.
Vanmar St.
River Rd.

Dayton Dr.
Reid Rd.
Stevenson
Higginson Rd.
Roy Ave.

South
Sumas Rd.
South Sumas Rd.
Insley Ave.
Chilliwack Track Complex
Kinkora Golf Course
Bailey Rd.

Unsworth Rd.
Evans Rd.
Tyson Rd.
Balmoral Ave.
Roseberry Ave.
Tzeachten IR 13
Chilliwack
Matheson Rd.
Teskey Wy.
Ross Rd.

Watson Rd.
Wilkins Dr.
Arlington Dr.
Sappers' Wy.
Garrison Blvd.
Promontory Rd.
Mount Thom Park

Lickman Rd.
Unsworth Rd.
Cumberland Ave.
Carter Rd.
Janis St.
Watson Glen Park
Thomas Rd.
Promontory Wy.
Jinkerson Dr.
Sylvan Dr.

Elsie Pl.
Keith Wilson Rd.
Webster Rd.
Peach Rd.
Canterbury Dr.
Keith
UFV (Trades & Technology Centre)
Wilson Rd.
Korea
Caen Rd.
Sicily Rd.
Vedder
Mullins Teskey
Teskey
Goldspring Pl.
Extrom Rd.

Festubert
Vimy Ave.
Petawawa
Dyke Rd.
Sylvan Dr.
Valleyview Rd.
Thornton Rd.
Forester Rd.

Vedder River
Chilliwack Lake Rd.
Teskey Rd.

N

Vedder Mountain Rd.
Cultus Lk. Rd.
Sweltzer Ck.
Soowahlie IR 14
Greenhill Rd.

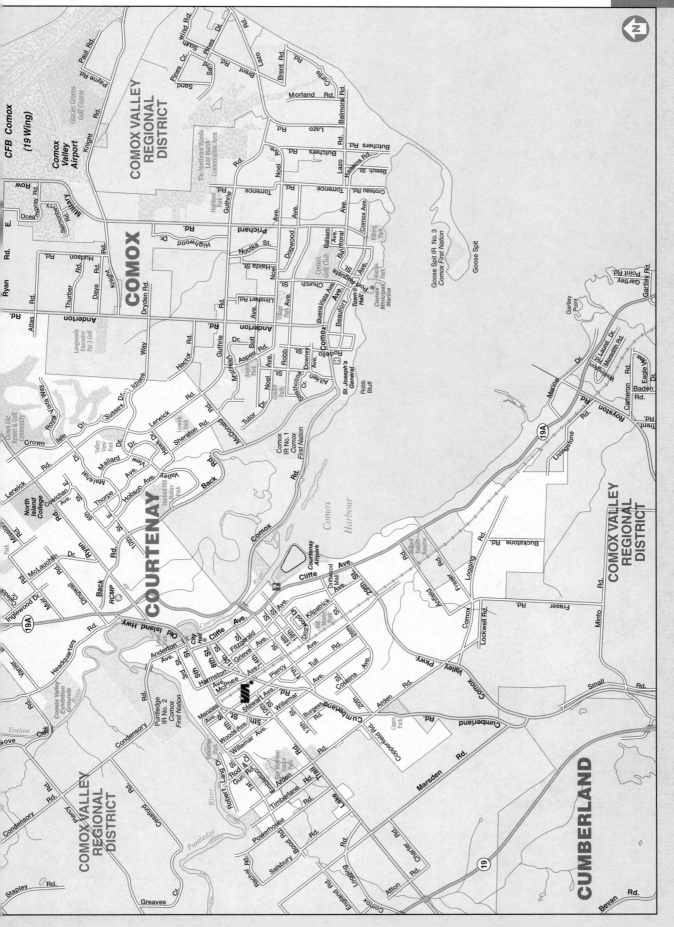

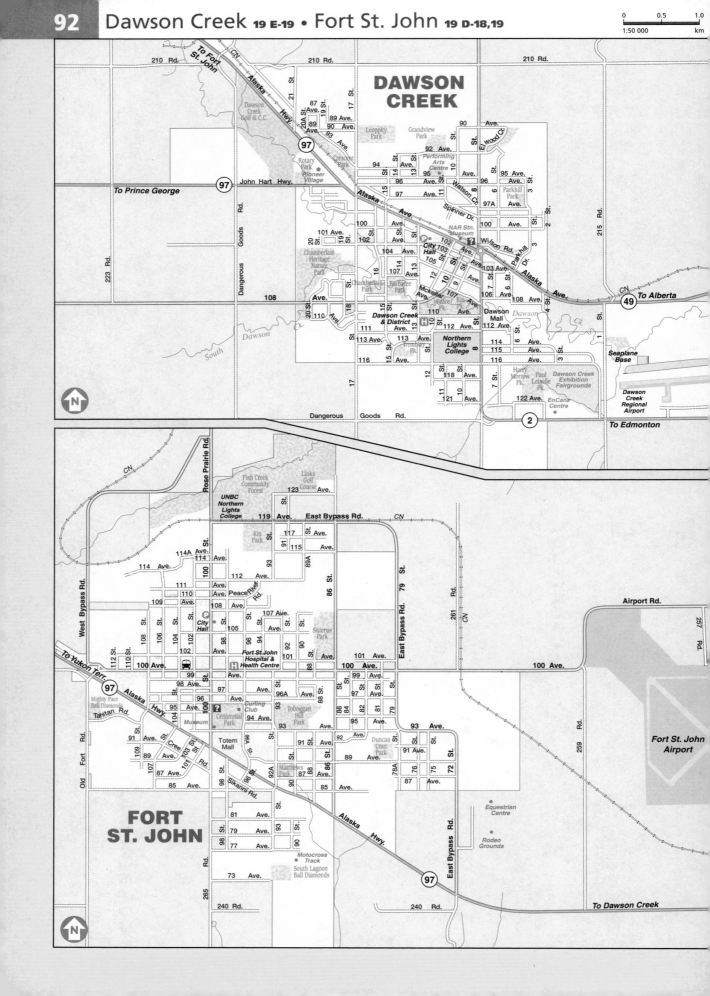

DAWSON CREEK

210 Rd.

To Prince George

John Hart Hwy.

Alaska Hwy.

Chamberlain Heritage Nature Park

Dawson Creek & District

Northern Lights College

Dawson Creek Exhibition Fairgrounds

Dawson Mall

NAR Stn. Museum

City Hall

Leoppky Park

Grandview Park

Performing Arts Centre

Parkhill Park

Dawson Creek Golf & C.C.

Rotary Park

Pioneer Village

To Alberta

Seaplane Base

Dawson Creek Regional Airport

To Edmonton

EnCana Centre

Dangerous Goods Rd.

FORT ST. JOHN

Rose Prairie Rd.

Fish Creek Community Forest

Links Golf Course

UNBC Northern Lights College

East Bypass Rd.

Kin Park

West Bypass Rd.

To Yukon Terr.

Alaska Hwy.

Mighty Pace Ball Diamonds

Tahitan Rd.

Old Fort Rd.

Museum

Centennial Park

Totem Mall

City Hall

Fort St. John Hospital & Health Centre

Curling Club

Surerus Park

Toboggan Hill Park

Duncan Cran Park

Matthews Park

Sikanni Rd.

Motocross Track

South Lagoon Ball Diamonds

Equestrian Centre

Rodeo Grounds

East Bypass Rd.

Airport Rd.

Fort St. John Airport

To Dawson Creek

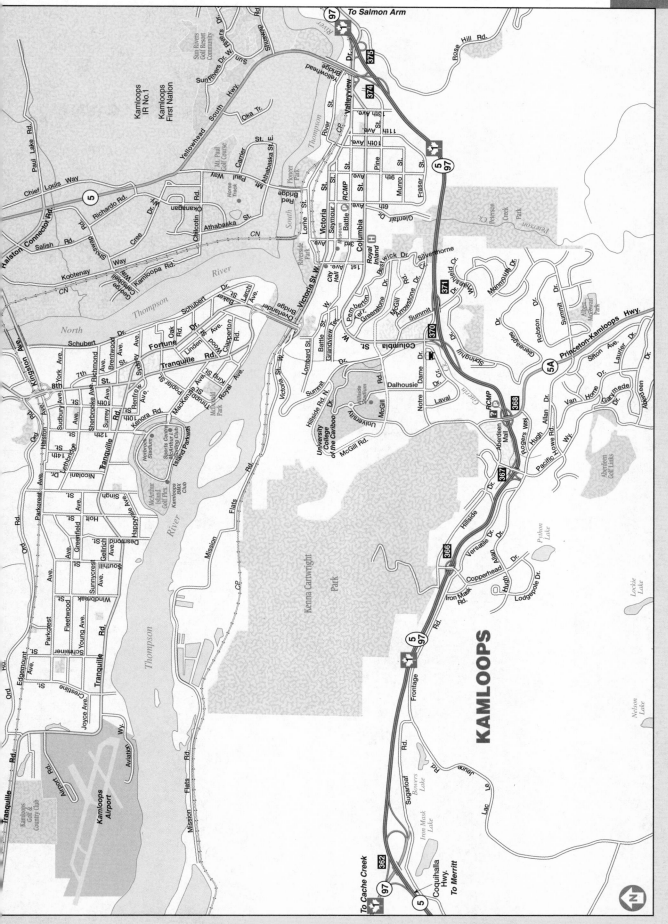

KAMLOOPS

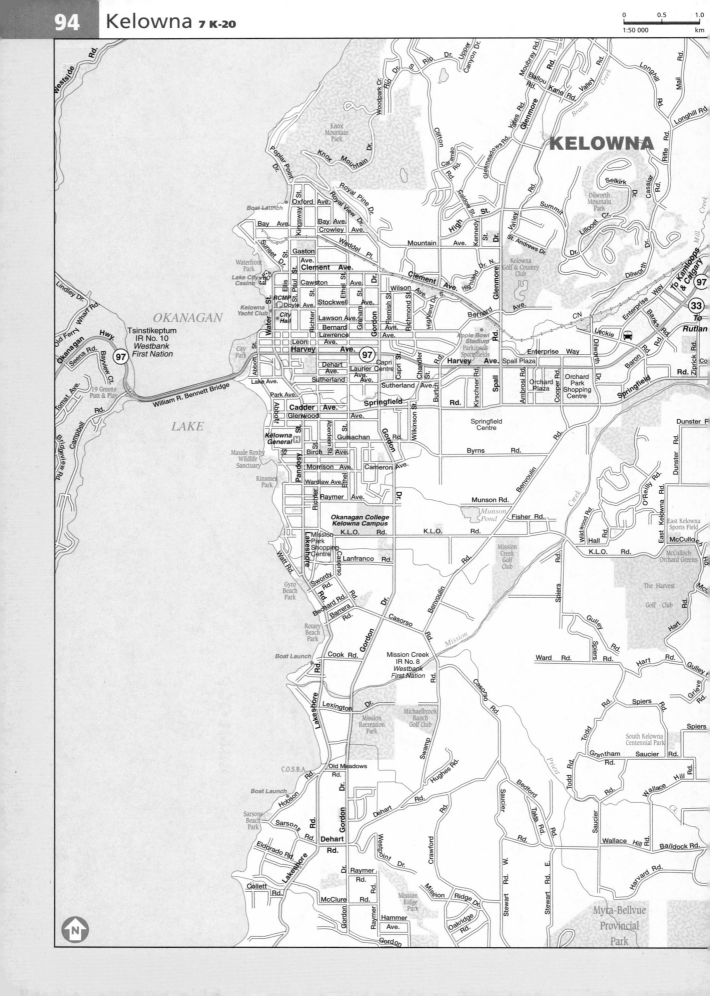

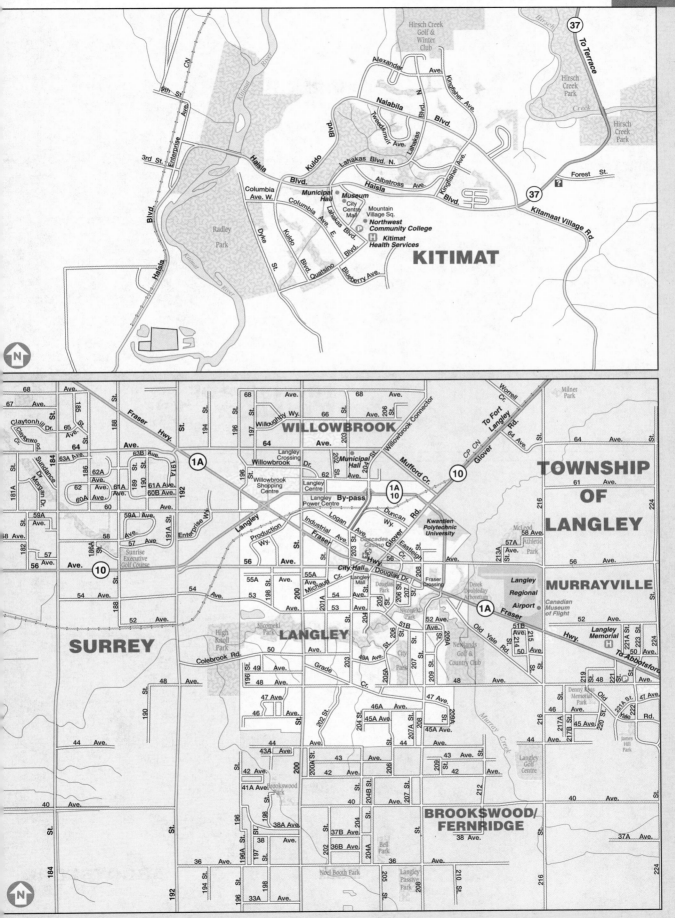

KITIMAT

SURREY

LANGLEY

WILLOWBROOK

TOWNSHIP OF LANGLEY

MURRAYVILLE

BROOKSWOOD/ FERNRIDGE

0   0.5   1.0
1:50 000   km

PITT MEADOWS

MAPLE RIDGE

132 Ave.

To Port Coquitlam

Lougheed Hwy.

Golden Ears Way

Meadow Gardens Golf Club

Harris Park

Park Rd.

North Bonson Park

Meadowtown Centre

CP WCE

Westgate Centre

Meadow Ridge Shopping Centre

Dewdney Trunk Rd.

Lougheed Hwy.

Ridge Meadows

Hammond Stadium

Westfield

Maple Ridge Golf Course

Pitt Meadows Athletic Park Airport

Katzie IR No.1
Katzie First Nation

Golden Ears Bridge

Fraser River

Bishops Reach

Barnston Island

SURREY

Katzie IR No.2
Katzie First Nation

Derby Reach Regional Park

TOWNSHIP OF LANGLEY

Derby Reach Regional Park

Municipal Hall

ValleyFair Mall

Brickwood Park

Port Haney Wharf

Maple Ridge Museum

Haney By-pass

Thomas Haney Centre & Telosky Stadium

CP WCE

Kanaka Creek Regional Park

To Mission

Horseman's Park

Maple Ridge Park

Dogwood A

Abbernethy

MISSION

To Maple Ridge Lougheed Hwy.

Mission Golf and Country Club

Mission Rotary Sports Park

Mission Memorial

Dewdney Trunk Rd.

Ferndale Ave.

Correctional Service Canada

Mission Institution

Ferndale Institution

Municipal Hall

Dewdney Trunk Rd.

Westminister Abbey

UFV (Mission Campus)

Fraser River Heritage Park

Lougheed Hwy.

To Kent

The Junction London

Mission Bridge Bar Park

Fraser River

ABBOTSFORD

MATSQUI ISLAND

Three Islands IR No.3
Matsqui First Nation

Mission Raceway Park

Abbotsford-Mission Bridge

To Abbotsford

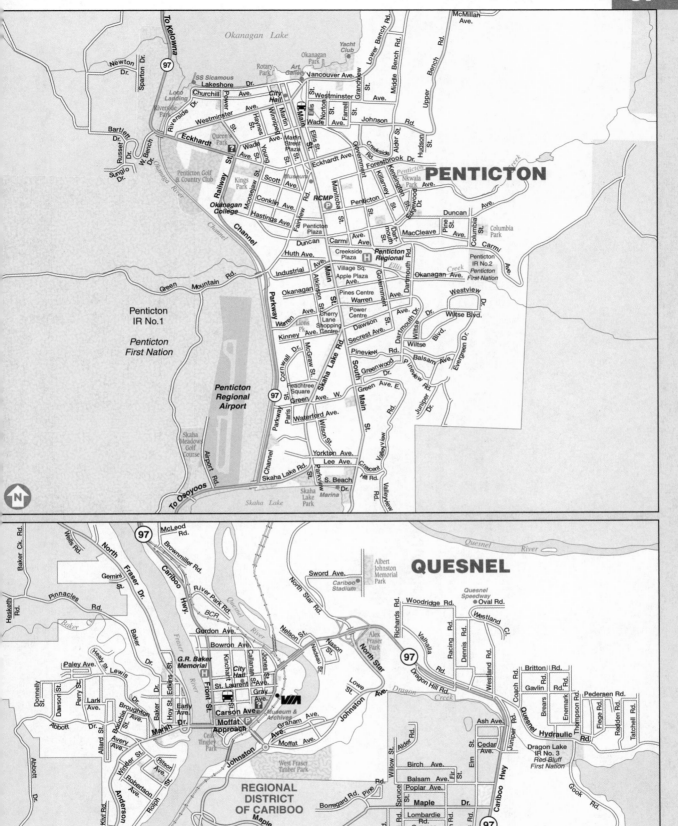

PENTICTON

To Kelowna
97

Okanagan Lake

Yacht Club

Okanagan Park

Rotary Park

Art Gallery

SS Sicamous

Loco Landing

Riverside Park

Churchill Ave.
Power Ave.
City Hall
Westminster Ave.
Vancouver Ave.
Lower Bench Rd.
Middle Bench Rd.
Upper Bench Rd.
Grandview
McMillan Ave.

Lakeshore Dr.

Westminster
Haynes St.
Winnipeg St.
Martin St.
Main St.
Ellis St.
Wade
Norton
Farrell
Johnson Rd.

Eckhardt
Queen's Park
Wade Ave.
Young St.
Eckhardt Ave.
Creekside
Alder St.
Hudson St.
Government
Forestbrook Dr.

Bartlett Dr.
Russet Dr.
Sunglo Dr.
W. Bench Dr.
Railway St.
Fairview Rd.
Scott Ave.
Swaillewan
Manitoba St.
Killarney
Nkwala Park Ave.
Kinshngth

Penticton Golf & Country Club
Kings Park
Conklin Ave.
Penticton
Duncan Ave.
Nanaimo Ave.
MacCleave
Pine St.
Columbia St.
Columbia Park

Okanagan College
Hastings Ave.
RCMP
Penticton Plaza
Carmi Ave.
Dartmouth
Ridgewood Dr.
Duncan Ave.
Carmi

Channel
Channel
Huth Ave.
Creekside Plaza
Penticton Regional H
Okanagan Ave.
Ellis
Penticton IR No.2 Penticton First Nation

Green Mountain Rd.
Industrial Ave.
Village Sq.
Apple Plaza Ave.
Government
Creek

Penticton IR No.1

Penticton First Nation

Parkway
Okanagan Ave.
Warren St.
Pines Centre
Warren
Power Centre
Westview Dr.
Wiltse Blvd.

Lions Pk.
Cherry Lane Shopping Centre
Dawson Ave.
Dartmouth Dr.
Wiltse Blvd.

Warren
Kinney Ave.
Secrest Ave.
Wiltse Dr.
Balsam Ave.
Evergreen Dr.

Cornwall St.
McGraw St.
Pineview Rd.
Greenwood Dr.
Pineview Rd.

Penticton Regional Airport
97
Peachtree Square
Paris St.
Green Ave. W.
South Main St.
Green Ave. E.
Juniper

Skaha Meadows Golf Course
Waterford Ave.
Wilson St.
Crescent

Airport Rd.
Yorkton Ave.
Lee Ave.
Valleyview
Valleyview Dr.

Channel
Skaha Lake Rd.
Skaha Lake Park
S. Beach Dr.
Marina

To Osoyoos
Skaha Lake

QUESNEL

97
McLeod Rd.
Quesnel River

Baker Ck. Rd.
Wells Rd.
North Fraser Dr.
Brownmiller Rd.
Cariboo Hwy.
River Park Rd.
Sword Ave.
Cariboo Stadium
Albert Johnston Memorial Park

Hesketh Rd.
Gemini St.
Pinnacles Rd.
BCR
Gordon Ave.
Nelson St.
North Star Rd.
Quesnel Speedway
Oval Rd.
Woodridge Rd.
Westland Ct.

Baker Cr.
Paley Ave.
Healy St.
Lewis
Baker Dr.
Bowron Ave.
Callanan St.
Nason St.
Alex Fraser Park
97
Richards Rd.
Valhalla Rd.
Racing Rd.
Dennis Rd.
Westland Rd.
Britton Rd.

Donnelly St.
Dawson St.
Lark Ave.
Perry St.
Broughton Ave.
Bodachi Dr.
G.R. Baker Memorial H
Kinchant St.
City Hall
St. Laurent
Gray
VIA
Lowe St.
North Star
Dragon Hill Rd.
Coach Rd.
Gavlin Rd.
Brears
Enemark
Thompson Rd.
Pedersen Rd.

Abbott Dr.
Allard St.
Avery Ave.
Winder St.
Ritson
Robertson Ave.
Baker Dr.
Hoy St.
Edkins St.
Early Ave.
Front St.
Carson Ave.
Moffat Approach
Museum & Archives
Graham Ave.
Moffat Ave.
Johnston St.
Johnston
Dragon Creek
Ash Ave.
Cedar Ave.
Juniper St.
Quesnel Hwy.
Hydraulic
Fiege Rd.
Redden Rd.
Tatchell Rd.

Kiwi Rd.
Anderson Dr.
Rolph
Johnston
Cen Tingley Park
West Fraser Timber Park
Birch Ave.
Willow St.
Alder Rd.
Elm St.
Dragon Lake IR No. 3 Red Bluff First Nation

REGIONAL DISTRICT OF CARIBOO
Maple Dr.
Borregard Rd.
Pine St.
Balsam Ave.
Fir St.
Poplar Ave.
Maple Dr.

Veneer Rd.
Plywood
Ellison Rd.
Oak Ave.
Laurel St.
Spruce St.
Lombardie Rd.
Cypress Ave.
Dogwood Rd.
Mountain Ash Rd.
Maple Heights Rd.
97
Sing St.
Spruce Ridge Rd.

Caragana Rd.
Marsh
Butterfield Rd.
Lust Rd.
Red Bluff Rd.
Brist
Lust Rd.
Adbutus
Gook Rd.
Jade Rd.
Beryl Rd.
Croft St.
Jay Rd.
Beach
Lakeview Cr.

Fraser River
CN
Quesnel IR No. 1 Red Bluff First Nation
Dragon Lake Golf Course
Dragon Lake

1:50 000

km

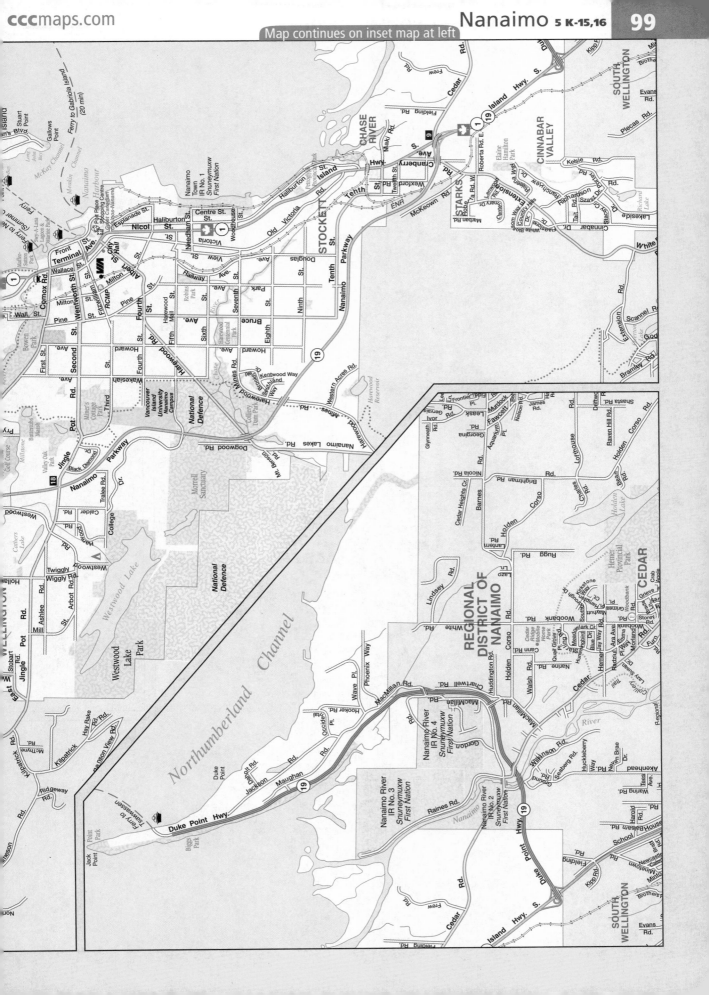

0   0.5   1.0
1:50 000   km

POWELL RIVER

Poplar St.
Lombardy
Crown Ave.
Cranberry St.
Mowat Ave.
Warner
Cranberry
Haslam
Drake St.
Marlatt St.
Yukon
Maple Ave.
Church St.
Bird
Timberlane Ave.
Nelson
Park Ave.
Manson Ave.
Sanctuary
Cranberry Lake
Timberlane Park

Smith Rd.

Batty Rd.

Marine Ave.

Cypress Blvd.

Best Rd.

Malaspina

101

Powell River General H

Willingdon Beach Park

Museum Alberni
?
Joyce
Kiwanis Ave.
Saskatchewan
Lamarque Rd.
Fayette Rd.
Kellow Rd.
Walker
Lamarque Rd.
Willingdon Ave.

ALBERNI-CLAYOQUOT REGIONAL DISTRICT

Alberni Golf Club

Strait

Barnet
Harvie
Michigan
Ontario
A
St.
Manson Park
Karen Pl.
Wadena Rd.
Withers Rd.
Drinkwater Rd.
Saunders Rd. N.
Cowley Rd.
Milligan Rd.
P
Courtenay St.
Duncan
Burnaby St.
Fenwood
Manson
Bowness
Tanner

Malabar Rd.
Cherry
Margot Rd.
Rumsby Rd.
Municipal Hall
?
Powell River Airport
Joyce
Field
Lugrin Rd.
Mersey Rd.
Chapman
Strick
Gordon Ave.
Maplehurst Park
Moore
Fairmont St.
Ontario
Manson

Paper Mill Dam Park
Georgia Rd.
Glacier
Westview
Pierce Rd.
Grandview Ave.
Indian Ave.
Strathcona St.
Willow St.
Bishop Cr.
Kamloops

Compton Rd.
Golden St.
Brown Rd.
Compton Rd.
McEachern
Marpole St.
Compton Rd.
Michigan Rd.
Mozart Rd.
Maebelle Rd.
Lytton St.
Massett Ave.
Selkirk Ave.
Gordon Pk.

Tsahaheh IR No. 1
Tseshaht First Nation
Mission Rd.
River
Airport Rd.
Golden St.
Josephine St.
Mary St.
Lacson St.
Beaver Creek
Margaret
Gertrude St.
Leslie Ave.
Ian St.
Tebo Ave.
Glenside Rd.
Johnston Rd.
Alberni Mall
Highmoor Rd.
Vancouver Island University
Nootka St.
Oliver St.
Nutana Cr.

4
Ahahswinis IR No. 1
Hupacasath First Nation
Lathom
Arrowsmith St.
4
The Hollies Executive Golf Course
Gordon St.
Penticton St.
Quesnel St.

ALBERNI-CLAYOQUOT REGIONAL DISTRICT
Stitkee Park
Somass River
PORT ALBERNI
Hollywood St.
Glenwood Centre
Alberni Valley Multiplex
North Island College
Victoria Dr.
Port Alberni Highway
Richmond St.
Terrace St.
Teakerne Ave.
Cariboo St.
Theodosia

Clutesi Haven Marina
Glenwood
10th
Bob Dailey Stadium
Roger St.
Kendall
McIntyre Dr.
21st Ave.
Hernando Ave.
Toba St.
Tofino

J.V. Cline Bird Sanctuary
Stamp Ave.
RCMP
P
Roger
Echo Park Alberni Valley Museum
Wood St.
Anderson
West Coast General H
Grief Point
Windsor
Thunder Bay St.

Port Alberni Harbour
Wallace
Maitland Ave.
Russell Park
16th St.
Beach Gardens Resort & Marina

Lupsi Cuspi Point
3rd
4th
5th
6th
8th
10th
Redford St.
Burde St.
North Park Dr.
Burde Rd.

N

Paper Dock
Dunbar St.
Divatcha Creek

Fisherman's Harbour Marina
Kingsway
3rd
Argyle
North Cr.
Argyle
18th St.
Black Sheep Rugby Field

Harbour Quay Marina / Maritime Discovery Centre
2nd
Mar
City Hall
Rollin Art Centre
China Creek Rd.

Alberni
Hohm Island
Montrose
6th
8th
10th
Ave.
ALBERNI-CLAYOQUOT REGIONAL DISTRICT

Inlet
Bruce
4th
5th
6th
8th
10th
Bruce
15th
Foxtie Cr.

Neill St.
Anderson
Scott St.
3rd
11th
Ravenhill Ave.

Katharine Point
Mallory Dr.
Cameron Dr.
Ship Creek
Ship Creek Rd.

Polly Point
Alberni IR No. 2
Tseshaht First Nation
Stamp Point

Creek

N

PRINCE
GEORGE

To Prince Rupert

Otway Rd.
CN
Foothills Blvd.
North Nechako Rd.
To Fort St. John
Bellamy Rd.
Northwood Pulpmill Rd.
Aberdeen Glen Golf Course
BCR
Fraser River

Fish Traps Island Park
Foothills Bridge
Ospika Blvd.
Nechako
Wilson Park
Parkhill Centre
Theatre North West
John Hart Bridge
Cameron Bridge
Hart Hwy.
River
97
Aberdeen
McMillan Regional Park
Aintree Dr.
Rd.
Hoferkamp Rd.

Moore's Meadow Park
Otway Rd.
McDermid Dr.
Gordon Bryant Park
1st Ave.
Hammond Ave.
2nd Ave.
2nd Ave.
3rd Ave.
River
1st Ave.
River
McMillan Regional Park
Prince George Pulpmill Rd.
Cottonwood Island Park
Prince George Railway & Forestry Museum
Grand Trunk Pacific Bridge

Russman Rd.
1st Ave.
Anderson St.
5th Ave.
Ospika Quinn St.
Ogilvie St.
Moffat St.
Kelly St.
5th Ave.
5th Ave.
CN
3
Ave.
1st
2nd Ave.
4th Ave.
Yellowhead Bridge
Pickering Rd.
Prince George Regional Correctional Centre

Cranbrook Hill Rd.
Foothills Blvd.
5th Ave.
Lakewood Park
Rainbow Park
Stuart Dr.
Urbon St.
Rainbow
Kerry St.
Liard Dr.
Hatry Loder Pk.
Ahbau St.
Central St. W.
Central St.
Carney St.
8th Ave.
10th Ave.
Wells Ave.
Freeman St.
Alward St.
9th Ave.
11th Ave.
Prince George Regional H
Edmonton St.
Winnipeg St.
Victoria St.
Vancouver St.
Quebec St.
Brunswick St.
George St.
Dominion St.
1st Ave.
City Hall
Elm St.
Cedar St.
Ash St.

Crest Rd.
Kueng Rd.
University Way
Tabor Blvd.
15th Ave.
18th Ave.
Ospika Blvd.
Freeman Park
Central St.
15th Ave.
Parkwood Place
Patricia Blvd.
Connaught Hill Pk.
17th
Ingledew St.
Gorse St.
The Exploration Place
Fort George Park
LC Gunn Park

Exhibition Park
22nd Ave.
Quinn St.
Nicholson St.
College of New Caledonia
Ave.
Masich Place Stadium
Carrey Jane Grey Park
YMCA
Winnipeg St.
97
Upland St.
Spruce St.
20th
Oak St.
Maple St.
Juniper St.
Strathcona
Pine St.
Victoria St.
Hudson's Bay Slough Nature Park
Youth Custody Centre

Forests for the World
Massey Dr.
Vanier Dr.
Pine Centre
Westwood Dr.
Pinewood Ave.
Yellowhead Hwy.
Abbott Cr.
Milburn Ave.
Diefenbaker Dr.
Pearson Ave.
Moss Ave.
Queensway
Ford Ave.
River
CN

University of Northern British Columbia
Ospika Blvd.
Prince George Golf & Curling Club
Ferry Ave.
Recreation Place
Treasure Cove Casino
Upland St.
Ferry Ave.
Simon Fraser Bridge
Fraser River
Prince George Airport

Tyner Blvd.
Ospika Blvd.
Baker Rd.
Range Rd.
Pine Valley Golf Centre
Vance Rd.
Wiebe Rd.
Lansdown
Covart Rd.
Railway
Industrial
Great St.
Terminal Blvd.
Pacific
Cariboo Hwy.

McGill Cr.
Simon Fraser Ave.
BCR

Domano Blvd.
College Hts. Plaza
O'Grady Rd.
97

To Prince Rupert
Kimball Rd.
Bear Rd.
Henry Rd.
Bunce Rd.
Aldeen Rd.
16
Yellowhead Hwy.
Southridge Ave.
Marleau Rd.
Parent Rd.
Bernard Rd.
St. Patrick Ave.
Lawrence Ave.
Gladstone Dr.
Gladstone Dr.
Domano Blvd.
Malaspina Ave.
Pacific St.
Industrial Wy.
To Vancouver
97

N

0 0.5 1.0
1:50 000
km

PRINCE RUPERT map

Bacon Cove
Vigilant Island
Hays Cove
Ritchie Point
David Point
Curling Club
Seal Cove
Bacon Point
Douglas Point
Melville Arm
Prince Rupert Harbour
Seal Cove Rd.
Sourdough Bay
Shoowahtlans IR No. 4
Russell Point
Cow Bay
George Hills Wy.
Ambrose Ave.
6 Ave.
7 Ave.
8 Ave.
Immanuel St.
11 Ave.
Prince Rupert Blvd.
Fern St.
Shawatlans Rd.
Wilnaskancaud IR No. 3
Prince Rupert
Museum
Museum
City Hall
McBride Ave.
Hays Cove Ave.
Alfred St.
4 Ave.
Green Ave.
8
11 Ave.
Yellowhead Hwy.
Prince Rupert Blvd.
Prince George St.
Kaien Island
To Terrace
RCMP
Borden
2 Ave.
5 6 Ave.
8 Ave.
Performing Arts Centre
Prince Rupert Golf Club
PRINCE RUPERT
Mount Oldfield △ 575m
16
Roosevelt Park
Summit
Prince Rupert Region
Graham Ave.
Atlin Ave.
Park
Kootenay St.
Sloan Ave.
Prince Rupert Airport
Phillsbury Point
Pillsbury Ave.
Fairview
16
N

SALMON ARM map

Boat Launch
Canoe Beach Park
Public Beach
Engineer's Point
Marina
Canoe Beach Dr.
William Baker Park
Ganoe Beach Dr.
Marina
70 Ave. NE
Lakeshore Rd.
Park Hill Rd.
John Lund Park
50 St.
Shannon's Recreation Park
60 Ave. NE
Mallard Point
Coyote Park
60 Ave. NE
30 St.
35 St.
55 Ave. NE
Shuswap
25 St.
50 Ave. NE
45 Ave. NE
30 St.
SALMON ARM
Lake
20 St.
Lakeshore Rd.
CP
30 Ave. NE
25 St.
30 St.
40 Ave.
26 Ave. NE
20 Ave. NE
Switsemalph IR No. 6
1
Sandy Point
Public Wharf
Promenade Pier
15 Ave. NE
Haney Heritage Village & Museum
Haney Heritage House Park
10 Ave. NE
Switsemalph IR No. 3
Salmon Arm Waterfront Park
Harbour Front Dr. NE
Lakeshore Dr.
18 St. NE
12 St. NE
Boat Launch
Marine Park
Shuswap Lake General
6 Ave. NE
27 St. NE
22 St. NE
28 St. NE
Curling Club
5 Ave. NE
1
Grindrod - Salmon Arm Hwy.
Okanagan Ave.
CP
Beatty Ave.
Lakeshore Ave.
2 Ave. NE
City Hall
11 St. NE
4 Ave. SE
27 St. NE
33 St.
Okanagan College
Little Mountain Park
60 St.
Sports Complex
5 Ave. SW
3 St. SW
Shuswap St.
16 St. SE
Auto Rd.
4 Ave. SE
Okanagan Ave.
Switsemalph IR No. 7
Blackburn Park & Fair Grounds
3 St.
12 St.
Auto Rd. SE
8 Ave. SE
33 St.
10 Ave. SE
Salmon Arm Hwy.
10 Ave. SE
1
10 Ave. SW
30 St. SW
14 Ave. SE
15 St. SE
15 Ave. SE
30 St. SE
10 Ave. SE
18 Ave. SE
Salmon Arm Airport
Salmon Arm Golf Club
20 Ave. SE
20 Ave. SE
20 Ave. SE
N

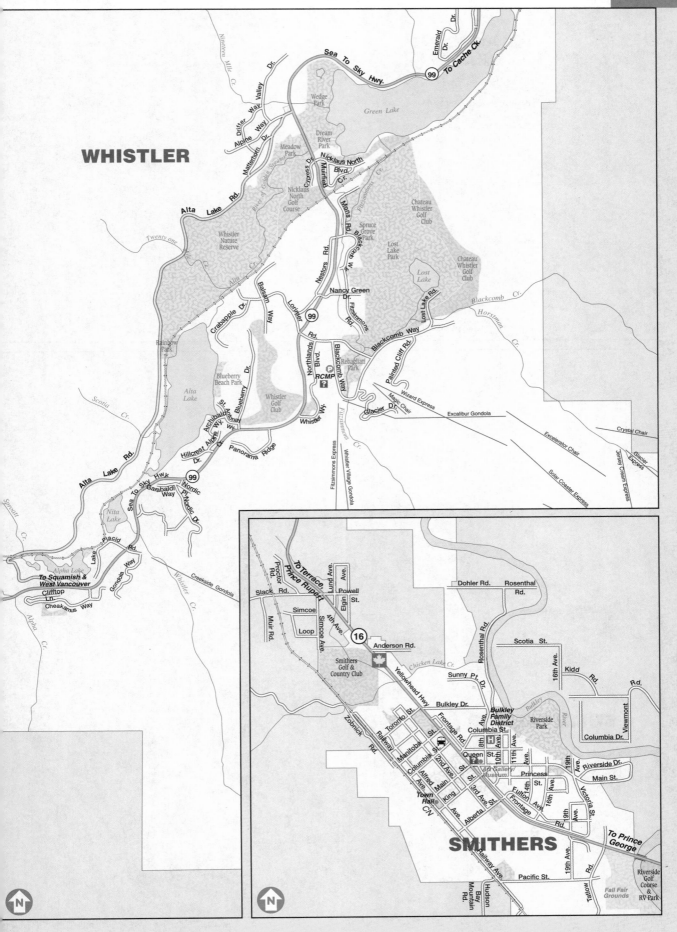

WHISTLER

Sea To Sky Hwy. 99 To Cache Ck.

Green Lake

Wedge Park

Dream River Park

Meadow Park

Nicklaus North Blvd.

Nicklaus North Golf Course

Chateau Whistler Golf Club

Alta Lake Rd.

Whistler Nature Reserve

Spruce Grove Park

Lost Lake Park

Chateau Whistler Golf Club

Lost Lake

Blackcomb Cr.

Horstman Cr.

Twenty one Mile Cr.

Nancy Green Dr.

Crabapple Dr.

Rainbow Park

Blueberry Beach Park

Alta Lake

Blueberry Dr.

Whistler Golf Club

Northlands Blvd.

RCMP

Rebagliati Park

Blackcomb Way

Painted Cliff Rd.

Wizard Express

Magic Chair

Glacier Dr.

Excalibur Gondola

Excelerator Chair

Crystal Chair

Solar Coaster Express

Jersey Cream Express

Glacier Express

Scotia Cr.

Hillcrest Dr.

Sea To Sky Hwy. 99

Garibaldi Way

Nordic Pl. Nordic Dr.

Nita Lake

Sproatt Cr.

Placid Lake Rd.

Gondola Way

Alpha Lake

Creekside Gondola

Whistler Cr.

Fitzsimmons Express

Whistler Village Gondola

Alpha Cr.

Clifftop Ln.

Cheakamus Way

To Squamish & West Vancouver

SMITHERS

To Terrace Prince Rupert

Proctor Rd.

Slack Rd.

Muir Rd.

Simcoe

Loop

Lund Ave.

Powell St.

Elgin St.

16 Anderson Rd.

Smithers Golf & Country Club

Dohler Rd. Rosenthal Rd.

Rosenthal Rd.

Scotia St.

16th Ave. Kidd Rd.

Sunny Pt. Dr.

Yellowhead Hwy.

Chicken Lake Cr.

Bulkley Dr.

Bulkley Family District

Bulkley River

Riverside Park

Columbia Dr.

Viewmont

Zobnick Rd.

Railway Ave.

Toronto St.

Manitoba St.

Columbia St.

Frontage Rd.

Columbia St.

Riverside Dr.

Main St.

Alfred Ave.

Main Ave.

King Ave.

Queen St.

Art Gallery/ Museum

Princess St.

Fulton St.

Victoria St.

9th Ave.

Town Hall

CN

Alberta Ave.

Frontage Rd.

To Prince George

Railway Ave.

19th Ave.

Pacific St.

Bay Mountain Rd.

Hudson St.

Tallow

Fall Fair Grounds

Riverside Golf Course & RV Park

0   0.5   1.0
1:50 000
km

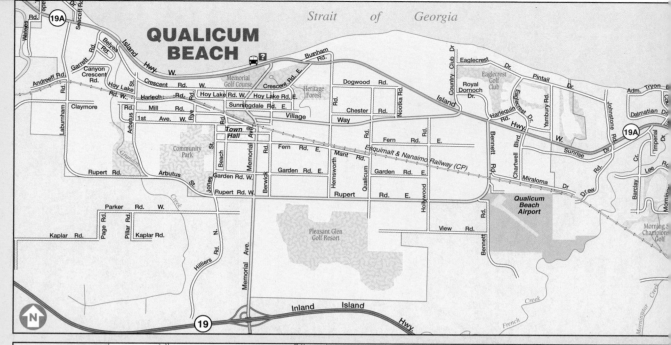

Strait of Georgia

QUALICUM BEACH

19A

Island Hwy. W.

Weilers Rd.

Andreeff Rd.

Belvel Rd.
Garrett Rd.
Canyon Crescent Rd.
Hoy Lake St.
Rd. W.
Harlech Rd.
Mill Rd.
Arbutus St.
1st Ave. W.

Laburnham

Claymore

Rd.

Crescent Rd. W.
Hoy Lake Rd. W.
Sunningdale Rd. E.

Bunham Rd.

Memorial Golf Course

Crescent Rd. E.
Hoy Lake Rd. E.

Heritage Forest

Dogwood Rd.

Village

Chester Rd.

Way

Nootka Rd.

Country Club Dr.

Eaglecrest Dr.

Royal Dornoch Dr.

Eaglecrest Golf Club

Pintail Dr.

Eaglecrest Dr.
Yambury Rd.

Adm. Tryon Rd.

Dalmatian Dr.

Johnstone Rd.

Imperial

Barclay Cr.

Lee

Morningstar

Island Hwy.

Town Hall

Community Park

Rupert Rd.
Arbutus St.

Garden Rd. W.
Rupert Rd. W.

Jones St.
Beach Ave.
Berwick Rd.
Memorial Ave.

Fern Rd. E.
Garden Rd. E.

Hemsworth Rd.

Mant Rd.

Fern Rd. E.

Esquimalt & Nanaimo Railway (CP)

Qualicum Rd.

Garden Rd. E.

Rupert Rd. E.

Hollywood Rd.

Bennett Rd.

Chartwell Blvd.
Harlequin Rd.

Sunrise Dr.

Miraloma Dr.

Drew Rd.

Qualicum Beach Airport

Parker Rd. W.

Kaplar Rd.

Page Rd. N.
Pillar Rd.

Kaplar Rd.

Hilliers Rd.

Memorial Ave.

Pleasant Glen Golf Resort

View Rd.

Bennett Rd.

French Creek

Morningstar Creek

N

Inland Island Hwy.

19

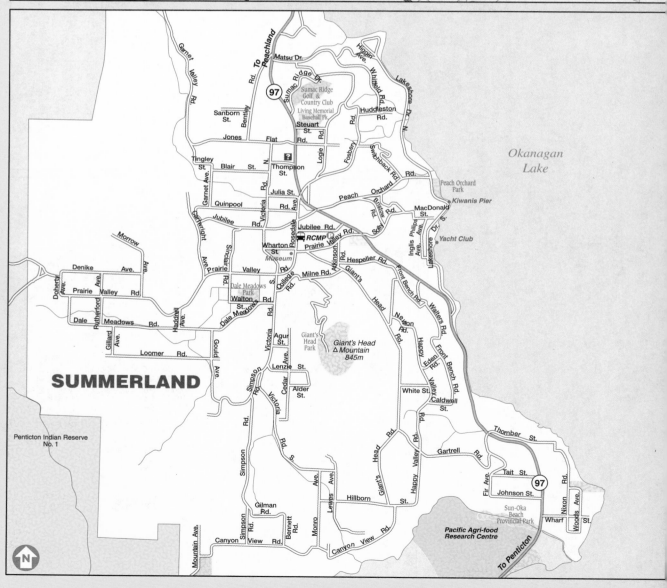

Garnet Valley Rd.

To Peachland

Matsu Dr.

Sumac Ridge Dr.

97

Higgin Ave.

Whitfield Rd.

Lakeshore Dr. N.

Sanborn St.

Bentley Rd. N.

Sumac Ridge Golf & Country Club

Living Memorial Baseball Pk.

Steuart St.

Huddleston Rd.

Okanagan Lake

Jones

Flat Rd.

Logie

Fosbery

Switchback Rd.

Rd.

Tingley St.

Blair St.

Thompson St.

Garnet Ave.

Victoria Rd. N.

Julia St.

Peach

Orchard Rd.

Peach Orchard Park

Kiwanis Pier

Quinpool

Jubilee

Cartwright Ave.

Jubilee Rd.

Biston Rd.

Solly Rd.

MacDonald St.

Inglis Ave.
Phillips Ave.

Lakeshore Dr. S.

Yacht Club

Morrow

Sinclair Rd.

Rosedale Ave.

RCMP

Wharton St.

Museum

Prairie Valley Rd.

Prairie Valley Rd.

Atkinson Rd.

Hespeller Rd.

Giant's Head Rd.

Front Bench Rd.

Walters Rd.

Denike Ave.

Doherty Ave.

Prairie Valley Rd.

Dale Meadows Park

College Rd.

Milne Rd.

Rutherford

Dale Meadows Rd.

Walton St.

Victoria Rd. S.

Nelson Rd.

Front Bench Rd.

Dale Meadows Rd.

Haddrell Ave.

Gillard Ave.

Loomer Rd.

Gould Ave.

Agur St.

Lenzie St.

Giant's Head Park

Giant's Head Mountain 845m

Happy Valley Rd.

Eden Rd.

SUMMERLAND

Simpson Rd. S.

Victoria Rd. S.

Cedar St.

Alder St.

White St.

Caldwell St.

Thomber St.

Penticton Indian Reserve No. 1

Gilman Rd.

Simpson Rd. S.

Mountain Ave.

Canyon View Rd.

Bennett Rd.

Monro Ave.

Lewes Ave.

Hillborn

Canyon View Rd.

Giant's Head Rd.

Happy Valley Rd.

Gartrell Rd.

Fir Ave.

Tait St.

97

Johnson St.

Nixon Rd.

Woods St.

Wharf

Sun-Oka Beach Provincial Park

Pacific Agri-food Research Centre

To Penticton

N

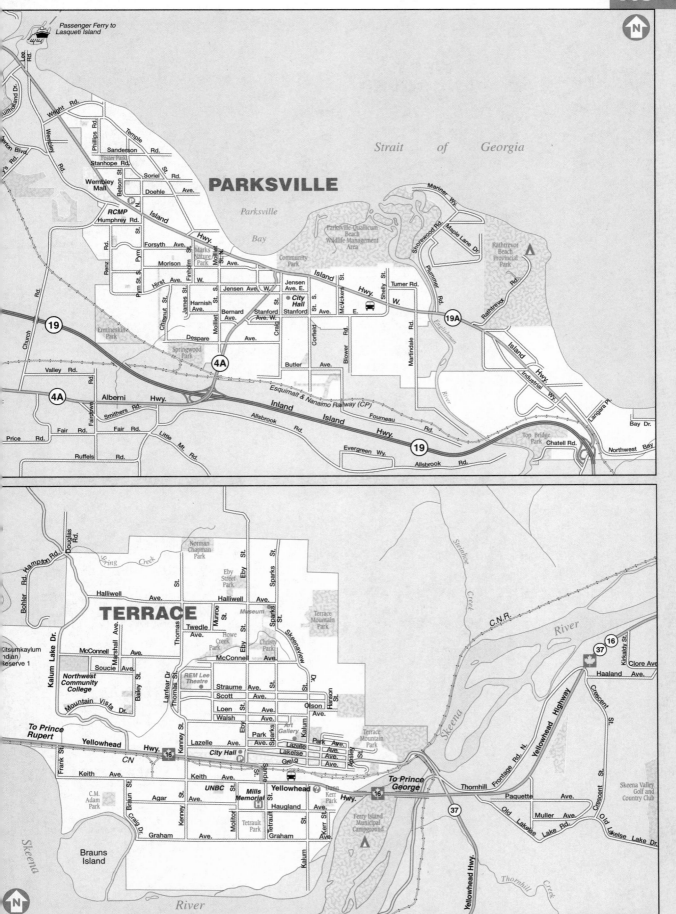

Marine Dr.

Sea to Sky Highway

1
99
1
2
2

Batchelor Cove

Howe Sound

Gleneagles Golf Course

Nelson Canyon Park

WEST VANCOUVER

Eagle Lake

Cypress Provincial Park

Capilano Lake

Larsen Bay

West Vancouver Yacht Club

Westport Rd.

Woodley Dr.

Cypress Bowl Rd.

Ballantrae Park

Ballantrae Dr.

Capilano River Regional Park

Eagle Island

Cypress Falls Park

Woodgreen Dr.

Chartwell Dr.

Millstream Rd.

Eyremount Dr.

Groveland Rd.

Capilano Golf and Country Club

Irwin Bluff

Greenleaf Dr.

Caulfeild Dr.

Rockridge Rd.

4

Woodgreen Dr.

Pinoe Rd.

Westridge Ave.

Upper Levels Hwy.

7

8

Westhill Dr.

Chippendale Rd.

Cross Ck. Rd.

Eyremount Dr.

Southborough Dr.

Stevens

Hollyburn Country Club

Capilano Suspension Bridge

Capilano

Indian Bluff

Headland Dr.

Bayridge Ave.

Marine Dr.

Mathers

Roseberry Ave.

27th St.

1

99

10

11

13

Burley Dr.

Inglewood Ave.

14

Levels

Water Ln.

Pilot Cove

Sandy Cove

West Bay

Queens

Mathers

Ave.

Ave.

21st St.

15th St.

11th St.

Taylor

Keith Rd.

22nd St.

Lighthouse Park

Caulfield Cove

Marine Dr.

Park Royal

Marine Dr.

15th St. W.

Pemberton Ave.

17th

Starboat Cove

Navvy Jack Pt.

Ambleside Beach

Capilano I.R. No.5

Welch St.

Stewart St.

Pt. Atkinson

Prospect Pt.

First Narrows

Calamity Point

Burrard

Siwash Rock

Third Beach

Stanley Park

Pipeline Rd.

Stanley Park Nat'l. Historic Site

Vancouver Aquarium

Brockton Point

Inlet

Ferguson Point

Lions Gate Bridge Rd.

Beaver Lake

Lost Lagoon

Stanley Park

1A

99

Hallelujah Po

Deadman's Island

Royal Vancouver Yacht Club

Coal Harbour

Second Beach

Beach Ave.

Denman St.

Barclay St.

Robson St.

Georgia St. W.

Vanco & Exh

Waterfro

Water

Comox St.

Jervis St.

Davie St.

Bute St.

Thurlow St.

Burrard St.

Hornby St.

Nelson

Has St.

English Bay Beach

Pacific St.

St. Paul's Hos

Seymour St.

Stac

English Bay

Hadden Park

Vanier Park

Yaletown Roundhouse

P Place

Main St.

Tower Beach

Spanish Banks Beach

N.W. Marine Dr.

Acadia Rd.

Chancellor Blvd.

Drummond Dr.

2nd Ave. W.

Jericho Beach Park

Point Grey Rd.

Cornwall Ave.

1st Ave.

Pacific Blvd.

Olympic Village

2nd

6th Ave. W.

Museum of Anthropology

Newton Wynd

Westbrook Rd.

University Blvd.

4th Ave. W.

8th Ave. W.

Nat. Defence

Alma St.

4th Ave.

MacDonald

Broadway

6th Ave. W.

Broadway

City Hall

U.B.C. Health Sciences Centre

Agronomy Rd.

Thunderbird Blvd.

East Mall

West Mall

University Blvd.

Golf Club

10th Ave. W.

13th Ave. W.

16th Ave. W.

Blanca St.

Dunbar St.

Blenheim St.

12th Ave.

16th

Kitsilano

Burrard St.

Fir St.

Birch St.

Oak St.

Cedar Cr.

Granville St.

Matthews

Wolfe St.

Vancouver Hospital & Health Sciences

20th Ave. W.

Wreck Beach

Thunderbird Stadium

Stadium Rd.

16th Ave.

20th Ave. W.

Crown St.

King Edward Ave. W.

Puget Dr.

MacDonald St.

Abbutus St.

King Edward Ave.

Nanton Ave.

Heather St.

Cambie St.

King Edward

29th Ave.

Midlothian

University of British Columbia

Imperial Rd.

29th Ave.

29th Ave.

Eddington Dr.

Yew St.

Angus Dr.

B.C. Children's

B.C. Women's

Van Dusen Botanical Gardens

Pacific Spirit Regional Park

South West Marine Dr.

33rd Ave.

Dunbar St.

37th Ave.

Larch St.

West Blvd.

33rd Ave. W.

Queen Elizabeth Park

Shaughnessy Golf and Country Club

Juculta Cr.

Crown St.

41st Ave. W.

MacKenzie St.

37th Ave. W.

Strait

51st Ave. W.

Marine Dr.

45th Ave. W.

99

41st Ave. W.

Oakridge Mall

Oakridge-41st Ave.

Of

Dunbar St.

Blenheim St.

Balaclava St.

49th Ave. W.

S.W. Marine Dr.

West Blvd.

49th Ave. W.

Langara College

Georgia

Point Grey Golf And Country Club

54th Ave. W.

Angus Dr.

55th Ave. W.

McCleery Golf Course

Marine Drive Golf Club

59th Ave. W.

Granville St.

Heather St.

Langara Golf Course

VANCOUVER

Iona Island

60th Ave. W.

64th Ave. W.

Oak St.

Marine Dr.

70th Ave. W.

Cambie St.

Marine Drive

North Arm Fraser River

Twin Isla

N

0   1.0   2.0
1:80 000   km

BELCARRA

ANMORE

Bedwell Bay

Sasamat Lake

Belcarra Regional Park

Westwood Plateau Golf Academy

Westwood Plateau Golf & Country Club

Pinecone Burke Provincial Park

Bedwell Bay Rd.

Belcarra Regional Park

PORT MOODY

Crown Park Blvd.

Plateau Blvd.

Coy Ave.

Martin St.

Burns Point

Carraholly Point

Port Moody

Reed Point

Marina

Barnet Hwy.

7A

Pinetree Way

Coquitlam River

Oxford St.

Coast Meridian Rd.

Hyde Creek Nature Reserve

mon Fraser University

University Dr.

Burnaby Mountain Conservation Area

North Rd.

Clarke Rd.

Broadway

St. Johns St.

St. George St.

City Hall

Eagle Ridge

Barnet Hwy.

7A

Mariner Way

City Hall

7

Lougheed Highway

Coquitlam Ave.

Westminster Ave.

Riverwood Gt.

Victoria Dr.

Prarie Ave.

Lincoln Ave.

Oxford St.

Riverside

Dominion Ave.

COQUITLAM

Como Lake Ave.

Mundy Park

Austin Ave.

Austin Ave.

PORT COQUITLAM

Mclean Ave.

Langan Ave.

Pitt River Rd.

Broadway St.

Coast Meridian Rd.

Kebet Way

Pitt River

Coquitlam I.R. 2

Riverview

Coquitlam Colony Farm Regional Park

Lougheed Highway

Lougheed Town Centre

George Derby Centre

37

Braid St.

United Blvd.

1

Mary Hill - Pass

7B

Windsor Rd.

Ford Rd.

Queen's Park Care Centre

99A

1A

Sapperton Channel

Sapperton Channel

Fraser   River

Douglas Island

Fraser River Islands Regional Park

Helmcken Point

Sebastian Point

NSTER

99A

1A

116 Ave.

King Rd.

Surrey Rd.

South Fraser Perimeter Rd.

Surrey Bend Regional Park

114 Ave.

115 Ave.

114 Ave.

McBride Dr.

112 Ave.

110 Ave.

DELTA

SURREY

Surrey Memorial

King George Hwy.

Fraser Hwy.

Green Timbers Urban Forest

Tynehead Regional Park

1

RCMP

15

1A

99

99A

Bear Creek Park

80 Ave.

N

Vancouver International Airport
YVR Airport
Coast Guard Station
Float Plane Base
Sea Island Centre
Middle Arm Fraser River

North Arm Fraser River

70th Ave. W.
S.W. Marine Dr.
Drive
Kent Ave. N.
Mitchell Rd.
S.E. Marine Dr.
Marine Way
Marine Dr.
Kent Ave. N.
North Fraser Wy.
Riverway
River Rd.

Marine Dr.
Grant McConachie Wy.
Grauer Rd.
Templeton St.
Bridgeport
Van Thorne Wy.
No. 4 Rd.
River Rd.
Twigg Island
Twigg Pl.
Mitchell Island
Knight St.
River Rd.
River Rd.

Miller Rd.
Russ Baker Wy.
Middle Arm
No. 3 Rd.
Sea Island Wy.
Kil by Dr.
St. Edwards Dr.
Shell Rd.
Bridgeport Rd.
No. 5 Rd.
No. 6 Rd.
No. 7 Rd.

Jericho Ave.
Gilbert Rd.
Capstan Way
Cambie
King George Park
Jacombs Rd.
Mikasa Golf Centre

River Rd.
Elmbridge Way
Aberdeen
Lansdowne Park Shopping Centre
38
Alderbridge Wy.
Greenacres Golf Club
91
Mayfair Lakes Golf & Country Club

Westminster Hwy.
Lansdowne Rd.
Garden City Rd.
Cooney Rd.
37
Richmond Nature Park W.
Richmond Nature Park E.
Westminster Hwy.
Nelson Rd.
No. 9 Rd. (Ewen Rd.)

No. 1 Rd.
No. 2. Rd.
Richmond **H**
Minoru Park **P**
Lansdowne Way
Minoru Blvd.
36
99

Granville Ave.
City Hall
Granville Ave.
Richmond Go-Cart Track
Pacific Coast Golf Academy

RICHMOND

Blundell Rd.
Railway Ave.
No. 3. Rd.
Mof fatt Rd.
St. Albans Rd.
General Currie Rd.
Lulu Island
Blundell Rd.
No. 5 Rd.
Sidaway Rd.
Country Meadows Golf Course

Francis Rd.
No. 1. Rd.
No. 2. Rd.
Gilbert Rd.
No. 4 Rd.
Mylora Golf Course
No. 6 Rd.
Richmond Horsemen's Club

Williams Rd.
Railway Ave.
South Arm Park
Williams Rd.
Shell Rd.
Triangle Rd.
Fraser River Gravesend Reach
Hopcott Rd.
River Rd.
98 St.

No. 1 Rd.
London Park
Gilbert Rd.
Steveston Hwy.
Richmond Country Club
Green Slough
Richmond Ice Centre & Watermania
Progress Way
72 St.

Moncton St.
Trites Rd.
No. 2. Rd.
Finn Rd.
Horseshoe Slough
Hammersmith Wy.
Horseshoe Wy.
Rice Mill Rd.
Deas Thruway
32
Deas Island
68 St.
62B St.

Cannery Channel
Steveston Island
Dyke Rd.
Finn Rd.
Dyke Rd.
Woodward Slough
Woodward Reach
Deas Island Regional Park
Vasey Rd.
60 A ve.
64 St.

River
Sea Reach
Reifel Island
Woodward Island
Rose Island
Kirkland Island
Williamson Slough
Williamson Slough
Cove Links Golf Course
29
28
Burns Dr.
99
72 St.

George C. Reifel Migratory Bird Sanctuary
Duck Island
Gunn Island
Ladner Reach
Ferry Rd.
60 St.
LADNER

Robertson Rd.
Westham Island Rd.
Savage Rd.
Barber Island
Ladner Harbour Park
Bridge St.
Westminster A ve.
Central A ve.
Grove Ave.
Linden Dr.
10
Ladner Trunk Rd.

WESTHAM ISLAND
Westham Island Rd.
Tamboline Rd.
River Rd. W.
Elliott St.
52
53 St.
57 St.
H **Delta**
64 St.
66 St.
80 St.

ROBERTS BANK
Canoe Passage
46B St.
44A Ave.
48B St.
44 A ve.
Harvest Dr.
Arthur Dr.
DELTA
Churchill St.
Boundary Bay Airport

River Rd. W.
46A St.
36 Ave.
17
34B Ave.
36 A ve.
72 St.

Musqueam IR No.4
41B St.
33A A ve.
Deltaport Wy.
53 St.
57B St.
60 St.
64 St.

BCR
27B A ve.
28 A ve.
60 St.

Tsawwassen IR
52 St.
56 St.
Tsawwassen Dr.
52nd St. Pk. Res.

N
16 Ave.
Tsawwassen Golf & C.C.
17A Ave.
57 St.
16 A ve.

1:50 000

km

HIGHLANDS

Fizzle Lake

Prospect Lake

Beaver Lake

Woodridge Pl.

West Ridge Pl.

Kerryview Dr.

Perworth Dr.

Stevens Rd.

Goward Rd.

Excelsior Ave.

Old West Rd.

17A

Elk / Beaver Lake Regional Park

Elk Lake

17

Falaise Dr.

Munns Rd.

Prospect Lake Golf Course

Mountain Rd.

Quayle Rd.

Spring Rd.

Elk Rd.

Beaver Lake Rd.

West Saanich River

Royal Oak Golf Club

Commonwealth Place Park

Royal Oak

Broad Villa

17A

Thetis Lake Regional Park

Maltby Lake

Calvert Park

Viaduct Ave. W.

Logan Park

Stratford Rd.

Interurban Rd.

Glendale Gardens & Woodlands

Quick's Bottom Park

Markham Rd.

Greenlea Dr.

Viaduct Ave. E.

Viewmont Ave.

Chatterton Way

Westoby Rd.

Thetis Rd.

Barker Rd.

Highland Rd.

Pike Lake

Conway Rd.

Ivor Rd.

Hector Rd.

Liberto Rd.

Camosun College (Interurban Campus)

Layritz Park

Lindsay St.

Casa Linda Rd.

Royal Oak Shopping Centre

McKenzie Lake

Munns Rd.

Prospect Lake Rd.

Charlton Rd.

Vancouver I. Regional Correctional Centre

Wilkinson Rd.

Mann Ave.

Vanalman Ave.

Glanford Ave.

Douglas

Patricia Bay Highway

Frances/King Regional Park

Charlton Rd.

Granville Ave.

Hastings St.

Holland Ave.

Santa Anita Rd.

Roy Rd.

Interurban Rd.

Carey Rd.

Panama Hill Park

Copley Park

Baker St.

Tait St.

Glanford Ave.

Prior Lake

Highland Pacific Golf

Burnside Rd. W.

Watkiss Way

Helmcken Rd.

Knockan Hill Park

Wilkinson Rd.

Tulip Ave.

Grange Rd.

Hyacinth Park

McKenzie Ave.

Interurban Rd.

Tillicum Rd.

Carey

Thetis Lake

Highland Rd.

VIEW ROYAL

1

Six Mile Rd.

Victoria General H

Way

Burnside Rd.

Marigold Rd.

Burnside Rd.

ENR.

Gourman Pl.

Goldie Ave.

Bellamy Rd.

Phelps Ave.

Selwyn Rd.

Millhill Rd.

Langvista Dr.

Hansen Ave.

Mill Hill Regional Park

Atkins Ave.

Price Bay

Heddle Ave.

Helmcken Rd.

Hedgeview

Craigflower Creek Park

King Rd.

Werra Rd.

Midwood Rd.

Portage Inlet

Admirals Rd.

Cuthbert Holmes Park

Cowper Ave.

Colquitz Rd.

Ker Ave.

Tillicum Centre

Hampton Rd.

1

Burnside Rd.

LANGFORD Ave.

1A

Highway

Wilfert Rd.

Beaumont Ave.

Royal Ave.

Sitmont Ave.

Municipal Hall

Admirals Rd.

Gorge Rd. W.

Gorge Rd.

Dysart Rd.

Obed Ave.

Maddock Ave.

Milgrove St.

Harriet Rd.

Burnside Rd. W.

Gorge Rd. W.

Balfour Ave.

Gorge

Hoffman Ave.

Atkins Ave.

Goldstream Ave.

Island Highway

Ocean Blvd.

Rosebank Rd.

Juan de Fuca Recreation Park

Portage Park

Craigflower Rd.

Cooper Rd.

Gorge Waters

Esquimalt Gorge Park

1A

The Gorge

Gorgeview

Royal Colwood Golf Club

College Dr.

Aldeane Ave.

Chagel Rd.

14

CFB Esquimalt Blvd.

Esquimalt Harbour

Thetis Cove

New Songhees IR No. 1A

Parkland Dr.

Gorge Vale Golf Club

Tillicum Rd.

Selkirk Ave.

Craigflower Rd.

Skinner St.

Selkirk Water

Banfield Park

Mount View Ave.

Sooke Rd.

Leaming Rd.

University Dr.

College Dr.

Belmont Rd.

ESQUIMALT

Admirals Rd.

CFB Esquimalt (Naden)

Colville Rd.

Rockheights Ave.

Lampson St.

Highrock Park

Devonshire Rd.

Dominion Rd.

Hereward Rd.

ENR.

Wilson St.

Esquimalt Rd.

Kelly Rd.

Langholme Dr.

Royal Roads University

Pilgrim Cove

Constance Cove

Fort Rodd Hill and Fisgard Lighthouse National Historic Sites

Lang Cove

CFB Esquimalt (Dockyard)

Esquimalt Rd.

Old Esquimalt Rd.

Municipal Hall P

Esquimalt Rd.

West Bay

Lime Bay

Metchosin Rd.

Wishart Rd.

Cottonwood Rd.

Fisgard Lighthouse

Esquimalt Lagoon

Lyall St.

Lyall St.

Lampson St.

Greenwood Ave.

Bewdley Ave.

Munro St.

Rose Bay

Shoal Point

Allandale Rd.

Heatherbell Rd.

Coburg Peninsula Park

Ocean Blvd.

Saxe Point Park

Saxe Point

Inspiration Cove

Fraser St.

McAuley St.

CFB Esquimalt (Work Point)

Dallas Rd.

Owens Rd.

Lagoon Rd.

Milburn Dr.

MacAulay Point Park

MacAulay Point

McLoughlin Point

Ogden Point

Wishart Rd.

Dressler Rd.

Cotlow Rd.

Latoria Rd.

COLWOOD

Royal Roads

Ferry to Port Angeles

Passenger Ferry to Pt. Angeles & Seattle

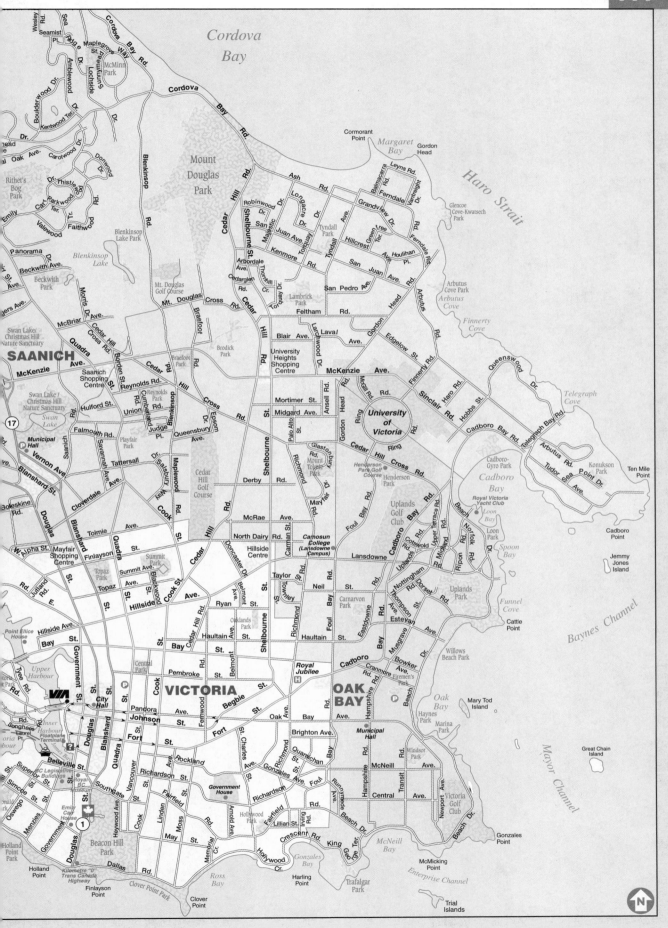

0   0.5   1.0

1:50 000   km

REGIONAL DISTRICT OF NORTH OKANAGAN

COLDSTREAM

VERNON

Okanagan Lake

Okanagan Indian Reserve 1

Okanagan Lake

Kalamalka Lake

To Armstrong/Kamloops
Okanagan Hwy.

To Lumby

To Lumby

Dixon Dam Rd.
Harben Creek Rd.
Silver Star Rd.
Star Rd.
Silver Star Rd.
Dedecker East Rd.
Dedecker West Rd.
L & A Rd.
Rimer Rd.
Rimer Rd.
MacDonald Rd.
Pleasant Valley Rd.
Old Kamloops Rd.
Vernon Rd.
Briggs Rd.
Ploeger Rd.
BX Rd.
Mutrie Rd.
Cascade Dr.
Reservoir
Black Rock Rd.
Francis St.
East Vernon Rd.
East Vernon Rd.
Ballou Rd.
Phillips Rd.
Gallano Rd.
Pottery Rd.
Shantz Rd.
Pottery Rd.
Mountview Rd.
Hillview Golf
Sarsons Rd.
Sarsons Rd.
Middleton Wy.
Cypress Dr.
Upland Dr.
Buchanan Rd.
Aberdeen Rd.
Municipal Hall
Grey Rd.
Kalamalka Lake Rd.
Howe Dr.
Gile Dr.

46 Ave.
43 Ave.
39 Ave.
35 Ave.
30 Ave.
14 Ave.
37 Ave.
32 Ave.
15 St.
18 St.
19 St.
24 Ave.
23 Ave.
25 Ave.
20 Ave.
22 St.
23 St.
25 St.
26 St.
27 St.
28 St.
29 St.
30 St.
31 St.
32 St.
33 St.
34 St.
55 St.
24 St.
48 St.
45 St.
42 St.
27 St.
29 St.
41
35 Ave.
37 Ave.
39
42 Ave.
30 Ave.
37
27 Ave.
25 Ave.
24 Ave.
15 Ave.
34 Ave.
33 Ave.
Alexis Park Rd.

Village Green Mall
Lake City Casinos
Kin Race Track
Performing Arts Centre
Polson Park
Vernon Jubilee
RCMP City Hall

Okanagan Ave.
Davison Rd.
Bella Vista Rd.
Bella Vista Rd.
Hemitage Dr.
Allenby Way
27 Ave.
Okanagan Landing Rd.
43 St.
Fulton Rd.
Okanagan Hills Blvd.
Cameo Dr.
Scott Rd.
Tronson Rd.
Tronson Rd.
Landing Rd.
Longacre Dr.
Lakeshore Rd.
Bench Row Rd.
Commonage Rd.

Vernon Creek

Priests Valley IR No. 6
Vernon Regional Airport
Marshall Field Complex

Okanagan Lake
Marina
Marina
Boat Launch

Waddington Dr.
Middleton Wy.
Kalamalka Lake Rd.
CN
97
6
29 St.
W Addington Dr.
Vernon Golf and Country Club
Kalamalka Research Station
Alan Brooks Nature Centre
Vernon Military Camp
Okanagan College (Kalamalka Campus)
College Wy.
Reservoir Rd.
Mission Rd.
Derke Rd.
Husband Rd.
Postill Dr.
Westkal Rd.
Coldstream Rd.
Coldonie Rd.
Kidston Rd.
Juniffer Rd.
Postill Dr.

97
6

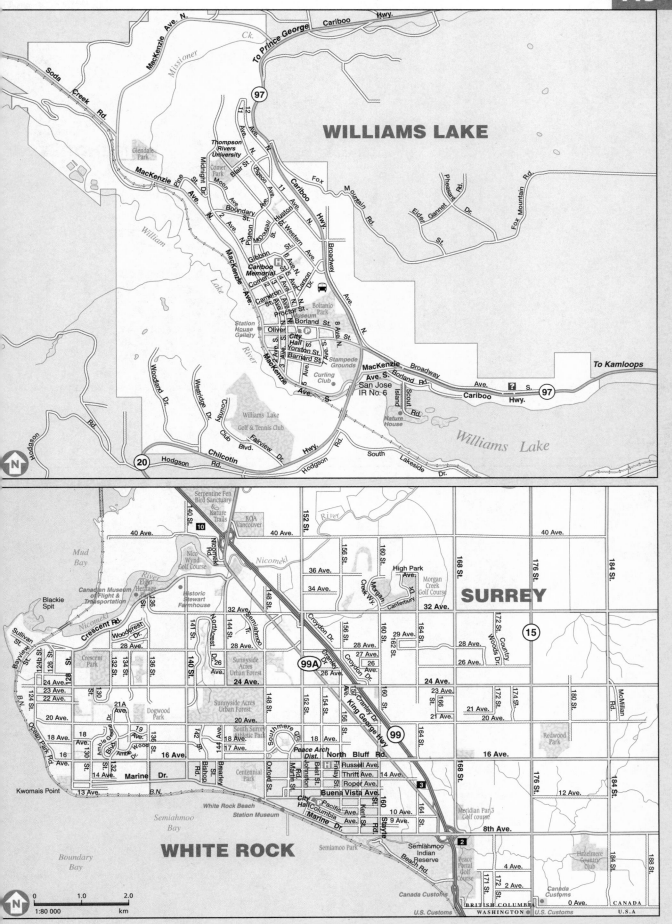

WILLIAMS LAKE

To Prince George
Cariboo Hwy.
97

Soda Creek Rd.

Missioner Ck.

MacKenzie Ave. N.

Glendale Park

Thompson Rivers University

Comer Park

Pine St.

Midnight Dr.

Blair St.

Pigeon Ave.

Moon

Boundary St.

McDonald

Huston St.

Western Ave.

Cariboo Hwy.

Broadway

Fox St.

Mountain Rd.

Pheasant Rd.

Elder St.

Gannet Dr.

Fox Mountain Rd.

MacKenzie Ave.

William Lake

Gibbon St.

Cariboo Memorial

Comer

Cameron Ave.

Carson Ave.

Proctor St.

Boitanio Park

Museum

Borland St.

Station House Gallery

City Hall

Oliver St.

Yorston St.

Barnard St.

8 Ave. N.

Stampede Grounds

MacKenzie Ave. S.

Borland Rd.

Broadway

Ave.

Cariboo Hwy. 97

To Kamloops

Curling Club

San Jose IR No. 6

Island

Scout Rd.

Nature House

Williams Lake

Williams Lake Golf & Tennis Club

Woodland Dr.

Westridge Dr.

Country Club Blvd.

Fairview Dr.

MacKenzie Ave. S.

Hodgson Rd.

Chilcotin Rd.
20 Hodgson Rd.

Hwy.

South Lakeside Dr.

WHITE ROCK

SURREY

Serpentine Fen Bird Sanctuary & Nature Trails

140 St.

10

KOA Vancouver

152 St.

River

40 Ave.

40 Ave.

40 Ave.

Mud Bay

Nico Wynd Golf Course

Nicomekl River

Nicomekl

156 St.

160 St.

High Park

36 Ave.

Morgan Creek Golf Course

168 St.

176 St.

184 St.

Blackie Spit

Canadian Museum of Flight & Transportation

Elgin Heritage Park

136 St.

Historic Stewart Farmhouse

34 Ave.

Morgan Creek Wy.

Canterbury

32 Ave.

Crescent Rd.

32 Ave.

Semiahmoo Tr.

148 St.

Croydon Dr.

Camley

156 St.

160 St.

162 St.

164 St.

29 Ave.

172 St. Country

15

Woods Dr.

Crescent Park

141 St.

144 St.

28 Ave.

28 Ave.

Northcrest Dr.

28 Ave.

Sunnyside Acres Urban Forest

Croydon Dr.

27 Ave.

26 Ave.

26 Ave.

28 Ave.

166

26 Ave.

172 St.

174 St.

180 St.

McMillan Rd.

Sullivan

Bayview St.

124 St.

126 St.

134 St.

132 St.

130

136 St.

140 St.

24 Ave.

99A

24 Ave.

154 St.

152 St.

156 St.

23 Ave.

166

21 Ave.

20 Ave.

Redwood Park

24 Ave.

23 Ave.

22 Ave.

21A Ave.

Dogwood Park

Sunnyside Acres Urban Forest

148 St.

20 Ave.

152 St.

King George Hwy.

160 St.

21 Ave.

20 Ave.

99

B.N.

18 Ave.

16 Ave.

Ocean Park Rd.

124 St.

130 St.

132 St.

14 Ave.

Amble

Wood Dr.

19 St.

142 St.

136 St.

South Surrey Athletic Park

18 Ave.

17 Ave.

18 Ave.

Southmere Crt.

Peace Arch Dist.

18 Ave.

North Bluff Rd.

164 St.

160 St.

16 Ave.

168 St.

176 St.

184 St.

188 St.

Kwomais Point

Marine Dr.

B.N.

13 Ave.

Centennial Park

Brearley St.

Bishop Rd.

Oxford St.

Johnston Rd.

Best St.

Finlay St.

Martin St.

Russell Ave.

Thrift Ave.

Roper Ave.

14 Ave.

3

Meridian Par 3 Golf course

Hazelmere Country Club

Boundary Bay

White Rock Beach Station Museum

City Hall

Columbia

Pacific

Buena Vista Ave.

Marine Dr.

160 St.

Stayte Rd.

Kent St.

10 Ave.

9 Ave.

164

12 Ave.

8th Ave.

Semiahmoo Bay

Semiahmoo Park

Semiahmoo Indian Beach Rd.

Semiahmoo Indian Reserve

Peace Portal Golf Course

2

4 Ave.

171 St.

172

2 Ave.

Canada Customs

188 St.

CANADA

Canada Customs

Canada Customs

U.S. Customs

BRITISH COLUMBIA
WASHINGTON U.S. Customs U.S.A.

0 Ave.

N

0   1.0   2.0
1:80 000   km

0   0.5   1.0
1:50 000
km

WHITEHORSE

To Alaska

1

Range Rd.

Two Mile Hill

Industrial Rd.

Quartz Rd.

Yukon River

VALLEYVIEW

Alaska Hwy.

Ogilvie St.

Fourth

Sixth

Eighth Ave.

Strickland

Wood St.

Second Ave.

First St.

Wickstrom

Main Ave.

City Hall

Hanson St.

Whitehorse General H

Whitehorse Airport

Transportation Museum

HILLCREST

Hamilton Blvd.

Hillcrest Dr.

Falcon Dr.

Hamilton Blvd. Dr.

Falcon

Robert Service Way

Lewes Blvd.

Nisutlin

Alsek

Teslin

Lewes Blvd.

Alsek

RIVERDALE

Chadburn Lake Rd.

To Watson Lake
Hwy. 97 B.C.

Schwatka Lake

N

YELLOWKNIFE

Fox Lake

To Rae / Edzo

Long Lake

Fred Henne Territorial Park

3

3

Jackfish Lake

To Giant Mine

4

Fault L.

Latham Island

Back Bay

Morrison Dr.

Old Town

Wiley Rd.

Jolliffe I.

Niven L.

Yellowknife Airport

Old Airport Rd.

Frame Lake

48th St.

Franklin Ave.

44th St.

Draw Ave.

City Hall

51 St.

51 St.

Ave.

54th St.

54th Ave.

School Ave.

Yellowknife Bay

Stanton Regional H

Range L.

Lake Rd.

Byrne Rd.

Franklin Ave.

Forrest Dr.

Con Rd.

Finlayson Dr.

Range

Kam Lake Rd.

Taylor Rd.

Deh Cho Blvd.

Enterprise Dr.

Coronation Dr.

Curry Dr.

Kam Lake

Pud Lake

YELLOWKNIFE

N

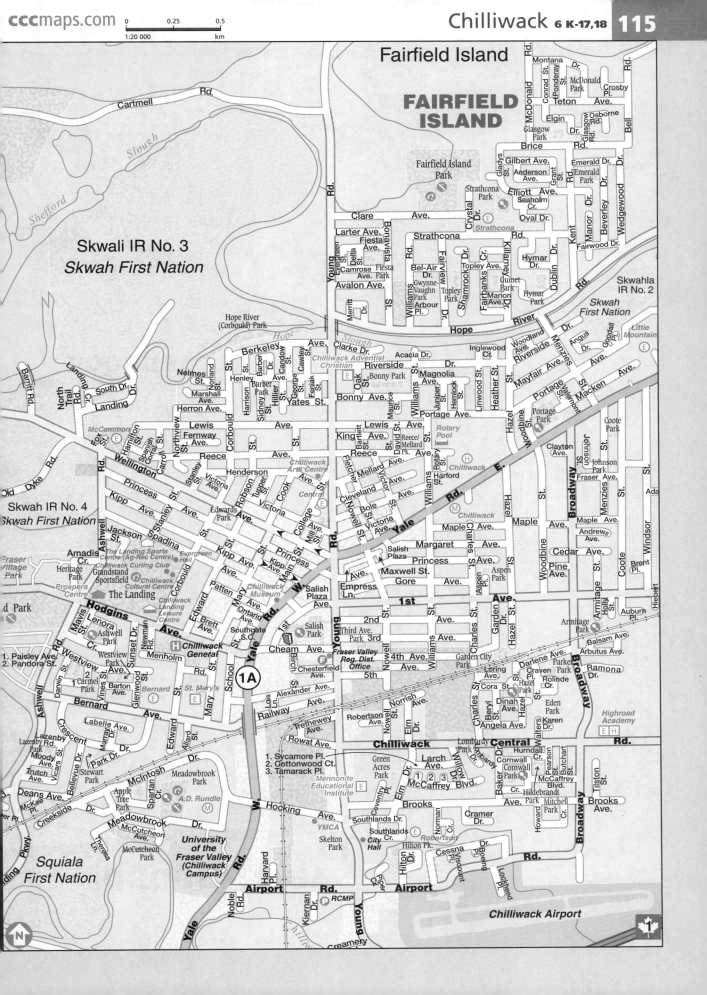

0   0.25   0.5
1:20 000   km

Fairfield Island

FAIRFIELD ISLAND

Skwali IR No. 3
Skwah First Nation

Skwahla IR No. 2

Skwah First Nation

Skwah IR No. 4
Skwah First Nation

Squiala First Nation

University of the Fraser Valley (Chilliwack Campus)

Chilliwack Airport

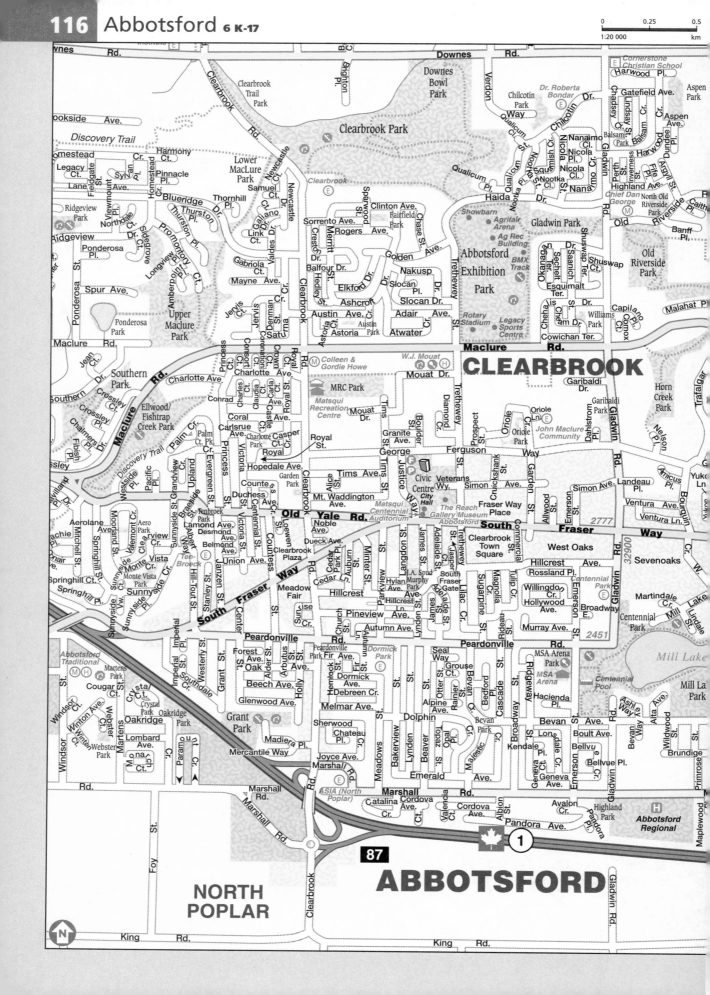

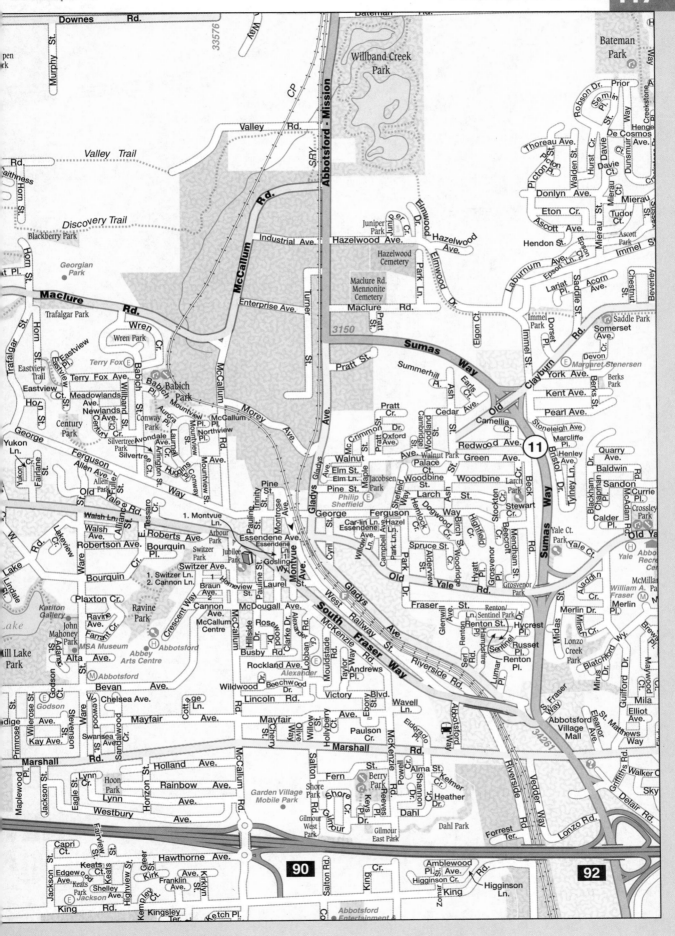

0   0.25   0.5
1:20 000   km

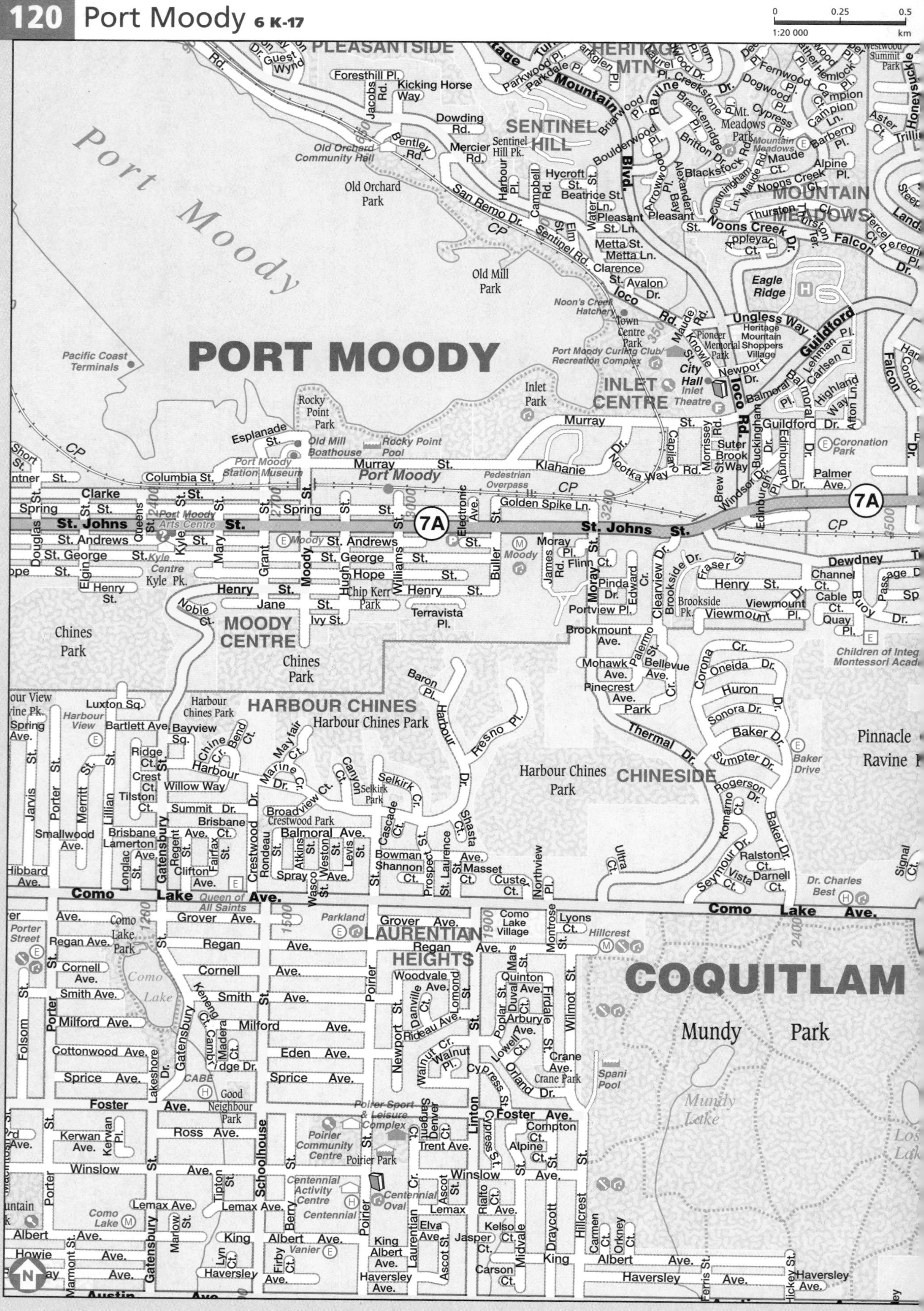

0   0.25   0.5
1:20 000   km

PLEASANTSIDE

HERITAGE MTN

SENTINEL HILL

PORT MOODY

MOUNTAIN MEADOWS

Pacific Coast Terminals

INLET CENTRE

City Hall

MOODY CENTRE

HARBOUR CHINES

Chines Park

Harbour Chines Park

CHINESIDE

Pinnacle Ravine

LAURENTIAN HEIGHTS

COQUITLAM

Mundy   Park

Como Lake

Mundy Lake

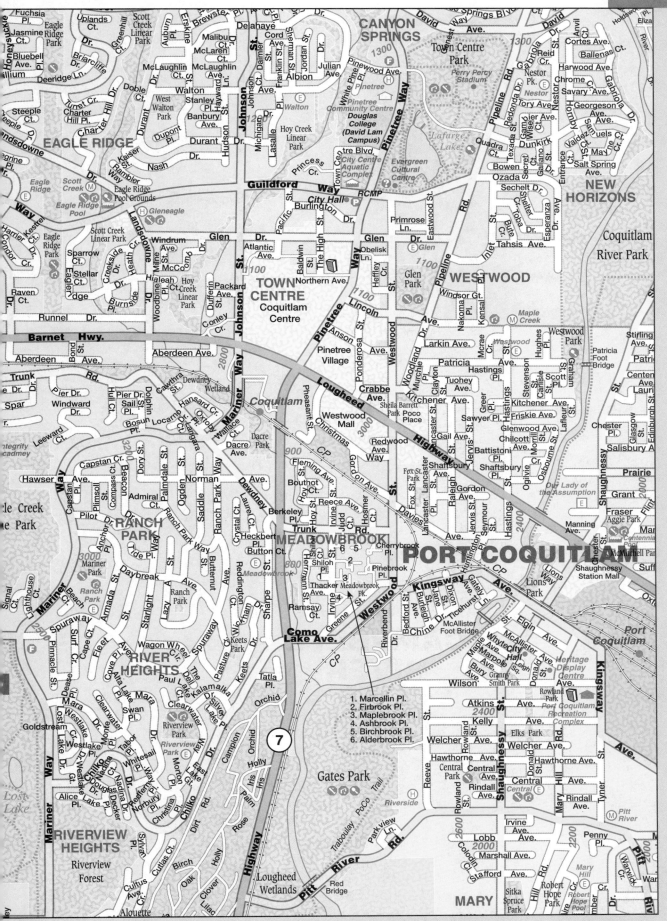

1. Marcellin Pl.
2. Firbrook Pl.
3. Maplebrook Pl.
4. Ashbrook Pl.
5. Birchbrook Pl.
6. Alderbrook Pl.

0   0.25   0.5
1:20 000
km

Elk Falls Provincial Park

28

19

Baikie Island

Dick Murphy Park

Thunderbird RV Park & Campground

Spit Rd.

Chum Rd. Rambow Rd. Vargo Rd. Vigar Rd. Coulter Rd. Baikie Rd. Alice Rd. Meredith Rd. Antonelli Rd.

Dolly Varden Rd. Coho Spring Rd. Woodburn Rd. Robinson Rd.

O'Leary Ave. Doyle Rd. Detweiler Rd. Charleville Rd. Quinsam Rd.

Steelhead Park Rd. Ida Rd. Ebert Rd. Enns Rd.

CAMPBELLTON

Campbell River

Raven Park

Campbell River Indian Reserve No. 11
Campbell River First Nation

Discovery Harbour Centre

Henderson Ave.
Homayno Cr.
Matlaten Cr.
Loughborough Dr.
Eaglenest Cr.
Spit

Willow St. Tamarac St. Island Hwy.
19A
19th Ave. 20th Ave.
16th Ave. 17th Ave. 15th Ave.
Spruce 16th Ave. 15th Ave. 14th Ave.
Redwood St. Petersen Ave. Maple Ave.
Campbellton Park
Pease Rd.
16th Ave.
Old Island Hwy. Captain John Cr. Quattell Ave. Cliffe Ave. Drake St. Roberts Cr. Weiwalkum Rd. Ferry Rd.

19A
Island Hwy. 19A
Old Spit Rd.
Discovery Harbour Marina

Sequoia Dr.
QUINSAM
Tree Lane Bear Pl. Cheviot Westmore Rd. Sandtrap Pl. Watson Rd. Northmore Rd. Highland Rd. Hopton Rd. Marguerite Rd. Kathleen
Troon Dr. Antigua Ripple Rock Pinehurst Dr. Augusta Fairway Pl.
Magnolia Dr.
Spruce St. Marwalk Cr.

Homewood Rd.

Nunn's Creek Park

Campbell River Common

Mariner Square Shopping Centre

1500

14th Ave. Cedar St. Dogwood St. Shoppers Row Roberts Reach

Tyee Plaza

Ferry to Quadra Island (10 min)

Campbell River Art Gallery
Tidemark Theatre
Campbell River Community Centre
Cypress St. 13th Ave. 11th Ave.
Dubeau Rd.

Coast Marina

Sequoia Springs Golf Club

Petersen Rd.
Shetland Rd.
Walworth Rd.

13th Ave. 12th Ave. 10th Ave. 9th Ave. 8th Ave.
Ironwood St. Hemlock St. Greenwood St. Fir St. Elm St. Cedar St. Birch St. Alder St. Thulin St.
Maple Rd.
Strathcona Regional District Office
Beech St. St. Ann's Rd. 9th Ave. 10th Ave.
City Hall
798

Robert Ostler Park

Fisherman's Wharf

Willis Rd.
Fisher Rd.
Carolyn Rd. Anne Rd.
Lynn Rd.
Douglas Rd.
Petersen Rd.
Old Petersen Rd.

Homewood Rd. Otter Rd. Smith Rd. Warden Rd. Westmere Rd.
7th Ave.
Des Deux Mondes
Phoenix M
7th Ave. 6th Ave. 7th Ave.
Frederick Cr. Charles Pl. Maria Gr.
Thulin St.

Discovery Pier
Maritime Heritage Museum

CAMPBELL RIVER

Holmstrom Rd.
Croation Rd.
Croation Mobile Home Park
Evergreen Rd.
Franzen Rd. Clerke Rd. Greta Rd. Mo Rd. Petersen Rd. Dolora Rd.
Franzen Park
Pinecrest Rd.
Jacqueline Rd.
Mer et montagne

Berne Rd.
2nd Ave.
Lonsdale Cr.
McPhedran Cr.
Taylor Way
Masters Rd. Nelson Pl. Thanet St. Munson St.
Panorama Dr.
11

Victoria Cr. Alpine Rd. Elkhorn Rd. Ridge Rd. 4th Ave.
Carihi H
Campbell River Curling Club
Leishman Rd.
Whitmore Ln. Cedar
Campbell River & District General H
Dogwood St.
Colwyn St. 5th Ave. 4th Ave. McCarthy St.
Centennial Park
Centennial Pool
Museum at Campbell River
Coronation Cr. Coronation Park
1st Ave.
Birch St. Alder St. McLean St. Thulin St. Murphy St.
McLean St. 3rd Ave. 2nd Ave. 5th Ave. 6th Ave.

Yaculta Bank
Sequoia Park

Nicholls Rd.
Willowcrest Rd.
Pinecrest
South Elk River Rd.
McPhedran Rd.
Elizabeth Rd. Jesmar Pl. Jones Rd. Velvecchio Rd. Lutod Rd.
Evergreen Dr.
Bathurst St.

Hidden Harbour Park North
Hidden Harbour Park South

Discovery Passage

N

Duncan (top map)

Stonehaven Park
Cowichan District
Holmesdale
Creek Park
Mayo Park
Baker Rd.
Cornerstone Pl.
Brownsey
Queen Ave.
Margaret's School
Cedar
Arbutus Ave. W
Dogwood Ave.
Hemlock Ave.
Gibbins
Banks Rd.
Wilson Ave.
Kinch Ave.
Watts Rd.
Lashman Ave.
Cliffs Rd.
Government St.
College
Nagle
Islay St.
Holmes St.
Cairnsmore
Herbert
McDonald
Cavell
White Rd.
Lukaitis Ln.
Pine Ave.
Spruce
Vista Ave.
Duncan
Beverly St.
Canada Hwy.
2749
Duncan
Vancouver Island University (Cowichan Campus)
Island Savings Centre
Quamichan
Alexander
Beverly St.
Lewis St.
Heather St.
Clair St.
Dingwall St.
York Rd.
2355
5859
Fourth St.
Third St.
Second St.
First
Vian St.
Clements
Cowichan Theatre
James St.
Garden St.
Alderlea St.
Elvins St.
Kinsmen Park
Cowichan Aquatic Centre
Cowichan
Alexander
Powell St.
Whistler St.
Bundock Ave.
Howard Ave.
Charlotte St.
Chesterfield
Duncan
Georgina Dr.
Olson Rd.
Lakes Rd.
400
Tzouh
Centennial Park
Jubilee St.
Boundary
Evans St.
Ingram St.
CVRD Office
Lois Ln.
Kenneth
Queens Rd.
Julian St.
Brae Rd.
Coronation
Ypres
Festubert
Robertson St.
Coronation Mall
Bundock Ave.
Marchmont
Beech Ave.
Lomas Rd.
Prevost
Lakes Rd.
Cowic
Gabourie Pl.
Cowichan River
Khowhemun
Station St.
Craig St.
City Hall
Cowichan Valley Museum
Trunk Rd.
Underwood St.
281
Duncan Mall
Central
Watson St.
Oak St.
Chaster St.
Dobson Rd.
McKinstry
Wharncliffe
Castle St.
Lee St.
1. Khowhemun Rd.
2. Georgetown Rd.
3. Club St.
4. Somenos St.
5. Kakalatza Rd.
6. August Rd.
Whut'stun Rd.
Willies Rd.
Seymour Rd.
River Rd.
Thorne Rd.
Church Rd.
Qwulshemut Rd.
Indian Rd.
Miller Rd.
Allenby Rd.
Laurel Gv.
Shmaqwuthut Rd.
Cowichan IR No. 1
Cowichan First Nation
Way
Price Rd.
McKinstry Pl.
Al Wilson Gv.
McAdam Park
Campbell Pl.
Castle Park Pl.
Beech Rd.
Campbell Rd.
DUNCAN
5460
Boys Rd.
Khowutzun Wy.
Daniels Rd.
Muladu Rd.
Stoltou Cr.
Rogers Ln.
Smith Rd.
Jacob Rd.
Frontage Rd.
SVI
3025
Boys Rd.
2699
5460

N

Fort St. John (bottom map)

West Bypass Rd.
C.M. Finch
W.I. Park
Peace River
Princess Crescent Park
110 Ave.
109 Ave.
108 Ave.
107 St.
106
105 St.
104 St.
108 St.
106
105 Ave.
104
103
102
101
100 Ave.
Pickell Park
112 St.
110 St.
City Hall 107
North Gate Mall
North Peace Cultural Centre
Fort St. John Central
Bert Bowes
99
98
97
96
95
104 Rd.
94
93
91
Alaska Rd.
Alaska Hwy.
Fort Rd.
115 St.
Old Rd.
Mighty Peace Ball Diamonds
Tahltan Rd.
111 St.
112 St.
Beaver Rd.
Cree Rd.
89
107 Rd.
103 Rd.
FORT ST. JOHN
Peace Ave.
109 Ave.
Princess
Dr. Kearney
Alwin Holland
107A Ave.
106 Ave.
105 Ave.
104 Ave.
103A Ave.
103 Ave.
102 Ave.
101 Ave.
88A St.
86A St.
Surerus Park
Fort St. John Hospital & Health Centre
The Fort St. John Cemetery
100 Ave.
91A St.
88 St.
Robert Ogilvie
98A Ave.
97 Ave.
96A
96 Ave.
North Peace Leisure Pool
North Peace Arena
Kids Arena
Curling Club
Enerplex
Centennial Park
Fort St. John North Peace Museum
94A St.
93A St.
Toboggan Hill Park
North Peace
Totem Mall
93 Ave.
94A St.
91 Ave.
89 Ave.
87 St.
88 St.
86A St.
86 St.
92 St.
Mathews Park
92A St.

N

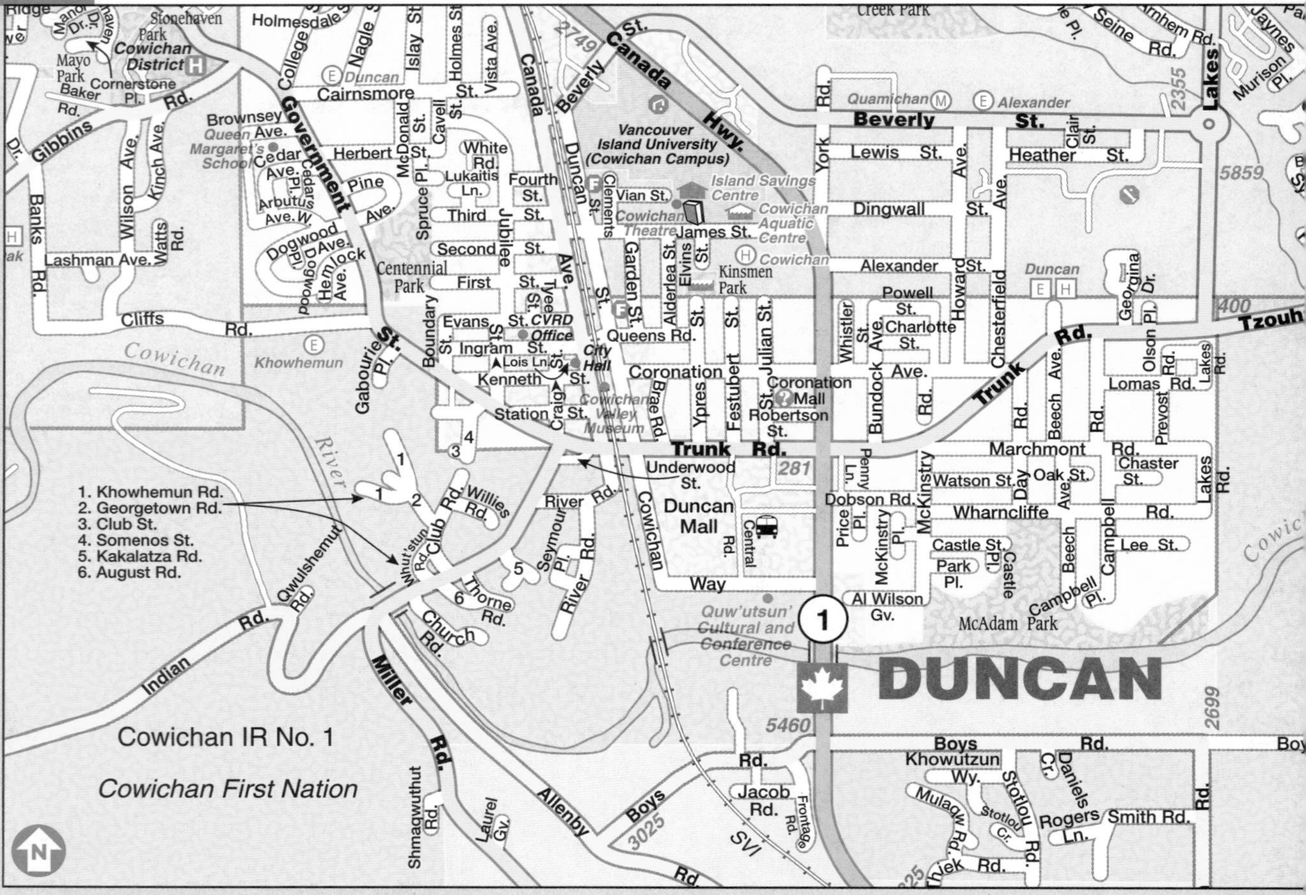

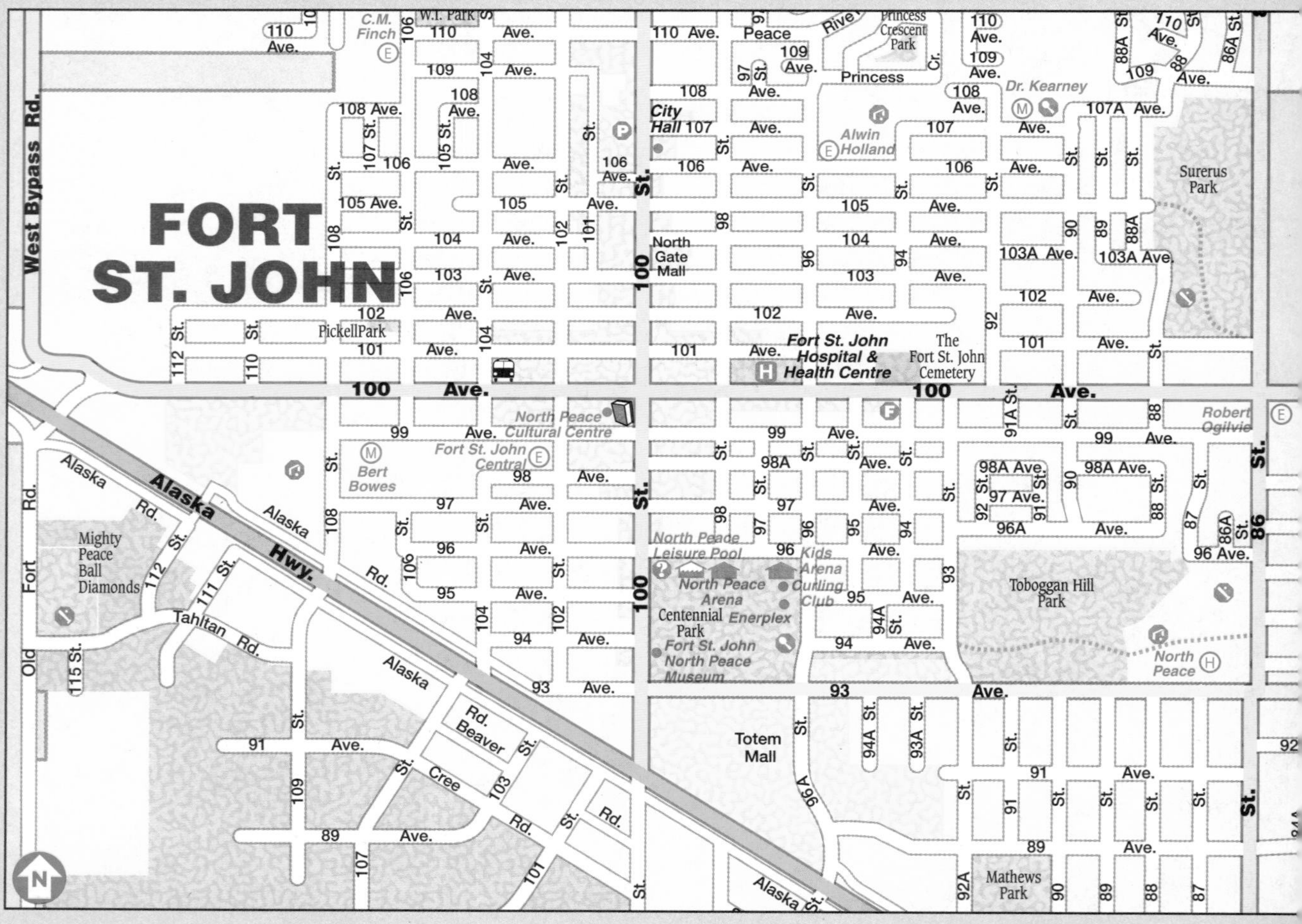

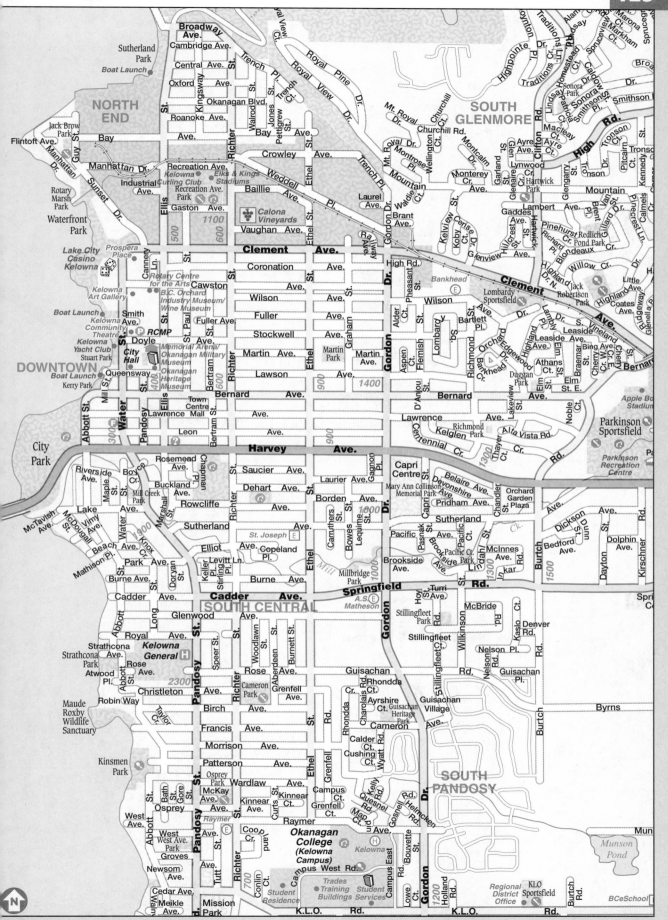

0   0.25   0.5
1:20 000
km

Kamloops map (top)

Thompson River

Overlander Park

Silver Sage Rd.
Silver Sage Trailer Park

Riverside Park
Interior Savings Centre
Kamloops Heritage Railway
Waterfront Park
Pioneer Park
Waterfront Park
Pioneer Cemetery

Strathcona Park

Victoria St. W.
City Hall
Lorne St.
Lansdowne Village
Lansdowne St.
Lake City Casino
Kamloops Curling Club
Memorial Arena
Skateboard Park

Seymour St.
Victoria Ave.
Art Gallery
Regional District Office
CITY CENTRE
Pavilion Theatre
Exhibition Park
Charles Anderson Stadium

Memorial Hill Park
Kamloops Museum & Archives
St. Paul St.
YMCA
Battle St.
Nicola St.
Columbia St.

St. Ann's Academy
Royal Inland
KAMLOOPS
Dominion St.
Pine St.
Pleasant St.
Lloyd George
Prince Charles Park
Crescent Heights Park

Sahali Centre Mall
McGill Rd.
Sa-Hali Terrace Park
Provincial Home Cemetery
Douglas St.
Pleasant St. Cemetery

Summit Shopping Centre
Columbia Place
Columbia Square
Tudor Village
LOWER SAHALI
Munro St.
Cowan St.
Sagebrush Theatre
South Kamloops
Fraser St.

Peterson Creek Park

370
Springhill Dr.
Whiteshield Pl.
1 **97**

Langley map (bottom)

64 Ave.
Langley Crossing
Municipal Hall
Willowbrook Recreation Centre
WILLOWBROOK
Mufford Cr.
Glover

Willowbrook Dr.
Willowbrook Shopping Centre
Langley Centre
62 Ave.
National Training Rink
10

1A
Langley By-pass
Langley Power Centre
1A 10
CP CN

LANGLEY
Landmark Wy.
Fraser Hwy.
Logan Ave.
Duncan Wy.
Logan Creek Park
Kwantlen Polytechnic University

Production Wy.
200A St.
Industrial Ave.
Locke Ln.
Whytecliff Agile Learning Centre
Dumais Park
Glover Rd.
By-pass
Canlan Ice Sports Langley Twin Rinks

Langley College
Cascades Casino
Innes Corners
57 Ave.
1A

56 Ave.
The Global School
DOUGLAS
City Hall
Rotary Centennial Park
Fraser Crossing

NICOMEKL
Linwood Park
Michaud Park
Timms Comm. Centre
Langley Mall
Park Ave.
Douglas Park
Derek Doubleday Arboretum

Brydon Park
54A Ave.
Douglas Recreation Centre
Douglas Park Community

Nicomekl Community
Nicomekl Park
52 Ave.
51A Ave.

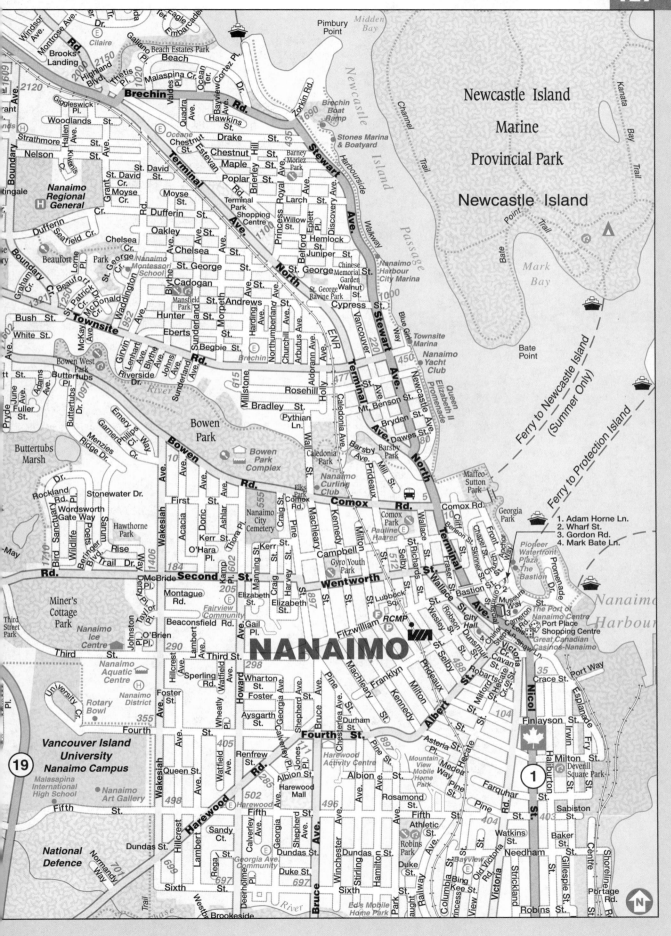

0   0.25   0.5
1:20 000
km

MacKay Creek Park
Beaconsfield Rd.
Wavertree Rd.
Mosquito Creek Park
Granada
Saville Ct.
Lucerne Pl.
Cartier
Cartier Pl.
Monte Vista Ct.
St. Albans
St. Pauls
Tamarack Pl.
St. Marys
Sunnycrest
Highland Blvd.
Wentworth Ave.
Trenton Pl.
Verona Pl.
Croydon Pl.
Delbrook
Croydon Pl.
Rockland Rd. W.
Norwood
Woodbury
Rockland Rd. W.
Rockland Park
Rockland Rd. E.
Braemar Rd. E.
Beaumont
Evergreen Pl.
Leovista Ave.
Delbrook Plaza
Silverdale
Balmoral Rd. W.
Runnymede Rd.
Carisbrooke
Braemar Dr.
Wellington Dr.
Braemar Rd.
Melbourne Ave.
Glenview Dr.
Evergreen Pl.
Kerry
Sharon
Entree
Calder Ave.
Sandringham
Carnarvon
Kensington Ave.
Kensington Rd.
Carisbrooke
Forest Hills Dr.
Glenora Ave.
The Del
Redfern
Holyrood
Osborne Rd. W.
Osborne
Carisbrooke Rd. E.
Carisbrooke Park
Carisbrooke Rd. E.
St. Kilda Ave.
Kennedy
Arlington Cr.
Belmont Ave.
Birchwood Dr.
James Rd. W.
St. James Rd. W.
St. James
St. Andrews E.
Regent
Canfield
Beverley
Highlands
Fairmont Park
Windsor Rd.
Kings Rd.
Andre Piolat
Windsor Rd.
Kings Rd.
Queens Rd. E.
Queens Rd. E.
Markham
Colwood
Woodbine
Griffin
Del Rio Dr.
Delbrook Park
Delbrook RecCentre
Queens Rd. W.
District Hall
W. 29th
Holy Trinity
Eastern Ave.
E. 28th St.
E. 27th St.
E. 25th St.
Somerset St.
Princess
Edgemont
William Griffin RecCentre
William Griffin Park
Westview Park
Westview Shopping Centre
W. 29th St.
28th
27th
26th
25th
2600
E. 26th St.
Tempe
Maitland
Tempe Heights Park
Dudley Place Park
W. 23rd St.
W. 24th St.
Larson Park
1 ⚜
17
Upper Levels Hwy.
18
W. 24th St.
Norseman Park
Centennial Theatre
Mickey McDougall RecCentre
McDougall Field
Greenwood Park
Sowden Park
Windsor House Alternate
Westmoreland Cr.
Larson Cr.
Carson Graham
W. 23rd
W. 22nd
23rd
22nd
Rey Sargent Park
Harry Jerome RecCentre
Memorial RecCentre
E. 24th St.
E. 23rd
E. 22nd St.
Hamilton Park
W. 21st St.
Larson Dr.
W. 22nd
W. 21st St.
21st
Rodger Burnes Green
21st
E. 21st St.
Queensbury
Kea Wood Cr.
Macleod Park
W. 20th St.
Wolfe
W. 20th St.
Wagg Creek Park
W. 20th St.
20th
Grand Blvd.
E. 20th St.
E. 18th St.
Boundary
Heywood Park
W. 19th St.
Mosquito Creek Park
W. 19th St.
Kinsman Park
19th
Lonsdale Ave.
1900
19th
Moody
Cumberland Cr.
Fir St.
Chris Zuelke Park
18th
Chesterfield
18th
Ridgeway
St. Andrew's
Tobruck Ave.
W. 17th St.
Westview
Mahon Park
17th
17th
Hyak Park
W. 16th St.
16th
16th
Capilano Mall
Marine Dr.
W. 15th St.
W. 14th St.
Delbruck
Forbes
15th
14th
14th St. Civic Plaza
1400
Lions Gate H
15th
14th
Boulevard Park
W. 3rd St.
W. Keith Rd. W.
13th St.
St. Thomas Aquinas
W. 8th St.
City Hall
RCMP P
F
E. 13th St.
13th St.
Copping St.
Automall Dr.
Mission IR No. 1 Squamish First Nation
Mahon
Delbruck
McEvoy
W. Chief Joseph Ct.
St. Edmund's
Ottawa Gardens
Queen Mary
W. 12th St.
6th St.
Victoria Park
E. 8th St.
St. Andrew's Park
12th
1100
11th
St. George's
10th
Harbourside Dr.
Harbourside Pl.
Bewicke Park
Bodwell Academy
Kings Mill Walk
Mosquito Creek Marina
BCIT (Marine Campus)
Burrard Yacht Club
Gostick Pl.
Forbes
W. Esplanade
W. 1st
W. 2nd
W. 4th St.
W. 5th St.
Presentation House Museum
Chief August Jack Park
John Braithwaite Community Centre
St. George's Ave.
E. 6th St.
E. 5th St.
North Shore Neighbourhood House
Chief Mathias Joe Park
Ridgeway Annex
9th
8th
Lyon Pl.
E. 8th St.
Chief Dan George Park
NORTH VANCOUVER
Waterfront Park
Chesterfield Pl.
Cates
Chadwick
Semisch Park
Chief Mathias
John Braithwaite
Derek Inman Park
Emerald Park
E. 14th Ave.
7th
6th
SeaBus Terminal
Lonsdale Quay Market
Lonsdale Ave.
1100
St. George's
St. Patrick's Ave.
St. David's
Hamersley Park
E. 2nd St.
E. 3rd St.
5th
4th
Ridgeway
Moodyville Park
Burrard
Burrard Dry Dock Pier
North Vancouver Dry Docks
CN
Low Level Rd.
E. 1st St.
Low Level Rd.
Inlet
SeaBus (12 min)
Richardson International Terminal
Cargill Terminal
🧭 N

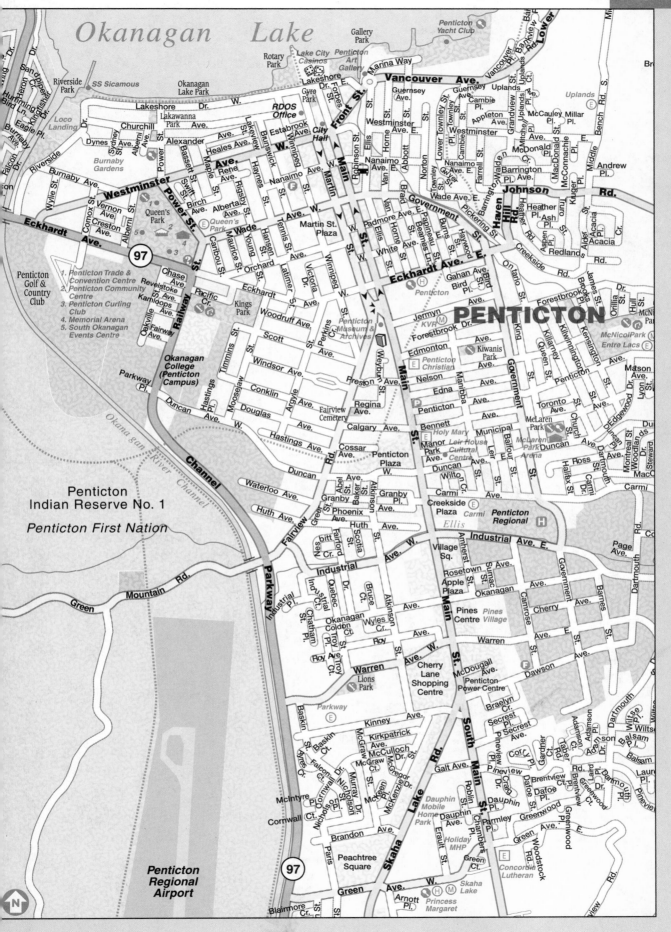

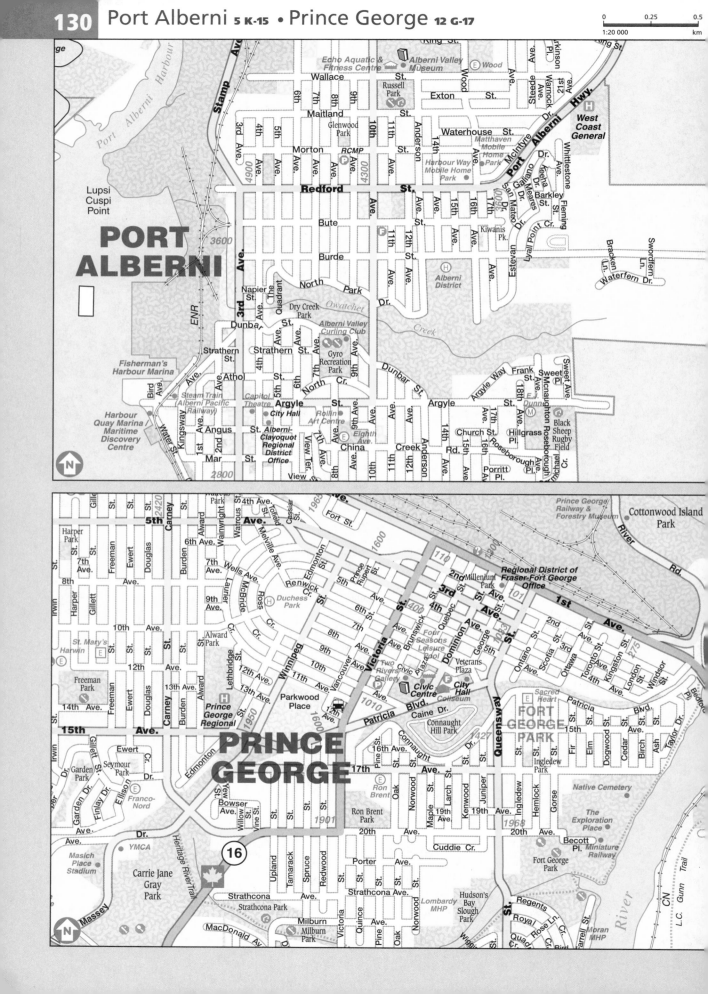

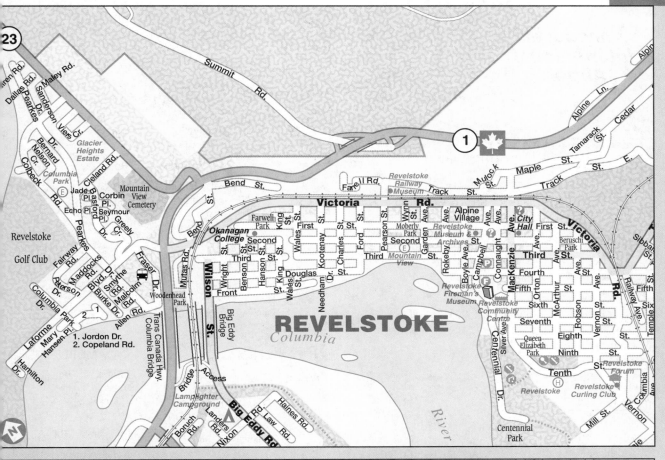

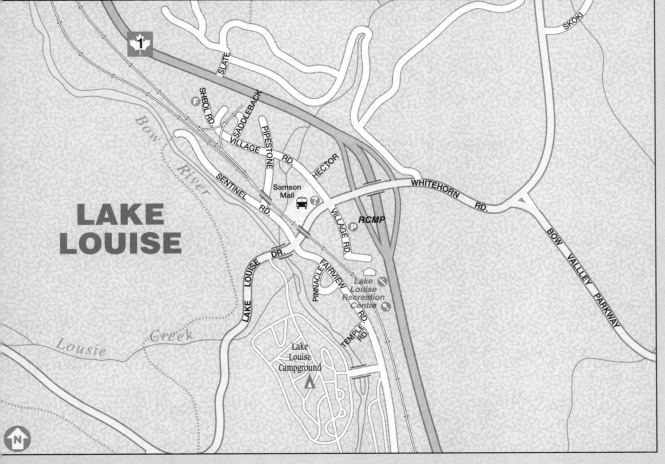

0   0.25   0.5
1:20 000
km

Vancouver International Airport

Grauer Rd.

Templeton

Templeton St.

Arthur Laing Bridge

River Rock Marina

River Dr.

River Horne

Van

No. 4 Rd.

Vancouver Marina/ Airport Yacht Club

River Rock Casino Resort

Bridgeport

River Rd.

SPY

River Rd. West

Charles St.

Beckwith

Smith

Garden City Rd.

Gage

39

Sea Island Centre

Miller Park

Airport Connector Bridge

Douglas St.

Bridgeport   Rd.

Grant   McConachi   Way

Miller   Rd.

BURKEVILLE

Sea Island Cr.

Sea Island C.O.

Stirling

Boeing Ave.

Hudson Ave.

Lysander Ln.

Moray Channel Bridge

Corvette Wy.

SPY

Sea   Island   Way

Patterson Rd.

Patterson   Rd.

99

Terrace Ave.

Jericho

Bella

R.C.A. Forum

Aylmer

Templeton Park

Templeton St.

Anson Ave.

Catalina Cr.

Burkeville Park

Cessna Dr.

Richmond Marina

Capstan Wy.

No. 3 Rd.

Capstan

Union Square

Walford St.

Kilby St.

Regina

Capella Dr.

Kilby

Tuttle Ave.

Garden City Rd.

9000

Talmey Park

Taimey

Kilby Ct.

Edwards St.

Wellington

Douglas

Airport Rd.

Handley Ave.

Lancaster

Baker   Way

Yaohan Centre

Hazelbridge

Cambie Field

Sexsmith

Wy.

Cunningham Pl.

McKay

McKay Pl.

Dougherty Rd.

B.C. Institute of Technology (Aerospace & Technology Campus)

Aberdeen

President Plaza

Cambie

Cunningham Dr.

Russ

Middle   Arm

Richmond Yacht Club

Aberdeen Centre

Browngate

Brownwood

Brownlea Rd.

Browndale Rd.

McKim Wy.

Odlin Rd.

Garden City

CAMBIE

Thomsett Park

McKim Wy.

Tomsett

Flight Path Park

Airport Rd. S.

Dinsmore Bridge

Aberdeen

No. 3   Rd.

Browngate

Brown

Parker Place

Brownell Rd.

Odlin Cr.

Northey Rd.

Sorenson Gt.

Odlin

Dubbert St.

Odlin   Rd.

Tomicki   Ave.

Inglis   Dr.

Gilbert

River   Rd.

SPY

Leslie

Leslie   Rd.

Alexandra   Rd.

No. 2 Road Bridge

BRIGHOUSE INDUSTRIAL PARK

Hazelbridge

Alexandra

RICHMOND

Way

Lansdowne

Alderbridge   Way

Richmond Olympic Oval

Hollybridge

Richmond Curling Club

Lansdowne Rd.

Cedarbridge Way

Blvd.

Lansdowne Centre

Kwantlen

Kwantlen Polytechnic University (Richmond Campus)

Brighouse Way

Oval Way

River Way

Alderbridge   Way

Lansdowne

Lansdowne   Rd.

THOMPSON   SEA   ISLAND

Elmbridge Way

Elmbridge Way

Ackroyd

Cooney

Arcadia

6000

Firbridge Way

Saba   Rd.

Lang Centre

Spires   Rd.

Alder St.

Birch

Birch Park

Thetis Pl.

Canim Pl.

7000

Azure Blvd.

Westminster

Bowling Green Rd.

Hwy.

BRIGHOUSE

Brighouse

Spires Gt.

Cook Cr.

Ferndale   Rd.

Katsura Park

Brighouse Park

Azure

Skaha

Alia

Richmond

Minoru

Richmond Centre

Cook

Cook Gt.

Garden City

9000

Hemlock   Dr.

Alder St.

Alberta   Rd.

Taseko Rd.

Brighouse

Minoru Chapel

Gateway Theatre

TOWN CENTRE

Cook

Cook Park Park

Pimlico Way

Christina Rd.

Drewry Cr.

Nadine

Nanika

Redfern

Adams Pl.

Minoru Park

Minoru Arenas

Minoru Sports Pavillion

Park

Buswell

Cooney

Eckersley Rd.

Citation Dr.

Garden City

Garden City Park

Anderson Park

MacNeill Park

Anderson

MacNeill / Incentive

Azure

Granville

Richmond Museum

RCMP

City Hall

Anderson   Ave.

Anderson Rd.

Granville   Ave.

Lechow St.

Livingstone Pl.

7000

Richmond Park

Brighouse Park

Bennett

Sills Ave.

Sills Ave.

Shields Ave.

Comstock   Rd.

Acheson Rd.

General   Currie   Rd.

Mang   Rd.

Udy   Rd.

No. 2   Rd.

Grandy

Chatterton Rd.

Gilbert   Rd.

Moffatt

Minoru   Blvd.

No. 3   Rd.

Currie

Turnill St.

General Currie

Paulik Park

Heather

Ash

Breden Ave.

Basset Rd.

Chatsworth Rd.

Chelsea Rd.

Garratt Park

Costain Ct.

Donald Rd.

Curzon St.

Chelmsford

Abercrombie Dr.

Abercrombie Pl.

General   Currie

General Currie Park

Jones

St. Albans

St. Albans   Rd.

Armstrong St.

Keefer   Ave.

N

Blundell   Rd.

8000

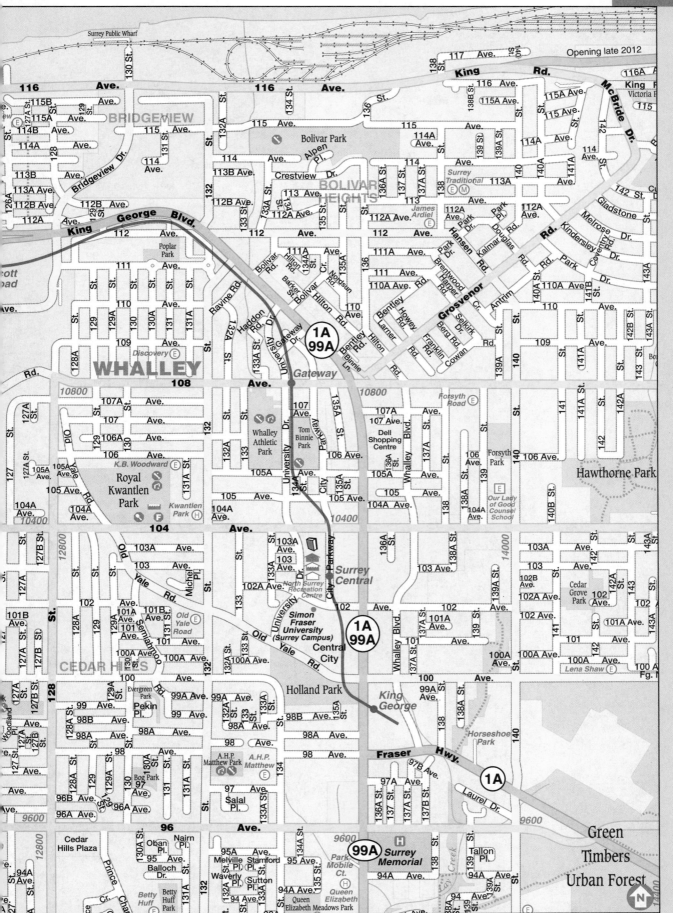

0   150   300
1:15 000   m

Second Beach Pool
Ceperley Meadow
Ceperley Field
Ceperley Meadow
Stanley Park Dr.
Stanley Park Pitch & Putt
Lost Lagoon
Nature House
Rhododendron Garden
Stanley Park Ln.
Lagoon   Dr.
Second Beach
Devonian Harbour Park
Royal Vancouver Yacht Club (Coal Harbour)
H M.C.S. Discovery
Deadman's Island
Bayshore West Marina
Cardero Park
Marina Square
Coal Harbour Marina
Coal Harbour Park
Harbour Green Park

Chilco St.
Comox
Pendrell
Gilford
Nelson
Barclay
Haro
Chilco
Denman
Bidwell
Alberni
Georgia
Bayshore Dr.
Menchions
Marina Square
Harbour Quay
Coal Harbour Quay
1900
1800
1700
1600
1500

Beach   Ave.
English Bay
English Bay Beach Park
English Bay Beach

WEST END
Morton Ave.
Morton Park
Bidwell
Davie
Alexandra Park
Cardero
Lord Roberts
Nicola
Comox
Nelson
Barclay
Jervis
Haro
King George
West End Community Centre
Cardero
Barclay Heritage Square
Barclay Manor
Roedde House Museum
Robson
St.
1400
1300
1A
99
Alberni
Broughton
Bute
Thurlow
Burr...
Christ... Cat...
Hotel Vancouver
1200
1100
1000
Melville
Pender
Hastings
Cordova
Coal...
Coal Harbour Community Centre

VANCOUVER

English Bay

Harwood
Nicola
Burnaby
Broughton St.
Pendrell
Nelson
Cardero
Sunset Beach Park
Seawall Walk
Beach   Ave.
Roberts Annex
Nelson Park
1000
YMCA
Robson Square Conference Centre
UBC (Robson Square)
St. Paul's
Thurlow
Pattison
900
800
700
Vogue Theatre

Jervis
Bute
Pacific   St.
Burrard
Davie
Drake
Hornby
Howe
Helmcken
Nelson
Seymour
Richards
Hamilton
1200
1100
1000
900
800
700
600
1300
1400
Vancouver Aquatic Centre
Anchor Point Montessori
Granville   St.
Ralston Ct.
Mainland
Pacific

Tiddly Cove Yacht Club
Vancouver Maritime Museum
Vanier Park
Vancouver Civic Marina
Burrard Civic Marina
Burrard Bridge
May & Lorne Brown Park
Seabreeze Wk.
Seawalk N.
Beach
Kinghorne Ms.
Strathmore Ms.
Homer
Yaletown-Roundhouse
Roundhouse
YALETOWN
David Lam Park
Elsie Roy
Round... Com... Cent...
1200

Hadden Park
Ogden   Ave.
McNicoll   Ave.
Whyte   Ave.
Creelman   Ave.
Greer   Ave.
Cypress
Maple
Laburnum St.
Walnut St.
Chestnut
Arbutus
H.R. Macmillan Space Centre/ Vancouver Museum
Burrard
Creekside Dr.
Pennyfarthing Dr.
Model Trains/ Model Ships/ Sportfishing Museums
Granville Island Public Market
Arts Club Theatre
Boatlift
Foreshore Wk.
Mast Tower Rd.
Maritime Mk.
Duranleau
Island
Johnston
George Wainborn Park
False Creek Yacht Club
Seymour Ms.
Homer
Pacific
David Lam Park

Kitsilano Beach Park
Cornwall   Ave.
2000
York   Ave.
Henry Hudson
Seaforth Peace Park
1st   Ave. W.
2nd   Ave. W.
3rd   Ave. W.
Cypress   St.
Burrard   St.
Fir   St.
Pine   St.
1st   Ave. W.
2nd   Ave. W.
3rd   Ave. W.
Marine... Wk.
Old Bridge Ct.
Hemlock
Foundry
Granville Island
Granville   St.
Old Bridge St.
Railway Alley
Waterfront Theatre
Cartwright St.
Sutcliffe Park
Performance Works
False Creek Community Centre
Pelican Bay
Granville Island Hotel
GRANVILLE ISLAND
Ironwork Ps.
Spruce Harbour Marina
False Creek
Charleson Park
False...

KITSILANO
Delamont Park
4th   Ave.   W.
5th   Ave. W.
6th   Ave. W.
7th   Ave. W.
8th   Ave. W.
Yew
Arbutus
Maple
Cypress St.
Pine
St. Augustine's
St. John's International
Granville Loop Park
2200
99
2300
2400
Broadway   W.
Century
Hemlock
Granville   St.
7th
8th
Birch
Alder
Family Montessori
The Foundry
Casting... Forge Qy.
The School Gn.
Sawcut
Greenh...
Ferry Ln.
Sawyer's Ln.
6th   Ave.   W.
Lamey's
Mill   Rd.
Charleson   St.
2200
Spruce
Oak
Laurel
Willow Park
Willow

N

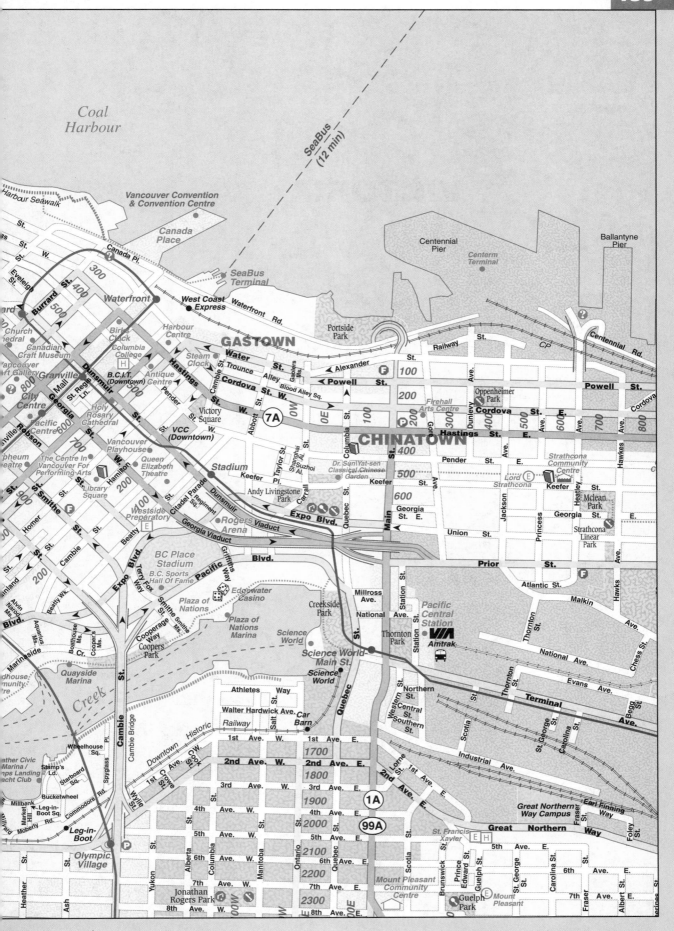

Coal Harbour

Harbour Seawalk

Vancouver Convention & Convention Centre

Canada Place

SeaBus (12 min)

SeaBus Terminal

Waterfront

West Coast Express · Waterfront Rd.

Canada Pl.

Burrard St.

300 · 400 · 500

Eveleigh St.

Church Cathedral

Canadian Craft Museum

Vancouver Art Gallery

Granville

City Centre

Pacific Centre

Robson

Orpheum Theatre

The Centre In Vancouver For Performing Arts

Library Square

Smithe

Homer

Cambie

Beatty Wk.

Aquarius Ms.

Boathouse Ms.

Cooper's Ms.

Marinaside

Quayside Marina

Boundhouse Community Centre

Creek

Heather Civic Marina / Stamps Landing Yacht Club

Stamp's Ld.

Starboard Sq.

Millbank

Leg-in-Boot Sq.

Bucketwheel

Market Hill

Moberly Rd.

Commodore Rd.

Leg-in-Boot

Heather St.

Ash St.

Olympic Village

Birks Clock

Columbia College

B.C.I.T. (Downtown)

Antique Centre

Holy Rosary Cathedral

VCC (Downtown)

Vancouver Playhouse

Queen Elizabeth Theatre

Westside Preparatory

Rogers Arena

BC Place Stadium

B.C. Sports Hall Of Fame

Plaza of Nations

Plaza of Nations Marina

Cooperage Way

Coopers Park

Wheelhouse Sq.

Spyglass Pl.

Dunsmuir

St. Regis Ln.

Georgia

Pender

Hastings

Cambie St.

Abbott St.

Victory Square

Citadel Parade Regiment Sq.

Georgia Viaduct

Dunsmuir

Griffiths Way

Terry Fox Way

Smithe Ms.

Cambie St.

Cambie Bridge

Wylie St.

Crowe St.

Downtown Historic Railway

1st Ave. W.

2nd Ave. W.

3rd Ave. W.

4th Ave. W.

5th Ave. W.

6th Ave. W.

7th Ave. W.

8th Ave. W.

Jonathan Rogers Park

Yukon St.

Alberta St.

Columbia St.

Manitoba St.

Ontario St.

Salt St.

Athletes Way

Walter Hardwick Ave.

Railway

Car Barn

Science World Main St.

Science World

Creekside Park

Steam Clock

Water St.

Trounce Alley

Cordova St. W.

Blood Alley Sq.

Gaolers

GASTOWN

7A

Stadium

Keefer

Taylor St.

Andy Livingstone Park

Carrall St.

Expo Blvd.

Shanghai Al.

Suzhoi Al.

Pacific Blvd.

Edgewater Casino

Expo Blvd.

Quebec St.

Portside Park

Alexander St.

Powell St.

Railway St.

CP

Centennial Pier

Centerm Terminal

Ballantyne Pier

Centennial Rd.

100

Powell St.

200

Firehall Arts Centre

Oppenheimer Park

Cordova St. E.

Hastings St. E.

CHINATOWN

Dr. Sun Yat-sen Classical Chinese Garden

Keefer St.

Pender

Georgia St. E.

Union St.

Prior St.

Main St.

Columbia St.

Gore Ave.

Dunlevy Ave.

Jackson Ave.

Princess Ave.

400 · 500 · 600 · 700 · 800

Cordova

Lord Strathcona

Heatley

Keefer St.

Strathcona Community Centre

Mclean Park

Strathcona Linear Park

Hawkes

Atlantic St.

Malkin

Thornton St.

Station St.

Pacific Central Station

VIA

Amtrak

National Ave.

Thornton Park

Millross Ave.

Terminal Ave.

Northern St.

Western St.

Central St.

Southern St.

Evans Ave.

Scotia St.

St. George St.

Carolina St.

Chess St.

Bagg St.

Industrial Ave.

1st Ave. E.

2nd Ave. E.

1700

3rd Ave. E.

1800

4th Ave. E.

1900

5th Ave. E.

2000

6th Ave. E.

2100

2200

7th Ave. E.

2300

8th Ave. E.

1A

99A

St. Francis Xavier

Great Northern Way Campus

Great Northern Way

Mount Pleasant Community Centre

Guelph Park

Mount Pleasant

Brunswick St.

Prince Edward St.

Guelph St.

St. George St.

Carolina St.

Fraser St.

Foley St.

Earl Finning Way

Scotia St.

5th Ave. E.

6th Ave. E.

7th Ave. E.

Albert St. E.

Lorne St.

1st Ave. E.

0   150   300
1:15 000   m

VICTORIA

Upper Harbour

Inner Harbour

Lime Bay

Victoria Harbour

James Bay

Shoal Point

Laurel Point

Laurel Point Park

Fishermans Wharf Park

Macdonald Park

Beacon Hill Park

Federal Marine Ecological Reserve

Holland Point Park

Holland Point

Finlayson Point

Clover Point Park

Regatta Point Park

Point Ellice House

Barclay Point

Ellice Point

Triangle Park

Victoria West Park

Vista Park

Lime Bay Park

Songhees Point

Swift St.

VIA

Johnson St.

Bridge

Wharf St.

Bastion Sq.

Heinckenn Alley

Langley St.

Waddington Alley

Commercial Alley

Trounce Alley

Fan Tan Alley

McPherson Playhouse

Capital Reg. District Headquarters

Centennial Square

City Hall

Save-On-Foods Memorial Arena

Victoria Curling Club

Intrepid Theatre

St. Andrews School

Royal Theatre

YMCA

Pioneer Square

Christ Church Cathedral School

The Bay Centre

Empress Hotel

Conference Centre

B.C. Legislative Buildings

Royal B.C. Museum

Cridge Park

South Park

Goodacre Lake

Irving Park

Emily Carr House

Lewis Park

Beacon Hill

Kilometre "0" Trans Canada Highway To St. John's Nfld. 7,349 km

Ferry to Port Angeles
Passenger Ferry to Port Angeles and Seattle

Floatplane Terminal

Crystal Pool and Fitness Centre

Central Park

Royal Athletic Park

Blanshard Community Centre

Wark St. Park

Mason St. Park

St. Andrews School

Opal St.

Rock Bay

Steamcrane Quay

Regatta Landing

Central Spur Rd.

Skinner St.

E&N Rail Trail

Street names

David St., Ellice St., Rock Bay Ave., Hillside Ave., Turner St., Pleasant St., John St., Bay St., Raynor Ave., Bella St., Edward St., Henry St., Dundas St., Russell St., Mary St., Catherine St., Esquimalt Rd., Harbour Rd., Tyee Rd., Sitkum Rd., Saghalie Rd., Kimta Rd., Paul Kane Pl., Cooperage Pl., Songhees Rd., Arthur Currie Ln., Alston St.

Store St., Discovery St., Chatham St., Herald St., Fisgard St., Pandora Ave., Johnson St., Yates St., View St., Fort St., Broad St., Government St., Douglas St., Blanshard St., Quadra St., Vancouver St., Cook St., Store St.

Queens Ave., Princess Ave., Pembroke St., Caledonia Ave., North Park St., Balmoral Rd., Mason St., Pandora Ave., Cormorant St., Fisgard St., Field St., Dowler Pl., Wark St., Empress Ave., Princess Ave., Green St., Kings Rd., Hillside Ave., Fifth St., Graham St., Prior St., Blackwood St., Vancouver St., Kings

Courtney St., Gordon St., Broughton St., Burdett Ave., Rockland Ave., Meares St., McClure St., Collinson St., Richardson St., Fairfield Rd., Rupert Ter., Penwell St., Humboldt St., Fairfield Rd., Academy Close, Southgate St., Convent Pl., Pakington St., Hilda St., Oscar St., McKenzie St., Chester St., Oxford St., Chapman St., May St., Leonard St., Faithful St., Woodstock Ave., Cambridge St., Wellington St., Linden Ave., Marlborough St.

Superior St., Michigan St., Simcoe St., Toronto St., Niagara St., Kingston St., Quebec St., Pendray St., Belleville St., Oswego St., Menzies St., Medana St., Clarence St., Rithet St., South Turner St., Government St., Battery St., Paddon Ave., Olympia Ave., Dallas Rd.

Huron St., Erie St., Lawrence St., Ontario St., Montreal St., Dock St., Pilot St., San Jose Ave., Sylvia St., Berwick St., Luxton Ave., Wynde Ln., Lewis St., Brotchie Ln., St. James St., Beckley Ave., Rendall St., Croft St., Parry St., Powell St., Heather St., Young St., Huntington St., Avalon Ave., Marifield Ave., St. Andrews St., Beacon St., Violet Ln., Thetis Ln., Ladysmith St., Simcoe St.

Heywood Ave., Arbutus St., Chestnut Row, Park Blvd., Oliphant Ave., Pendergast St., Sutlej St., Nursery Rd., Camas Cir., Beacon Hill Loop, Circle, Bridge Way, Clover Point

0   0.25   0.5
1:20 000
km

Park

Haney   Rd.

Norquay

Alain Rd.

Cunningham
Rd.

BX

Creek

Anderson

St.

Village
Green
Mall

53   Ave.

Lake
City
Casino

50
Ave.

Heron
Rookery

50 Ave.

Pleasant
Valley
Mobile
Home Park

Pearson Rd.

4800

48   Ave.

Silver   Sta

VERNON

4800

27

2600

48

47
Ave.

47   Ave.

BMX
Park

47
Ave.

Bx

46   Ave.

St.

46

46 Ave.

Bx
Ave.

Pleasant
Valley
Cemetery

Cascade

97

Vernon
Square

45
Ave.

45   Ave.

45   Ave.

Pleasant Valley
Academy

45
Ave.

Bighorn
Rd.

Cascade
Ct.

Wellington

Crystal Dr.

4240

Wesbild
Centre

Harwood

43A
Ave.

Cascade

43   Ave.

43   Ave.

43   Ave.

MacDonald
Park

Girouard Park

Mobile
Home
Park

43

42   Dr.

Reservoir

42A
Ave.

Alexis
Park

42
Ave.

42   Ave.

41

41 Ave.

41   Ave.

Cascade

41 Ave.

Windsor

40 Ave.

Alexis
Park

41 Ave.

34A St.

W.L.
Seaton

41   Ave.

41

Valley

40

39B
Ave.

39B

39A   Ave.

39   Ave.

39A
Ave.

39A

Hawks
Bill Pl.

Becker
Park

Vernon & District
Performing
Arts Centre

39

Rd.

Curling
Club

38   Ave.

Civic
Arena

38

38 Ave.

38 Ave.

Pleasant

EAST
HILL

Centennial

Greater
Vernon
Recreation
Centre

36

Powerhouse
Theatre

37

37   Ave.

37

Silver
Star

RCMP

36

36   Ave.

36

36   Ave.

3211

City
Hall

33

Bearisto

27

Pleasant

20A

34 Ave.

Discovery
Plaza

Greater Vernon
Museum &
Archives

33

32

3200

33

33 Ave.

33 Ave.

3211

Gateby
Pl.

Vernon
Art Gallery

31

Justice
Park

23 St.

3201

Lakeview
Park

17 St.

32 Ave.

30   Ave.

Coldstream Ave.

30   St.

30   Ave.

30

30

30 Ave.

29   Ave.

29

Coursier
Park

29

29 Ave.

28   Ave.

Fruit
Union
Plaza

28 Ave.

28

28 Ave.

25   Ave.

27

26   Ave.

Vernon
Community
Arts Centre/
Okanagan
Science Centre
Polson Park

2501

2500

24A Ave.

24   Ave.

24

24   Ave.

Okanagan   **Ave.**

24

Vernon

3907

23 Ave.

22 Ave.

6

Polson Place
Mall

Vernon
Jubilee

21 Ave.

21

19   Ave.

Armoury
Park

19 Ave.

Lake   Rd.

1801

18   Ave.

18   Ave.

Pottery

Mission   Hill
Park

Mission
Hill

16

15   Ave.

Pottery
Rd.

Mountview   Rd.

Commonage

Vimy
Rd.

14   Ave.

15   Ave.

Hillview
Golf

Commonage
Cr.

Verdun
Rd.

1201

Kosmina

Mt.
Baldur
Dr.

Caen Rd.

Hochwald
Rd.

Falaise
Rd.

Apres
Rd.

Arras Rd.

Ypres
Rd.

Vimy Rd.

Normandy Rd.

Sangro

Rimine

Camporasso
Ave.

Polson Dr.

Kalamalka

Fairweather
Dr.

Waddington

Middleton

Mt.
Fosthall
Dr.

Lindsay
Rd.

Dewdley Rd.

Fenwick

The Hook

Normandy
Rd.

Ghent Dr.

Mission   **Rd.**

20 Dr.

Vernon
Military
Camp

97

11. Lavenna Ave,.
12. Camme St.
13. Lanone Ave.
14. Liri Cr.
15. Nelson St.

1. Berardi St.
2. Adrano St.
3. Moro St.
4. Melfa St.
5. Regalbuto St.
6. Anzio St.
7. Casino St.
8. Saviord St.
9. Ortona St.
10. Coriano Ln.

Vernon
Golf and
Country
Club

Clubhouse

Browne

Creek

Sawicki
Park

Mt.
Atkinson
Ct.

Mt. Beaven
Ct.

Mt. Burnham
Rd.

Mt. Fosthall
Pl.

Mt. Bulman
Dr.

Mt. Ida

Quail
Vista Pl.

Cranbery
Ln.

Sarsons

N

0   0.25   0.5
1:20 000   km

Green Lake

Wedge
Park

ALPINE
MEADOWS
SOUTH

Fitzsimmons
Skateboard Park

Drifter Wy.
Needles Dr.
Alpine Way
Camino Dr.
Cedar Springs Rd.
Timber Ln.

Dream River
Park

Meadow Park
Sports Centre

Bear Pl.
Golden

Nicklaus North Blvd.
Murfield

NICKLAUS
NORTH
ESTATES

Glen Abbey Ln.
Mons Rd.

Forest Ridge Ct.
Lakewood Dr.
Matterhorn Dr.
Rainbow Dr.
Buckhorn
Fissile Ln.
Joywood Pl.

Meadow
Park

Dreams

Cypress Pl.
Murfield

Mons Ct.

Chateau
Whistler
Golf
Club

River of
Golden Dreams
Conservation
Area

Nicklaus
North
Golf
Course

MONS
CROSSING

BCR

Mons Rd.

Spruce
Grove
Park

Fitzsimmons Creek

Alta Lake Rd.

Whistler
Nature
Reserve

Valley Trail

WHISTLER

Whistler
Waldorf
School

SPRUCE
GROVE

Lost
Lake
Park

Lost
Lake

River of Golden

Creek

TAPLEY'S
FARM

Toad Hollow
Balsam Wy.

Myrtle Philip
Community

NESTERS

Kirkpatrick Wy.

Spruce Grove Cir.
Blackcomb

Spruce Grove Ln.

Nancy Greene Dr.

Fitzsimmons Rd. N.

Gate

Toni Sailer Ln.

Ambassador Cr. S.

WHITE
GOLD

Alta Creek

Tapley Pl.
Lorimer Rd.
Flute Pl.
Cedar Grove Ln.
Easy St.

Oboe
Piccolo Dr.
Seppos Way
Treetop Ln.
Nesters Rd.

Casabella Cr.

Fitzsimmons Rd.

Rainbow
Park

Crabapple Dr.
Daisy Ln.
Barnfield Pl.
Beaver Pl.
Gate
St. Andrews

Palmer Dr.
Wedge Ln.
Snowflake Pk.
Bishop Way

WHISTLER
CAY
ESTATES

Settebello Dr.
Montebello Pl.

MONTEBELLO

UPPER
VILLAGE

1. Whistler Museum
2. Maurice Young
   Millennium Place
3. Celebration Plaza
4. Squamish Lil'wat
   Cultural Centre

Chateau Whistler
Golf Club

HORSTMAN
ESTATES

Alta
Lake

Alta
Lake

Crabapple Dr.
Falcon Cr.
Falcon Ln.
Heron Pl.

WHISTLER
CAY
HEIGHTS

Fairway Dr.
Eagle Dr.
Par Rd.
Linkside Rd.

Whistler
Cay Dr.

Lorimer Rd.

Whistler
Health Care
Centre

Main St.

Blackcomb Wy.

Northlands Blvd.

Chateau Blvd.

Municipal
Hall

Rebagliati
Park

BLACKCOMB
BENCHLANDS

Spearhead Dr.
Horstman Dr.
Painted Cliff Rd.
Horstman Pl.

Blueberry Beach
Park North

BLUEBERRY
HILL

Blueberry
Beach
Park
South

Peak Dr.
Osprey Pl.
Nighthawk Ln.
Blueberry Dr.

Linkside Rd.
Eagle Ridge Cr.

Whistler
Golf
Club

RCMP
Village Gate Blvd.

WHISTLER
VILLAGE

Blackcomb
Base

Blackcomb Spearhead

Glacier Dr.
Magic Chair
Summit Ln.

Wizard Express

ALTA
VISTA

St. Moritz Cr.
St. Anton Way
Tyrol Cr.
Peak Dr.
Ptarmigan Pl.

Whistler Way

Whistler Golf
Club Driving
Range

Mountain Ln.
Springs Ln.

Blackcomb's Excalibur
Gondola Base

Whistler
Express
Gondola
Base

Glacier Ln.

Excalibur Gondola

Whistler
Sliding
Centre

Carleton Way
Archibald Cr.
Alta Vista Rd.
Lakeside Dr.

Brio Entrance
Arbutus Dr.
Hawthorne Pl.
Ridge

Tantalus Dr.

Sunridge Dr.

Lakeside
Park

Hillcrest Ln.
Hillcrest Dr.
Alpine Cr.
Juniper Pl.

BRIO

Sunridge Pl.

Panorama

SUNRIDGE
PLATEAU

Sea To Sky Hwy.

Fitzsimmons Express

Whistler Village Gondola

Fitzsimmons

N

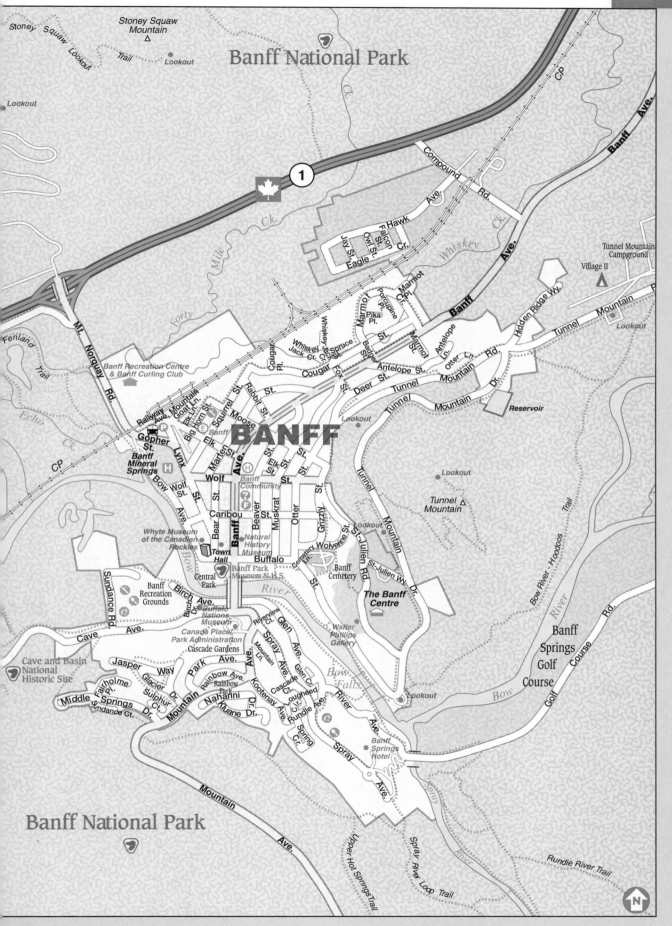

Banff National Park

Stoney Squaw Mountain

Stoney Squaw Lookout

Trail

Lookout

Lookout

Banff National Park

CP

Compound Rd.

Banff Ave.

1

Whiskey Ck.

Tunnel Mountain Campground

Village II

Tunnel Mountain Lookout

Hawk St.
Falcon St.
Owl St.
Jay St.
Eagle

Banff

Hidden Ridge Wy.

Tunnel Mountain Rd.

Mt. Norquay Rd.

Forty Mile Ck.

Fenland Trail

Marmot Cr.
Porcupine
Marmot Pl.
Pika Pl.
Marmot St.
Antelope Ln.
Otter Ln.

Banff Recreation Centre & Banff Curling Club

Whiskey Jack Ct.
Cougar Pl.
Spruce St.
Badger St.
Antelope St.
Deer St.
Fox St.
Cougar St.
Tunnel Mountain Dr.

Reservoir

Echo Ck.

CP

Railway Ave.
Mountain Ave.
Goat Ln.
Elk Ln.
Big Horn St.
Squirrel St.
Rabbit St.
Moose St.
Banff
Elk St.

Gopher St.
Banff Mineral Springs H
Lynx St.

BANFF

Lookout

Lookout

Marten St.
Elk St.
Elk St.
St.

Wolf St.

Banff Community

Tunnel Mountain Dr.

Tunnel Mountain

Bow Ave.
Wolf St.

Caribou St.

Bear St.
Banff Ave.
Beaver St.
Muskrat St.
Otter St.
Grizzly St.

Whyte Museum of the Canadian Rockies

Town Hall
Natural History Museum

Buffalo St.

Cemetery Ln.
Wolverine St.
St. Julien Rd.

Lookout

Tunnel Mountain

Banff Park Museum N.H.S.
Central Park

Banff Cemetery

Walter Phillips Gallery

St. Julien Wy.
St. Julien Dr.

The Banff Centre

Sundance Rd.

Bow River

Birch Ave.
Birch Dr.
Buffalo Nations Museum
Riverview Ct.
Glen Ave.
Glen Cr.

Banff Springs Golf Course

Banff Recreation Grounds

Canada Place, Park Administration
Cascade Gardens

Spray Ave.
Mountain Ln.
Cascade Ct.
Lougheed

Bow River - Hoodoos Trail

Cave Ave.

Jasper Way
Glacier Dr.
Park Ave.
Rainbow Ave.
Rainbow Park
Kootenay Ave.
Rundle Ave.

Bow Falls

Lookout

Bow River

Cave and Basin National Historic Site

Middle Springs Dr.
Fairholme Pl.
Sulphur Ct.
Mountain Dr.
Nahanni Dr.
Kluane Dr.
Spring Cr.

Banff Springs Hotel

Golf Course Rd.

Sundance Ct.

Spray Ave.

Banff National Park

Mountain Ave.

Upper Hot Springs Trail

Spray River Loop Trail

Spray River

Rundle River Trail

N

0   0.25   0.5
1:20 000
km

JASPER

Jasper
National
Park

Mina-Riley Lakes Loop

Jasper National Park

Jasper Par
Lodge

*Mildred
Lake*

*Trefoil
Lakes*

Athabasca River

Lodge Rd

16

*Lac
Beauvert*

Jasper Park
Lodge
Golf Club

Jasper
National
Park

Old For
Point

Juniper St.

St. Patricia Cir.

Aspen Cr.
Aspen Cr.
Bonhomme St.
Colin Cr.
Balsam St.
Aspen Ave.

Pyramid Lake Rd.

Connaught Dr.

Yellowhead Highway

Jasper
Information
Centre

VIA

Municipal Office
Jasper Curling Club
Jasper Activity Centre
Jasper Yellowhead
Museum & Archives

RCMP

Pyramid Ave.
Cedar Ave.
Desrochers
E
H
E
Geikie
Jasper
Patricia

The Den
*Jasper Wildlife
Museum*

Elm Ave.
Robson St.
Miette Ave.
Centennial
Park
Maligne Ave.
Pyramid St.
Birch Ave.
Turret St.
Miette Ave.
**Seton Jasper
Heathcare Centre**
Hazel Ave.

Tonquin St.
Turret St.
Geikie St.
Pine Ave.
Space Ave.
Willow St.

Creek Rd.
Poplar
Ash
Lodgepole
Brewster Cr.
J. Swift Cr.
Patricia
Cabin
Patricia Cr.

Connaught Dr.

CN
Sleepy Hollow Rd.

**Stan Wright
Industrial
Area**

Twin

Lakes

93A

Athabasca

River

16

93

Yellowhead Highway

Icefields

Miette

River

Parkway

Jasper
National
Park

*Tekarra
Creek*

Whistlers Rd.

The Whistlers
Campground

N

Provincial & Territorial Parks Facilities

BRITISH COLUMBIA

Park	Page Number	Coordinate	Vehicle / Tent Campsites	Wilderness Walk-In Camping	Picnic / Day Use	Sani-station	Showers	Wheelchair Access	Swimming	Fishing	Boat Launch	Hiking / Trails	Playground	Group Camping
Adams Lake (Bush Creek Site)	66	A-22	•						•	•	•	•		
Adams Lake-Poplar Point Site M	13	I-20		•					•	•				
Adams Lake-Spillman Beaches Site M	13	I-20		•					•	•				
Akamina-Kishinena	8	K-25		•						•		•		
Alexandra Bridge	6	K-18			•			•		•		•		
Alice Lake	33	Q-5,6	•	•	•	•	•	•	•	•		•	•	•
Allison Lake	48	L-17,18	•		•				•	•				
Alty Conservancy	10	G-10		•					•	•				
Anarchist Protected Area	42	R-24												
Anderson Bay	33	M-7								•		•		
Anderson Flats	17	E-12								•				
Anhluut'ukwsim Laxmihl Angwinga'asanskhl	17	E-11	•	•	•			•	•	•		•		
Anstey-Hunakwa	13	I-21		•					•	•				
Apodaca	33	P-7												
Arbutus Grove	33	M-8												
Arctic Pacific Lakes	18,19	F-18		•					•	•		•		
Arrow Lakes	69	D-32	•		•				•	•	•			
Arrowstone	6	J-18		•						•				
Artlish Caves	31	E-4		•						•		•		
Atlin Park & RA	22	A-5,6		•					•	•				•
Atna River	11	F,G-12		•					•	•		•		•
Babine Lake Marine - Pendleton Bay	17	F-14	•							•	•			
Babine Lake Marine - Smithers Landing	17	E-13	•		•					•	•			
Babine Mountains	17	F-13		•						•		•		
Babine River Corridor	17	E-12,13	•	•	•					•	•	•		
Bamberton	33	P-10	•		•			•	•	•				
Banana Island	66	D-22								•				
Bear Creek	50	J-23	•		•	•	•	•	•	•		•	•	
Bear Glacier	16	D-10												
Bearhole Lake Park & Protected Area	19	E-19	•	•	•				•	•	•			
Beatton	19	D-19	•		•			•	•	•	•	•	•	
Beatton River	19	D-19								•		•		
Beaumont	18	F-15	•		•	•		•	•	•	•	•		
Beaver Creek	45	R-34	•		•		•		•	•	•	•	•	
Bedard Aspen	6	J-18		•						•				
Bellhouse	33	Q-9			•					•		•		
Big Bar Lake	12	I-18	•		•				•	•	•	•	•	
Big Bunsby Marine	30	D-4		•					•	•				
Big Creek	12	I-16		•						•		•		
Bijoux Falls	18	E-17			•			•				•		
Birkenhead Lake	6	J-17	•		•			•	•	•	•	•		
Bishop Bay - Monkey Beach Conservancy	10	G-11		•	•				•	•				
Bishop Bay - Monkey Beach Corridor Conservancy	10	G-10,11		•	•				•	•				
Bishop River	5	J-15		•							•			
Blackcomb Glacier	33	Q-4										•		
Blanket Creek	68,69	B-31	•		•	•			•	•		•	•	

Park	Page Number	Coordinate	Vehicle / Tent Campsites	Wilderness Walk-In Camping	Picnic / Day Use	Sani-station	Showers	Wheelchair Access	Swimming	Fishing	Boat Launch	Hiking / Trails	Playground	Group Camping
Bligh Island Marine	31	F-6		•						•				
Blue Earth Lake	6	J-18	•							•	•	•		
Blue River Black Spruce	13	H-20								•				
Blue River Pine	13	H-20								•				
Bobtail Mountain	12	G-16								•		•		
Bocock Peak	18	E-16,17		•								•		
Bodega Ridge	33	P-9								•		•		
Bonaparte	13	I-19		•						•				
Boothman's Oxbow	44	R-30			•				•	•		•		
Border Lake	16	D-9		•						•				
Boulder Creek	17	E-12		•								•		
Boundary Creek	44	R-28	•							•				
Bowron Lake	12	G-18,19	•	•					•	•		•		•
Boya Lake	23	A-10,11	•					•		•		•		
Boyle Point	32	L-7			•							•		
Brackendale Eagles	33	Q-6								•				
Brandywine Falls	33	Q-4,5			•							•		
Brent Mountain Protected Area	41	N-21								•		•		
Bridal Veil Falls	38	Q-11			•			•				•		
Bridge Lake	13	I-19	•		•				•	•	•			
Brim River Hot Springs Protected Area	10	G-11		•					•	•				
Bromley Rock	41	O-19	•				•		•	•				
Brooks Peninsula/Muquin	30	C-4		•						•				
Broughton Archipelago Marine	4	J-13		•						•	•			
Browne Lake	51	K-25		•					•	•		•		
Buccaneer Bay	33	M,N-7		•					•	•				
Buckinghorse River Wayside	24	C-17	•		•			•	•	•	•	•		
Bugaboo	71	B-38,39		•	•							•		•
Bulkley Junction	17	E-12								•				
Bull Canyon	12	H-16	•		•		•			•		•		
Burges & James Gadsden	80	V-8,9			•							•		
Burgoyne Bay	33	P-9,10								•		•		
Burnie-Shea	17	P-9,10		•						•		•		
Burns Bog Ecological Conservancy	36	Q-3,4												
Burns Lake	17	F-14												
Buse Lake Protected Area	65	D-21										•		
Butler Ridge	18	D-17		•					•	•		•		
Caligata Lake	13	I-20								•		•		
Call Lake	17	F-12,13								•		•		
Callaghan Lake	33	Q-4	•		•					•	•	•		
Calvert Island Conservancy	10	I-11,12		•					•	•		•		
Canal Flats	8	J-24			•		•		•	•	•			
Canim Beach	12	I-18,19							•	•	•	•		
Cape Scott	30	B-2		•				•	•	•				
Cariboo Mountains	13	H-19	•	•					•	•				
Cariboo Nature	12	I-18												
Cariboo River	12	H-18		•						•	•			
Carmanah Walbran	34	L-10		•	•							•		
Carp Lake	18	F-16	•	•	•	•			•	•	•	•	•	•
Cascade RA	40	P-15,16		•						•		•		
Castle Rock Hoodoos	12	I-18,19												
Catala Island M	30	E-5		•						•	•			

Park	Page Number	Coordinate	Vehicle / Tent Campsites	Wilderness Walk-In Camping	Picnic / Day Use	Sani-station	Showers	Wheelchair Access	Swimming	Fishing	Boat Launch	Hiking / Trails	Playground	Group Camping
thedral Park & Protected Area	41	Q,R-20	•	•	•				•	•		•		
dar Point	12	H-18	•		•	•			•	•	•	•	•	•
ampion Lakes	45	Q-34	•		•	•		•	•	•	•	•	•	
arlie Lake	19	D-18,19	•		•	•		•	•	•	•	•		
ase	18	D-14,15		•					•	•		•		
asm	12	I-18			•					•		•		
emainus River	33	N-9			•			•	•	•		•		
illiwack Lake	39	R-12,13	•	•	•	•		•	•	•	•	•	•	
illiwack River	38	R-10										•		
inchaga Lakes Protected Area	25	C-19		•						•				
oquette Hot Springs	16	D-8		•						•				
ristie Memorial	42	O-23			•			•		•				
ristina Lake	44	R-31			•			•	•	•				
u Chua Cottonwood	13	I-19,20								•				
ukachida River Protected Area	23	C-12,13		•						•				
urn Creek Protected Area	12	I-17	•	•	•							•		
nemousun Narrows	67	A-26		•	•				•	•	•	•		
aud Elliott	31	F-3		•					•	•		•		
ayoquot Arm	32	J-8		•					•	•	•	•		
ayoquot Plateau	32	J-8		•										
endinning	33	N,P-3										•		
ose To The Edge Park & Protected Area	19	F-19										•		
dville Lagoon Marine	11	H-12		•					•	•		•		
dy Caves	55	L-38			•							•		
ldwater River	48	L-15								•		•		
llinson Point	33	P,Q-9												
lumbia Lake	72	UU-15			•			•	•	•		•		
nkle Lake	43	Q-26	•	•	•			•	•	•	•	•		•
peland Islands Marine	32	K,L-5		•					•	•				
quihalla Canyon	39	O-13			•			•				•		
quihalla River	39	N-13								•		•		
quihalla Summit RA	48	M-15		•						•		•		
rmorant Channel Marine	31	E-2		•					•	•				
rnwall Hills	6	J-18										•		
ste Rocks	10	G-11												
ttonwood River	12	G-17												
wichan River	35	N-10	•					•	•	•	•	•		•
ab Lake Conservancy	10	G-11		•					•	•				
aig Headwaters Protected Area	16	D-8,9		•						•				
oked River	18	F-17	•		•	•	•	•	•	•		•	•	
owsnest	8	K-25			•			•						
ltus Lake	38	R-9	•		•	•		•	•	•	•	•		•
mmins Lakes	13	H-21,22												
press	36	N,O-2		•	•			•				•		
hl Lake	12	G-16		•					•	•		•		
la-Kildala Rivers Estuaries	10	G-11		•						•				
ll River Old Growth	23	B-12		•						•		•		
mdochax Protected Area	17	D-12		•						•				
rke Lake	49	L-21,22	•							•				
vis Lake	37	P-8		•					•	•		•		
wley Passage	34	H-8		•						•				
netiah	23	B-12		•								•		

Park	Page Number	Coordinate	Vehicle / Tent Campsites	Wilderness Walk-In Camping	Picnic / Day Use	Sani-station	Showers	Wheelchair Access	Swimming	Fishing	Boat Launch	Hiking / Trails	Playground	Group Camping
Desolation Sound Marine	32	L-4		•					•	•		•		
Diana Lake	16	F-9			•			•	•	•		•		
Dionisio Point	33	P-9		•	•				•	•		•		
Discovery Island Marine	33	Q-11		•	•				•	•		•		
Dixie Cove Marine	30	D,E-4							•	•				
Downing	6	I,J-18	•		•				•	•	•			
Drewry Point	47	N,O-39		•	•				•	•				
Driftwood Canyon	17	F-12			•			•				•		
Drumbeg	33	P-8			•				•	•		•		
Dry Gulch	74	XX-14	•					•						
Duck Lake Protected Area	32	M-5							•	•				
Duffey Lake	6	J-17								•	•	•		
Dune Za Keyih Park & Protected Area	24	B-13								•				
Dunn Peak Protected Area	13	I-19,20								•		•		
Dzawadi/Klinaklini Estuary Conservancy	11	I-14												
Dzawadi/Upper Klinaklini River Conservancy	11	I-14		•						•		•		
E.C. Manning	40	Q-16	•	•	•	•	•	•	•	•		•		•
Eagle Bay	10	G-11		•					•					
Eakin Creek Canyon	13	I-19								•				
Eakin Creek Floodplain	13	I-19								•				
East Pine	19	E-18								•	•			
Echo Bay Marine	5	J-13		•	•					•				
Echo Lake	60	H-28							•	•				
Ed Bird-Estella Lakes	18	D-14	•	•					•	•		•		
Edge Hills	6	I,J-18		•								•		
Ekwan Lake Protected Area	25	B-19								•				
Elephant Hill	6	J-18												
Elk Falls	32	J-4,5	•		•	•		•	•	•		•	•	
Elk Lakes	74	WW-19		•	•				•	•		•		
Elk Valley	8	K-25			•			•		•				
Ellison	58	H-24	•		•	•		•	•	•		•	•	
Emar Lakes	13	I-19		•					•	•	•	•		
Emory Creek	39	N-12	•							•				
Enderby Cliffs	67	D-26								•		•		
Eneas Lakes	49	L-21	•	•						•		•		
English Lake	7	J-21												
Englishman River Falls	32	M-8	•		•			•	•	•		•	•	
Entiako	11	G-14		•						•		•		
Epper Passage	34	H-8		•					•	•				
Epsom	6	J-18							•	•		•		
Erg Mountain	12	G-18,19		•						•		•		
Eskers	18	F-16			•			•						
Ethel F. Wilson Memorial	17	F-14			•				•	•				
Europa Lake Conservancy	10	G-11		•					•	•				
Evanoff	19	F-18		•								•		
Exchamsiks River	16,17	F-10			•			•		•	•			
F.H. Barber	38	O,P-11												
Ferry Island	38	P-10												
Fillongley	32	L-6,7	•		•				•	•		•		
Finger-Tatuk	12	G-15	•	•						•		•		
Finlay-Russel Park & Protected Area	24	C-13		•						•		•		
Finn Creek	13	I-20								•				

Park	Page Number	Coordinate	Vehicle / Tent Campsites	Wilderness Walk-In Camping	Picnic / Day Use	Sani-station	Showers	Wheelchair Access	Swimming	Fishing	Boat Launch	Hiking / Trails	Playground	Group Camping
ntry Park & Protected Area	58	H-23	•		•		•	•	•	•		•	•	•
ordland Conservancy	10,11	H-11,12		•						•				
at Lake	12	I-18		•					•					
ores Island Marine	34	G-7		•					•	•		•		
och-Gilttoyees Park & Protected Area	10	G-10,11		•					•	•				
ort George Canyon	12	G-17			•					•		•		
ossli	32	K-8			•				•	•		•		
oster Arm Protected Area	13	H-21								•				
rancis Point	33	N-6			•									
ancois Lake	11	G-14	•	•	•				•	•	•			
raser River	12	G-17								•				
ench Beach	35	N-11	•		•	•		•	•	•		•	•	•
abriola Sands	33	N-8			•			•	•					
arden Bay Marine	33	N-6			•				•	•		•		
aribaldi	6	K-17		•	•				•	•		•		
ibson Marine	34	G-8		•					•	•		•		
ilnockie	8	K-24		•						•		•		
ilpin Grasslands	44	R-30,31							•			•		
iscome Portage Trail Protected Area	18	F-17								•				
itnadoiks River	17	F-10,11		•						•				
itxaala Nii Luutiksm/Kitkatla Conservancy	10	G-9												
ladstone (Texas Creek)	44	P-30,31	•	•	•			•	•	•		•		
oat Range	62	G,H-36		•						•		•		
od's Pocket Marine	30	D-1		•						•				
oguka Creek Protected Area	24	B-17												
old Muchalat	31	G-5		•						•		•		
olden Ears	37	N,O-7	•	•	•	•	•	•	•	•		•		•
oldpan	6	J-18	•		•				•	•				
oldstream	33	P-11	•		•	•	•	•	•			•		•
ordon Bay	35	M-9	•		•		•	•	•	•	•	•	•	•
owlland Tod	33	P-10,11			•				•			•		
raham-Laurier	18	D-16		•						•		•		
ranby	52	L-29,30		•						•		•		
raystokes	51	I,J-27								•				
reat Glacier	16	D-8		•						•				
reen Inlet Marine	10	H-11							•	•				
reen Lake	12	I-18	•		•	•		•	•	•	•	•	•	•
reenbush Lake Protected Area	7	J-21	•							•				
reenstone Mountain	64	D-17,18								•		•		
rohman Narrows	54	N-36												
willim Lake	19	E-18	•	•	•			•	•	•		•	•	
a'thayim (Von Donop) Marine	32	K-4		•					•	•				
ai Lake-Mount Herman	17	F-11		•					•					
akai Luxvbalis Conservancy	10	I-11		•						•				
alkett Bay	33	P,Q-7		•					•	•		•		
amber	13	H-22		•						•		•		
arbour Dudgeon Lakes	13	I-20							•	•				
ardy Island Marine	33	M-6		•					•	•				
armony Islands Marine	33	N-5							•	•				
arry Lake Aspen	6	J-18												
ay River Protected Area	25	B-19		•						•				
aynes Point	42	R-23,24	•		•			•	•		•	•		

146 British Columbia Parks

Park	Page Number	Coordinate	Vehicle / Tent Campsites	Wilderness Walk-In Camping	Picnic / Day Use	Sani-station	Showers	Wheelchair Access	Swimming	Fishing	Boat Launch	Hiking / Trails	Playground	
Heather-Dina Lakes	18	E-16	•	•					•	•	•	•		
Height of the Rockies	74	XX-18 WW-19		•					•	•		•		
Helliwell	32	L-7			•							•		
Hemer	35	N-8			•					•		•		
Herald	67	C-25	•		•	•	•	•	•	•	•	•		
Hesquiat Lake	31	F,G-7							•	•				
Hesquiat Peninsula	31	F-7		•					•	•				
High Lakes Basin	13	I-19		•						•		•		
Hitchie Creek	34	L-9,10		•						•		•		
Hole In The Wall	18	E-17,18		•								•		
Holliday Creek Arch Protected Area	13	G-20										•		
Homathko Estuary	5	J-15								•				
Homathko River-Tatlayoko P. Area	11	I-15		•					•	•				
Horne Lake Caves	32	L-7			•					•		•		
Horneline Creek	23	B-12		•								•		
Horsefly Lake	12	H-18	•	•	•		•	•	•	•	•	•	•	
Hunwadi/Ahnuhati-Bald Conservancy	5	J-13,14												
Hyland River	23	A-11												
Indian Arm	36	O-4		•	•				•	•	•	•		
Inkaneep	42	P-23,24	•							•		•		
Inland Lake	32	L,M-5	•	•	•			•	•	•	•	•		
Iskut River Hot Springs	23	C-9								•				
Itcha Ilgachuz	11	H-14,15		•						•		•		
Jackman Flats	13	H-20			•							•		
Jackpine Remnant	24	A-16		•										
Jackson Narrows Marine	10	H-11								•				
James Chabot	72	WW-14			•			•	•	•		•	•	
Jedediah Island Marine	33	M-7		•					•	•		•		
Jesse Falls Protected Area	10	G-11		•					•	•				
Jewel Lake	44	Q-29	•		•			•	•	•	•			
Jimsmith Lake	8	K-24	•		•			•	•	•				
Joffre Lakes	6	J-17		•						•		•		
John Dean	33	P-10			•							•		
Johnstone Creek	43	R-26	•									•		
Juan de Fuca	34,35	M-11	•	•				•	•	•		•		
Junction Sheep Range	12	I-17												
Juniper Beach	6	J-18	•		•	•	•	•	•	•		•		
K'distsausk/Turtle Point Conservancy	10	G-10		•					•					
K'nabiyaaxl/Ashdown Conservancy	10	G-10,11		•						•				
K'ootz/Khutze Conservancy	10	G-11		•						•	•			
K'wall Conservancy	10	G-10		•						•				
Kakwa Park & Protected Area	19	F,G-19		•						•		•		
Kalamalka Lake	59	H-25			•			•	•	•		•		
Kekuli Bay	59	H-25	•		•		•	•	•	•	•	•	•	
Kennedy Lake	34	J-9			•				•	•	•			
Kennedy River Bog	34	H,J-8												
Kentucky Alleyne	48	J-18	•							•	•			•
Keremeos Columns	42	P-22										•		
Kettle River RA	43	Q-27	•		•			•	•	•		•	•	•
Khutzeymateen Grizzly Bear Sanctuary	16	F-10												
Khutzeymateen Inlet Conservancy	16	F-9												
Kianuko	47	N-41								•		•		

Park	Page Number	Coordinate	Vehicle / Tent Campsites	Wilderness Walk-In Camping	Picnic / Day Use	Sani-station	Showers	Wheelchair Access	Swimming	Fishing	Boat Launch	Hiking / Trails	Playground	Group Camping
Lickininee	50	N-23			•			•	•	•	•			
Kikomun Creek	8	K-24	•		•	•	•	•	•	•	•	•	•	•
Kilby	38	P-9	•		•				•	•				
Kin Beach	32	K,L-6	•		•				•	•			•	
Kinaskan Lake	23	C-9	•		•			•	•	•	•			
King George VI	45	R-33												
Kingfisher Creek	67	C-27,28										•		
Kiskatinaw	19	E-19	•		•				•	•			•	
Kiskatinaw River Protected Area	19	D-19							•	•	•			
Kitasoo Spirit Bear Conservancy	10	H-11		•					•	•				
Kitimat River	17	F-11		•						•				
Kitlope Heritage Conservancy	11	G-12		•					•	•				
Kitson Island M	16	F-9		•						•				
Kitsumkalum	17	F-11	•		•				•	•				
Kitsumkalum Lake North Protected Area	17	F-11		•					•	•				
Kitty Coleman	32	K-6	•		•				•	•		•	•	•
Kitwanga Mountain	17	E-11		•								•		
Kleanza Creek	17	F-11	•		•			•				•		
Kledo Creek	24	B-16												
Klewnuggit Inlet Marine	10	G-10		•					•	•		•		
K'Igaan/Klekane Conservancy	10	G-11		•					•	•				
Klin-se-za Protected Area	18	E-17												
Klua Lakes Protected Area	24,25	B-17		•						•		•		
Kluskoil Lake	12	G-16		•					•	•				
Koeye Conservancy	11	I-12		•					•	•		•		
Kokanee Creek	54	M-37	•		•	•	•	•	•	•	•	•	•	•
Kokanee Glacier	54	K-37		•	•					•	•	•		
Koksilah River	35	N-10							•	•		•		
Kootenay Lake-Campbell Bay	55	J-39								•	•			
Kootenay Lake-Coffee Creek	55	L-38												
Kootenay Lake-Davis Creek	63	H-38	•					•	•	•	•			
Kootenay Lake-Lost Ledge	62,63	H,I-38	•					•	•	•	•	•		
Kootenay Lake-Midge Creek	47	O-39		•	•				•	•				
Kotcho Lake Village	25	A-18,19		•					•	•				
Ksi Xts'at'kw/Stagoo Conservancy	16	E-10												
K't'ii Racey Inlet Conservancy	16	E-10		•						•				
Ktisgaidz/MacDonald Bay Conservancy	10	G-10		•					•	•				
Kwadacha Wilderness	24	C-14,15		•						•		•		
Lac du Bois Grasslands Protected Area	64,65	C-18		•						•		•		
Lac La Hache	12	I-18	•		•	•		•	•	•	•	•	•	
Lac Le Jeune	65	E-18	•		•	•		•	•	•	•	•	•	
Lakelse Lake	17	F-11	•		•	•	•	•	•	•	•	•		•
Lakelse Lake Wetlands	17	F-11		•						•		•		
Lanz and Cox Islands	4	J-11		•						•				
Lava Forks	16	D-9		•						•				
Lawn Point	30	B-3		•					•					
Lax Ka'gaas/Campania Conservancy	10	H-10												
Lax Kwil Dziidz/Fin Conservancy	10	G-10		•						•				
Lax Lwax/Dundas and Melville Islands Conservancy	16	F-9												
Liard R. Corridor Pk. & Protected Area	24	A-14		•						•		•		
Liard River Hot Springs	24	A-13,14	•		•			•	•			•	•	
Little Andrews Bay M	11	G-13	•		•				•	•	•			

Park	Page Number	Coordinate	Vehicle / Tent Campsites	Wilderness Walk-In Camping	Picnic / Day Use	Sani-station	Showers	Wheelchair Access	Swimming	Fishing	Boat Launch	Hiking / Trails	Playground	Group Camping
Little Qualicum Falls	32	L-7,8	•		•			•	•	•		•	•	
Lockhart Beach	47	N-39	•		•				•	•		•		
Lockhart Creek	47	N-40										•		
Loveland Bay	32	J-4,5	•					•	•	•				•
Lowe Inlet Marine	10	G-10		•						•				
Lower Nimpkish	30	E-3		•					•	•				
Lower Raush Protected Area	13	G-19,20												
Lower Skeena River - Estew Site	17	F-10,11												
Lower Skeena River - Kasiks Site	16	F-10												
Lower Tsitika River	31	F-3		•						•				
Lundmark Bog Protected Area	17	F-11												
Mabel Lake	59,60	F-28	•		•	•		•	•	•	•	•	•	•
MacMillan	32	L-7,8						•						
Mahpahkum-Ahkwuna / Deserters-Walker Conservancy	30	D-1												
Main Lake	32	J-4		•					•	•	•	•		
Malaspina	32	L-5												
Mansons Landing	32	K-4			•			•	•	•	•	•		
Maquinna Marine	34	F,G-7		•	•				•	•		•		
Mara	67	C-26			•				•	•	•			
Marble Canyon	6	J-18	•		•				•	•		•		
Marble Range	12	I-18		•								•		
Marble River	30	D-2		•					•	•		•		
Marl Creek	79	U-8												
Martha Creek	78	X-2	•		•			•	•	•	•	•	•	
Maxhamish Lake Park & Protected Area	24	A-16		•					•	•				
McConnell Lake	65	E-18,19			•				•	•		•		
McDonald Creek	61	H-33	•		•			•	•	•	•	•		
Mehatl Creek	6	J-17,18								•		•		
Memory Island	33	P-10			•				•	•		•		
Meziadin Lake	16,17	D-10	•		•				•	•	•			
Milligan Hills	25	C-19		•										
Miracle Beach	32	K-5	•	•	•	•	•	•	•			•	•	•
Mitlenatch Island Nature	32	K-5							•	•		•		
Moberly Lake	18	E-18	•		•	•		•	•	•	•		•	
Moksgm'ol/Chapple - Cornwall Conservancy	10	G-10		•					•	•				
Momich Lakes	13	I-20	•						•	•				
Monashee	68	E-30,31		•	•					•		•		•
Monck	56	H-18	•		•	•		•	•	•	•	•	•	
Monkman	19	F-18	•	•	•			•		•		•		
Montague Harbour Marine	33	P-9	•	•	•			•	•	•	•	•		•
Monte Creek	65	D-21								•				
Monte Lake	66	E-22												
Moose Valley	12	I-18	•	•				•				•		
Morden Colliery Historic	35	N-8			•							•		
Morice Lake	11	G-12	•	•	•				•	•	•	•		
Morrissey	8	K-25												
Morton Lake	32	J-4	•		•			•	•	•	•	•		
Mount Assiniboine	83	Z,ZZ-16		•						•		•		•
Mount Blanchet	17	E-14								•		•		
Mount Edziza Park & RA	23	C-9		•						•		•		
Mount Elphinstone	33	P-7										•		
Mount Erskine	35	P-9										•		

Park	Page Number	Coordinate	Vehicle / Tent Campsites	Wilderness Walk-In Camping	Picnic / Day Use	Sani-station	Showers	Wheelchair Access	Swimming	Fishing	Boat Launch	Hiking / Trails	Playground	Group Camping
Mount Fernie	8	K-24	•		•					•		•		
Mount Geoffrey Escarpment	32	L-7							•	•		•		
Mount Griffin	7	J-21	•	•					•	•		•		
Mount Maxwell	33	P-9,10			•			•				•		
Mount Pope	18	F-15										•		
Mount Richardson	33	N,P-6	•	•					•	•		•		
Mount Robson	13	H-21	•	•	•	•	•	•	•	•	•	•	•	•
Mount Savona	64	C-16		•						•				
Mount Seymour	36	O-4		•	•				•	•		•		•
Mount Terry Fox	13	H-20			•							•		
Moyie Lake	8	K-24	•		•	•	•	•	•	•	•	•	•	
Mud Lake Delta	13	H-20,21								•				
Mudzenchoot	18	E-15								•				
Muncho Lake	24	B-14	•	•	•			•	•	•	•	•		
Murrin	33	Q-6			•			•	•	•		•		
Muscovite Lakes	18	D-15		•						•				
Myra-Bellevue	50	L-24										•		
Nadina Mountain	11	F-12,13		•								•		
Nahatlatch Park & Protected Area	6	K-18	•						•	•	•	•		
Naikoon-Agate Beach & Misty Meadows	4	G-8	•	•	•			•	•	•		•		•
Nairn Falls	6	J-17	•		•			•		•		•		•
Nalbeelah Creek Wetlands	17	F-11		•						•				
Nancy Greene	45	P-32	•		•				•	•		•		
Nation Lakes	18	E-15		•										
Nazko Lake	12	H-16	•	•					•	•		•		
Nechako Canyon Protected Area	11	G-14,15								•		•		
Negetl'/Nekite Estuary Conservancy	11	I-12												
Nenikëkh/Nanika-Kidprice	11	G-12		•					•	•		•		
Netalzul Meadows	17	E-13										•		
Newcastle Island Marine	33	N-8			•	•	•		•	•		•	•	•
Nickel Plate	41	O-21		•					•	•	•			
Nicolum River	39	O-13								•				
Nilkitkwa Lake	17	E-13		•						•				
Nimpkish Lake	30	E-3	•						•	•				
Ningunsaw	16	D-9		•						•				
Niskonlith Lake	66	B,C-22	•						•	•	•			
Nitinat River	34	L-9		•						•				
Norbury Lake	8	K-24	•		•				•	•		•		
North Thompson Islands	13	I-19,20								•				
North Thompson Oxbows East	13	H-20,21								•				
North Thompson Oxbows Jensen Island	65	B-19,20								•				
North Thompson Oxbows Manteau	13	H-20								•				
North Thompson River	13	I-19	•		•	•		•	•	•		•	•	
Northern Rocky Mountains	24	B-15		•						•		•		
Nuchatlitz	31	E-5,6		•					•	•				
Nuntsi	12	I-16		•						•				
Octopus Islands	32	J,K-4	•	•					•	•		•		
Okanagan Falls	42	O-23	•					•		•		•		
Okanagan Lake	50	L-22	•		•		•		•	•		•	•	
Okanagan Mountain	50	L-23		•	•				•	•		•		
Okeover Arm	32	L-5	•		•					•	•			
Old Man Lake	17	F-13							•	•				

Park	Page Number	Coordinate	Vehicle/Tent Campsites	Wilderness Walk-In Camping	Picnic / Day Use	Sani-station	Showers	Wheelchair Access	Swimming	Fishing	Boat Launch	Hiking / Trails	Playground	Group Camping
Oliver Cove Marine	10	H-11							•	•				
Omineca Park & Protected Area	18	E-14,15	•	•	•				•	•		•		•
One Island Lake	19	E-19	•		•				•	•	•	•	•	
Oregon Jack	6	J-18												
Otter Lake	48	M-16	•		•			•	•	•	•	•		
Owyacumish River	10	G-11		•					•	•				
Paarens Beach	18	F-15	•		•			•	•	•	•			
Painted Bluffs	64	C-17								•				
Paul Lake	65	C-20	•		•			•	•	•	•	•	•	•
Peace Arch	36	R-4,5			•			•						
Peace River Corridor	19	D-19		•						•		•		
Pennask Creek	49	J-20												
Pennask Lake	49	J-20	•						•	•	•			
Penrose Island Marine	11	I-12		•					•	•				
Petroglyph	33	N-8										•		
Pillar	66	D-23										•		
Pilot Bay	55	L,M-39		•	•				•	•				
Pine Le Moray	18	E-17	•	•	•				•	•		•		
Pine River Breaks	19	E-18		•						•		•		
Pinecone Burke	37	N-5,6		•	•				•	•		•		•
Pink Mountain	24	C-16,17		•								•		
Pinnacles	12	H-17										•		
Pirates Cove Marine	33	N-8		•	•				•	•				
Pitman River Protected Area	23	B-12		•						•				
Plumper Cove Marine	33	P-7		•					•	•		•		
Porcupine Meadows	64	A-18										•		
Porpoise Bay	33	N-7	•		•	•	•	•	•	•		•	•	•
Portage Brule Rapids Protected Area	24	A-13												
Porteau Cove	36	N-2	•	•	•	•	•	•	•	•	•	•		
Premier Lake	8	K-24	•		•	•	•	•	•	•		•		
Princess Louisa Marine	33	N-4		•	•				•		•	•		
Pritchard	66	C-22										•		
Prophet River Hotsprings	24	C-15,16		•						•				
Prophet River Wayside	24	B,C-17												
Prudhomme Lake	16	F-9,10	•					•	•	•				
Ptarmigan Creek Park & Protected Area	12	G-18,19		•						•		•		
Pukeashun	13	I-20		•						•		•		
Puntchesakut Lake	12	H-16,17			•				•	•	•			
Purcell Wilderness Conservancy Park & Protected Area	63	H-39,40		•					•	•				
Purden Lake	12	G-17,18	•		•	•		•	•	•	•	•	•	
Pure Lake	4	G-7			•				•	•		•		
Pyramid Creek Falls	13	H-20,21												
Q'altanaas/Aaltanhash Conservancy	10	G-11		•				•	•					
Quatsino	30	C-3		•					•	•		•		
Qwiquallaaq/Boat Bay Conservancy	31	F-3												
Raft Cove	30	B-2		•					•	•		•		
Rainbow Alley	17	E-13								•				
Rathtrevor Beach	33	M-7	•	•	•	•	•	•	•	•		•	•	•
Read Island	32	K-4		•					•	•				
Rearguard Falls	13	G-20								•		•		
Rebecca Spit Marine	32	K-4			•			•	•	•	•	•		
Red Bluff	17	F-13,14	•		•				•	•				

Park	Page Number	Coordinate	Vehicle / Tent Campsites	Wilderness Walk-In Camping	Picnic / Day Use	Sani-station	Showers	Wheelchair Access	Swimming	Fishing	Boat Launch	Hiking / Trails	Playground	Group Camping
Redfern-Keily	24	C-15,16		•					•			•		
Rendezvous Island South	32	K-4		•					•	•				
Roberts Creek	33	P-7	•		•	•		•	•	•		•		
Roberts Memorial	33	N-8			•					•		•		
Roche Lake	65	E-20	•	•					•	•	•	•		•
Rock Bay Marine	32	J-3								•				
Roderick Haig-Brown	66	A-23			•			•	•			•		
Rolley Lake	37	P-7	•		•	•	•	•	•	•		•	•	
Roscoe Bay	32	L-4		•					•	•				
Rosebery	62	I-35	•											
Rosewall Creek	32	K,L-7			•			•	•	•		•		
Ross Lake	17	E-12			•				•	•	•	•		
Rubyrock Lake	18	F-14								•				
Ruckle	33	P-9,10	•	•	•				•	•		•		•
Rugged Point Marine	30	D-5		•	•				•	•		•		
Ruth Lake	12	I-18			•				•	•	•			
Ryan	8	K-24			•									
Sabine Channel Marine	32	M-7		•					•	•				
Saltery Bay	33	M-5,6	•		•	•		•	•	•		•		
Sandwell	33	N-8			•				•	•		•		
Sandy Island Marine	32	L-6							•	•		•		
Santa Gertrudis-Boca del Infierno Marine	31	F-6		•						•				
Sargeant Bay	33	N-7			•			•	•	•		•		
Sasquatch	38	O-11	•		•	•		•	•	•		•	•	•
Scatter River Old Growth	24	A-15		•						•				
Schoen Lake	31	G-4	•	•	•				•	•	•	•		
Schoolhouse Lake	12	I-18		•						•				
Sechelt Inlets Marine	33	N-6		•	•				•					
Seeley Lake	17	E-12	•		•				•	•		•		
Seton Portage Historic	6	J-17												
Seven Sisters Park & Protected Area	17	F-11		•	•				•			•		
Shannon Falls	33	Q-6			•			•				•		
Shearwater Hot Springs Conservancy	10	G-11		•	•				•	•				
Shuswap Lake	66	B-24	•		•		•	•	•	•	•	•	•	•
Shuswap Lake Marine	67	A,B-26	•	•	•				•	•	•	•		
Shuswap River Islands	67	E-27												
Sikanni Chief Canyon Protected Area	25	C-17		•						•				
Sikanni Chief Falls Protected Area	24	C-16,17								•		•		
Sikanni Old Growth	25	B-18								•				
Silver Beach	13	I-20,21	•						•	•		•		
Silver Lake	39	O-12,13	•		•			•	•	•		•		
Silver Star	59	F-26										•		
Simson	33	N-7							•	•		•		
Sir Alexander Mackenzie	11	H-12								•		•		
Six Mile Hill Protected Area	64	C-17										•		
Skagit Valley	39	Q-14	•	•				•	•	•		•		•
Skaha Bluffs	42	N-23			•			•				•		
Skihist	6	J-18	•		•	•		•		•		•		
Skookumchuk Narrows	33	N-6								•		•		
Skookumchuk Rapids	67	D-28												
Sleeping Beauty Mountain	17	F-10,11		•								•		
Slim Creek	12	G-18									•			

Park	Page Number	Coordinate	Vehicle/Tent Campsites	Wilderness Walk-In Camping	Picnic/Day Use	Sani-station	Showers	Wheelchair Access	Swimming	Fishing	Boat Launch	Hiking/Trails	Playground	Group Camping
Small Inlet Marine	32	J,K-4		•					•	•		•		
Small River Caves	13	G-20												
Smelt Bay	32	K-5	•		•				•	•	•			
Smith River Falls-Fort Halkett	24	A-13			•					•		•		
Smuggler Cove Marine	33	N-7		•				•	•	•		•		
Snowy Protected Area	41	R-21		•						•		•		
Sooke Mountain	33	P-11		•						•		•		
Sooke Potholes	35	N-11			•				•	•				
South Okanagan Grasslands Protected Area	42	Q,R-23								•		•		
South Texada Island	33	M-7								•				
Sowchea Bay	18	F-15	•						•	•	•			
Spatsizi Headwaters	23	C-10,11		•						•				
Spatsizi Plateau Wilderness	23	C-11,12		•						•		•		
Spectacle Lake	33	P-10			•			•	•	•				
Spider Lake	32	L-7			•			•	•	•		•		
Spipiyus	33	N-6								•				
Sproat Lake	32	K-7,8	•		•		•	•	•	•	•	•		
Spruce Lake Protected Area	6	I,J-16,17		•					•	•		•		
Squitty Bay	33	M-7			•				•	•				
St. Mary's Alpine	55	K-41		•						•		•		
Stagleap	46	R-38								•		•		
Stair Creek Conservancy	10	G-10		•					•	•				
Stamp River	32	K-7	•							•		•		
Stawamus Chief	33	Q-6	•	•	•							•		
Steelhead	64	C-16	•		•	•	•	•	•	•	•	•		
Stein Valley Nlaka'pamux Heritage	6	J-17,18		•	•					•		•		•
Stemwinder	41	O-20	•					•		•				•
Stikine River	23	B,C-11		•						•	•			
Stone Mountain	24	B-14,15	•	•	•			•	•	•	•	•		
Strathcona	31	H-6	•	•	•			•	•	•	•	•	•	
Strathcona-Westmin	32,31	H,J-6		•						•		•		
Stuart Lake Marine	18	F-15		•					•	•				
Stuart River	18	F-15,16								•				
Sue Channel	10	G-11		•					•					
Sugarbowl-Grizzly Den Park & Protected Area	12	G-18		•						•		•		
Sukunka Falls	18	E-18		•						•		•		
Sulphur Passage	31	G,H-7		•					•	•				
Summit Lake	61	H-34	•		•			•	•	•	•	•		
Sun-Oka Beach	50	M-23			•			•	•	•			•	
Surge Narrows	32	K-4		•						•				
Sustut Park & Protected Area	17	D-13		•										
Sutherland River Park & Protected Area	18	F-14,15		•						•		•		
Swan Creek Protected Area	17	F-11		•						•				
Swan Lake	19	E-19,20	•		•			•	•	•	•		•	
Swan Lake/Kispiox River	17	E-11		•					•	•		•		
Sydney Inlet	31	G-7		•					•	•				
Syringa	45	O-33	•		•	•		•	•	•	•	•	•	•
Tahsish-Kwois	30	D,E-4		•					•	•				
Takla Lake Marine	17	E-14		•						•				
Tantalus	33	P,Q-5		•					•	•		•		
Tatlatui	23	C,D-12		•						•		•		
Tatshenshini-Alsek	28	J-2		•						•		•		

Park	Page Number	Coordinate	Vehicle / Tent Campsites	Wilderness Walk-In Camping	Picnic / Day Use	Sani-station	Showers	Wheelchair Access	Swimming	Fishing	Boat Launch	Hiking / Trails	Playground	Group Camping
Taweel	13	I-19								•				
Taylor Arm	32	K-8			•				•	•		•		•
Taylor Landing	19	D-19								•	•			
Teakerne Arm	32	K,L-4							•	•		•		
Ten Mile Lake	12	G-17	•		•	•	•		•	•	•	•	•	
Tetrahedron	33	P-6										•		•
Thinahtea Protected Area	25	A-19		•						•				
Three Sisters Lake	12	G-17								•		•		
Thurston Bay Marine	32	J-3		•					•	•				
Toad River Hot Springs	24	B-14		•										
Todagin South Slope	23	C-10		•						•		•		
Top of the World	8	K-24		•						•		•		
Topley Landing	17	F-13												
Tranquil Creek	32	J-7		•					•					
Trembleur Lake	18	F-14		•					•	•				
Trepanier	49	J-21,22		•						•		•		
Tribune Bay	32	L-6,7			•				•	•				
Truman Dagnus Locheed	58	H-24												
Ts'il-os	12	I-16	•	•	•				•	•		•		
Tsa-Latl'/Smokehouse Conservancy	11	I-12,13												
Tsintsunko Lakes	13	I-19								•		•		
Tudyah Lake	18	E-17	•		•			•	•	•	•	•		•
Tunkwa	64	D-16	•						•	•	•	•		•
Tuya Mountains	23	A-9								•		•		
Tweedsmuir North Park & Protected Area	11	G-13		•						•				
Tweedsmuir South	11	H-13,14	•	•	•	•			•	•		•		
Tyhee Lake	17	F-13	•		•	•	•	•	•	•	•	•	•	•
Ugwiwey/Cape Caution Conservancy	11	I-12												
Ugwiwey/Cape Caution–Blunden Bay Conservancy	10,11	I-11,12												
Uncha Mountain Red Hills	11	G-14		•						•		•		
Union Passage Marine	10	G-10		•						•				
Upper Adams River	13	I-20								•				
Upper Lillooet	5	J-16		•								•		
Upper Raush Protected Area	13	H-20												
Upper Seymour River	13	I-21								•		•		
Upper Violet Creek	67	C-26												
Valhalla	54	J-35		•	•				•	•		•		
Vargas Island	34	G-8		•					•	•				
Vaseux Lake	42	P-23,24	•		•			•	•	•		•		
Vaseux Protected Area	42	P-23,24												
Victor Lake	68	A-30								•				
Wakes Cove	33	P-8								•		•		
Walhachin Oxbows	64	C-16							•	•				
Wallace Island Marine	33	P-9		•	•				•	•				
Walloper Lake	64	E-18			•				•	•	•			
Walsh Cove	32	K,L-4							•	•				
Wapiti Lake	19	F-19		•						•				
Wardner Lake	8	K-24			•				•	•				
Wasa Lake	8	K-24	•		•	•		•	•	•		•	•	
Weewanie Hot Springs	10	G-11		•	•				•					
Wells Gray	13	H-19,20	•	•	•	•		•	•	•	•	•	•	
West Arm	54	N-37		•	•				•			•		

Park	Page Number	Coordinate	Vehicle / Tent Campsites	Wilderness Walk-In Camping	Picnic / Day Use	Sani-station	Showers	Wheelchair Access	Swimming	Fishing	Boat Launch	Hiking / Trails	Playground	Group Camping
West Lake	12	G-17			•			•	•	•	•	•		
West Shawnigan Lake	33	P-10			•				•	•				
West Twin Park & Protected Area	12,13	G-19		•	•							•		
Weymer Creek	31	F-5		•								•		
Whaleboat Island Marine	33	P-8									•			
Whiskers Point	18	F-16,17	•		•			•	•	•		•	•	
White Lake	67	B-25	•						•	•		•		
White Lake Grasslands Protected Area	42	O,P-23										•		
White Pelican	12	H-16												
White Ridge	31	H-6			•							•		
White River	31	G-4								•		•		
Whiteswan Lake	8	J-24	•	•	•	•		•	•	•		•		
Windermere Lake	72	VV-14												
Wire Cache	13	I-20								•				
Wistaria	11	G-13			•					•	•			
Woss Lake	31	F-4,5		•						•	•			
Wrinkly Face	59	I-25										•		
Yahk	8	K-23,24	•		•			•		•				
Yard Creek	67	B-27,28	•		•					•	•	•		

ALBERTA

Park	Page Number	Coordinate	Vehicle / Tent Campsites	Wilderness Walk-In Camping	Picnic / Day Use	Sani-station	Showers	Wheelchair Access	Swimming	Fishing	Boat Launch	Hiking / Trails	Playground	Group Camping
Aspen Beach	14	H-25,26	•		•	•	•		•	•	•	•	•	•
Aylmer RA	14	H-23,24	•							•		•		
Beauvais Lake	8	K-25	•	•	•	•				•	•	•	•	•
Beaver Lake RA	21	F-28	•				•	•	•	•	•			
Beaver Mines Lake RA	8	K-25	•		•			•	•	•	•	•		
Beaverdam RA	14	H-24	•		•					•		•		
Big Berland RA	13	G-21	•							•		•		
Big Elbow RA	74	YY-20,21		•						•		•		
Big Hill Springs	14	I-25			•							•		
Big Knife	15	H-27	•		•		•		•	•		•	•	
Big Mountain Creek RA	19	F-21								•		•		•
Bigelow Reservoir RA	14,15	I-26			•					•				
Birch Mountains Wildland	27	C-26,27		•						•		•		
Blackstone RA	14	H-23	•		•					•		•		
Bleriot Ferry RA	15	I-26,27	•							•				
Blue Rapids RA	14	G-24,25								•		•		
Bluerock Wildland	75	XX-21	•	•						•		•		
Bob Creek Wildland	8	J,K-25		•								•		
Bow Valley	8	I,J-24	•		•	•	•	•		•	•	•	•	•
Bow Valley Wildland	8	I,J-24		•	•					•		•		
Bragg Creek	8	J-25			•					•		•		
Brazeau Canyon Wildland	14	H-23		•						•		•		
Brazeau Reservoir RA	14	H-24	•						•	•	•	•		•
Brazeau River RA	14	H-23	•							•		•		

Park	Page Number	Coordinate	Vehicle / Tent Campsites	Wilderness Walk-In Camping	Picnic / Day Use	Sani-station	Showers	Wheelchair Access	Swimming	Fishing	Boat Launch	Hiking / Trails	Playground	Group Camping
Brown Creek RA	14	H-23	•							•				
Brown-Lowery	8	J-25			•							•		
Buck Lake RA	14	G,H-25	•		•					•	•			
Buffalo Lake RA	15	H-27	•						•	•			•	
Bullshead Reservoir RA	9	K-29			•					•	•			
Burnt Timber RA	14	I-24	•						•	•		•		
Calhoun Bay RA	14	H-25	•		•					•				
Calling Lake	21	E-26	•		•	•			•	•		•	•	
Canmore Nordic Centre	81	Y-17,18			•		•					•		
Caribou Mountains Wildland	26	A-24,25		•						•				
Carson-Pegasus	20	F-24	•		•	•	•	•	•	•	•	•	•	•
Cartier Creek RA	14	I-25	•							•				•
Castle Falls RA	8	K-25	•		•			•		•		•		
Castle River Bridge RA	8	K-25	•		•			•		•		•		
Cat Creek RA	75	VV-21			•							•		
Cataract Creek RA	75	UU-22	•		•					•		•		
Chain Lakes	8	J-25	•		•	•			•	•				•
Chain Lakes RA	21	F-26	•		•			•	•	•	•			
Chambers Creek RA	14	H-24	•		•					•		•		•
Chinchaga Wildland	25	C-20		•						•		•		
Chinook RA	8	K-25	•		•					•		•		
Chrystina Lake RA	20	F-24	•							•	•			
Coal Lake North RA	15	G-26			•					•	•			
Coal Lake South RA	15	G-26												
Coalspur RA	13	G-22												
Cobble Flats RA	8	J-25			•					•				
Cold Lake	21	F-29	•		•	•	•	•	•	•	•	•	•	•
Colin-Cornwall Lakes Wildland	27	A-29		•						•				
Cooking Lake-Blackfoot RA	15	G-27			•							•		
Crescent Falls RA	14	H-23	•		•					•		•		
Crimson Lake	14	H-24,25	•		•	•	•	•	•	•	•	•	•	•
Cross Lake	20,21	F-26	•		•	•	•	•	•	•	•	•	•	
Crow Lake	21	E-27												
Cypress Hills Interprovincial	9	K-29	•		•	•	•		•	•		•		•
Dawson RA	8	I-25	•							•		•		
Deer Creek RA	14	I-24								•				•
Dillberry Lake	15	H-29	•		•	•	•		•	•		•	•	•
Dinosaur	9	J-28	•		•	•	•					•	•	•
Don Getty Wildland	75	VV-22,23 YY-21		•						•		•		
Dry Haven RA	14	H-23	•							•		•		
Dry Island Buffalo Jump	15	I-27	•		•					•			•	
Dunvegan	19	E-21	•		•	•		•		•			•	
Dunvegan West Wildland	19	D-20		•						•		•		
Dutch Creek RA	8	K-25	•		•			•		•		•		
Eagle Point	14	G-24,25	•			•	•			•			•	
Elbow Falls RA	8	J-25	•		•			•		•				
Elbow River Launch RA	8	J-25								•				
Elbow River RA	8	J-25	•		•					•		•	•	•
Elbow-Sheep Wildland	8	J-24,25		•	•					•		•		
Elk Creek Fish Pond RA	14	H-24			•					•				
Elk Creek RA	14	H-24	•							•		•		
Elk River RA	14	G,H-23	•		•					•				

Park	Page Number	Coordinate	Vehicle / Tent Campsites	Wilderness Walk-In Camping	Picnic / Day Use	Sani-station	Showers	Wheelchair Access	Swimming	Fishing	Boat Launch	Hiking / Trails	Playground	Group Camping
English Bay RA	21	F-29							•	•	•			
Engstrom Lake RA	21	D-29			•					•		•		
Etherington Creek RA	75	UU-22	•		•					•		•		•
Evan-Thomas RA	8	J-24			•					•		•		
Eyrie Gap RA	75	VV-22			•					•		•		
Fairfax Lake RA	14	G,H-23	•							•	•			
Fallen Timber RA	14	I-25	•							•				
Fallen Timber South RA	14	I-24,25	•		•					•		•		
Fawcett Lake RA	20	E-25,26	•		•				•	•	•			•
Fickle Lake RA	14	G-23	•		•				•	•				
Fidler-Greywillow Wildland	27	A-29		•						•				
Figure Eight Lake RA	19,20	D-21,22	•		•				•	•		•		
Fish Creek	8	J-25,26			•		•	•	•	•		•	•	
Fish Lake RA	14	H-23,24	•		•				•	•		•		
Fisher Creek RA	8	J-25	•		•					•				
Fitzsimmons Creek RA	75	VV-21,22			•					•		•		
Fort Assiniboine Sandhills Wildland	20	F-25		•	•					•		•		
Fort Vermilion RA	26	B-23,24	•							•				
Franchere Bay RA	21	F-28,29	•		•	•	•		•	•			•	
Freeman River RA	20	F-24	•		•					•				
French Bay RA	21	F-29,30	•						•	•		•		
Garner Lake	21	F-28	•		•	•	•		•	•		•	•	
Ghost Airstrip RA	14	I-24	•							•		•		•
Ghost Reservoir RA	14	I-24	•		•					•		•		
Ghost River Wilderness Area	14	I-24		•								•		
Gipsy Lake Wildland	21	D-29		•										
Glenbow Ranch	14	I-25										•		
Gleniffer Reservoir RA	14	H-25	•		•				•	•	•			•
Goldeye Lake RA	14	H-23	•		•				•	•		•		
Gooseberry Lake	15	H-29	•		•	•	•			•			•	•
Gooseberry RA	8	J-25	•			•				•		•		
Grand Rapids Wildland	21	D-27		•						•		•		
Greene Valley	20	D-22			•							•		
Greenford RA	75	WW-23	•							•				
Gregoire Lake	21	D-28	•		•	•	•		•	•		•		•
Grizzly Ridge Wildland	20	E-24,25		•						•		•		
Hangingstone RA	21	D-28	•		•								•	
Harlech RA	14	H-24	•							•		•		
Hay-Zama Lakes Wildland	25	B-20												
Heart River Dam RA	20	E-23	•		•					•				
Highwood Junction RA	75	VV-22			•	•								
Highwood RA	75	VV-22								•				•
Hilliard's Bay	20	E-24	•			•	•		•	•	•	•	•	•
Honeymoon Creek RA	8	J-25						•						•
Horburg RA	14	H-24	•							•		•		
Hornbeck Creek RA	14	G-23	•								•			
Hubert Lake Wildland	20	F-25		•								•		
Indian Graves RA	75	UU-23	•							•		•	•	•
Ing's Mine RA	8	J-25			•									
Iosegun Lake RA	20	F-23	•		•				•	•	•			•
Island Lake RA	8	K-25	•					•	•	•				
Jackfish Lake RA	14	H-24	•		•					•	•			•

Park	Page Number	Coordinate	Vehicle / Tent Campsites	Wilderness Walk-In Camping	Picnic / Day Use	Sani-station	Showers	Wheelchair Access	Swimming	Fishing	Boat Launch	Hiking / Trails	Playground	Group Camping
James River Bridge RA	14	I-25												
James-Wilson RA	14	I-24	•		•					•		•		•
Jarvis Bay	14	H-25,26	•			•	•	•				•	•	•
Jensen Reservoir RA	9	K-27			•					•	•			
Kakwa River RA	19	F-21	•							•		•		
Kakwa Wildland	13	F,G-20		•								•		
Kehiwin RA	21	F-28,29	•							•	•			
Kinbrook Island	9	J-27,28	•		•	•	•		•	•	•		•	•
Kootenay Plains RA	85	P-12								•		•		•
La Biche River Wildland	21	E,F-27		•						•		•		
La Butte Creek Wildland	27	A-28		•								•		
Lake McGregor RA	9	J-27	•						•	•	•			
Lakeland	21	F-28		•	•					•		•		
Lakeland RA	21	F-28	•				•		•	•		•	•	
Lambert Creek RA	14	G-23								•				•
Lantern Creek RA	75	WW-21			•							•		
Lawrence Lake RA	20,21	F-26	•		•					•	•			
Lesser Slave Lake	20	E-25	•		•	•	•		•	•		•		
Lesser Slave Lake Wildland	20	E-24		•						•				
Lineham RA	75	WW-21			•									
Little Bow	9	J-26,27	•		•	•	•		•	•		•	•	•
Little Bow Reservoir RA	9	J-27	•		•				•	•	•			
Little Elbow RA	8	J-25	•			•				•		•		
Little Fish Lake	15	I-27	•											
Little Sundance Creek RA	13	G-22,23	•		•					•				
Livingstone Falls RA	8	J-25	•		•					•		•		
Lois Hole Centennial	14	G-26			•									
Long Lake	21	F-27	•		•	•	•	•	•	•		•	•	•
Lovett River RA	14	G-23	•							•		•		
Lundbreck Falls RA	8	K-25	•	•	•					•	•			
Lusk Creek RA	8	I-25			•					•		•		
Lynx Creek RA	8	K-25	•		•			•		•		•		
Machesis Lake RA	26	B-23	•		•					•	•			
Maqua Lake RA	21	D-28			•				•			•		•
Marguerite River Wildland	27	C-29		•								•		
Maybelle River Wildland	27	B-29		•								•		
Maycroft RA	8	K-25	•							•				
McLean Creek RA	8	J-25	•		•	•	•			•		•	•	
McLeod River RA	13	G-22	•							•				•
Medicine Lake RA	14	H-25	•		•				•	•	•		•	•
Mesa Butte RA	75	YY-22	•							•		•		
Michelle Reservoir RA	9	K-29			•					•				
Midland	15	I-27			•					•		•		
Minnow Lake RA	14	G-23,24	•							•	•			•
Miquelon Lake	15	G-27	•		•	•	•	•	•			•		•
Mist Creek RA	74,75	WW-21			•							•		
Mitchell Lake RA	14	H-24,25	•							•				
Moonshine Lake	19	E-20	•		•	•	•		•	•		•	•	•
Moose Lake	21	F-29	•		•	•			•	•	•			•
Muriel Lake RA	21	F-29												
Musreau Lake RA	19	F-21	•		•					•				•
Nojack RA	14	G-24	•											

Park	Page Number	Coordinate	Vehicle / Tent Campsites	Wilderness Walk-In Camping	Picnic / Day Use	Sani-station	Showers	Wheelchair Access	Swimming	Fishing	Boat Launch	Hiking / Trails	Playground	Group Camping
North Buck Lake RA	21	F-27	•						•	•	•		•	
North Fork RA	75	YY-22	•		•					•		•		
Notikewin	26	C-22,23	•		•					•		•		
O'Brien	19	E-21			•				•	•				
Obed Lake	13	G-22	•		•					•	•			
Oldman Dam RA	8	K-26	•		•	•	•			•	•			•	•
Oldman River North RA	8	K-25	•		•			•		•				•
Oldman River RA	8	K-26	•		•	•				•				
Ole's Lake RA	19	D-20	•		•				•	•		•		
Otter-Orloff Lakes Wildland	20,21	E-26		•								•		
Paddle River Dam RA	14	G-24,25							•	•	•			
Park Lake	9	K-26,27	•		•	•		•	•	•	•	•	•	•
Payne Lake RA	8	K-26	•		•					•				
Peace River Wildland	20	E-22		•						•		•		
Peaceful Valley RA	14	H-25			•			•				•		
Pembina Forks RA	14	H-23	•		•					•				
Pembina River	14	G-25	•		•	•	•	•	•	•		•	•	
Peppers Lake RA	14	H,I-24	•							•		•		
Peter Lougheed	74	YY-18	•	•	•	•	•	•	•	•		•		•
Phyllis Lake RA	14	H-24,25	•							•		•		
Picklejar RA	75	WW-21			•							•		
Pierre Grey's Lakes	13	G-21	•		•					•	•	•		•
Pigeon Lake	14	G-25	•		•	•	•	•	•	•			•	•
Pine Grove RA	8	I-25								•				•
Poachers' Landing RA	21	F-27	•							•				
Police Outpost	8	K-26	•		•	•				•		•		
Prairie Creek RA	14	H-24	•							•				
Queen Elizabeth	20	D-22	•		•	•		•	•	•				
Racehorse RA	8	K-25	•		•			•		•				
Rainbow Lake RA	25	B-20	•		•				•	•				
Ram Falls	14	H-24	•		•					•		•		•
Raven RA	14	H-25	•					•		•				
Red Deer River RA	14	I-24	•		•					•		•		•
Red Lodge	14	I-25	•		•	•	•		•	•			•	•
Richardson River Dunes Wildland	27	B-28		•								•		
Rochon Sands	15	H-27	•		•	•			•	•	•			•
Rock Lake	13	G-21	•		•				•	•	•	•		
Rock Lake-Solomon Creek Wildland	13	G-21,22		•						•		•		
Running Lake RA	19	D-20	•		•				•	•				
Saskatoon Island	19	E-20,21	•		•	•	•	•	•		•		•	•
Saunders RA	14	H-24	•							•		•		
Sentinel RA	75	VV-22			•					•		•		
Seven Mile RA	14	I-24	•		•					•		•		
Sheep Creek RA	19	F-21	•									•		
Sheep River	75	XX-21,22	•		•					•		•	•	•
Shunda Viewpoint RA	14	H-24												•
Shuttler Flats RA	19	F-20								•				•
Sibbald Lake RA	8	I-25	•		•					•		•	•	
Sibbald Meadows Pond RA	8	I,J-25			•					•		•		
Siffleur Wilderness Area	83	R-12		•								•		
Simonette River RA	19	E-21	•							•				
Sir Winston Churchill	21	F-28	•		•	•	•	•	•	•	•	•	•	•

Park	Page Number	Coordinate	Vehicle / Tent Campsites	Wilderness Walk-In Camping	Picnic / Day Use	Sani-station	Showers	Wheelchair Access	Swimming	Fishing	Boat Launch	Hiking / Trails	Playground	Group Camping
Smoke Lake RA	20	F-22,23	•		•				•	•	•			
Smoky River South RA	13	G-20	•							•	•			
Snow Creek RA	14	H-23								•		•		•
South Ghost RA	8	I-24,25			•									
Southview RA	19	F-21			•									
Spray Valley	8	J-24	•	•	•					•		•	•	
St. Mary Reservoir RA	9	K-26	•		•				•	•		•	•	•
Stoney Creek RA	8	J-24,25								•				•
Stoney Lake RA	19	D-21	•							•	•	•		
Stony Mountain Wildland	21	D-28		•								•		
Strachan RA	14	H-24	•		•					•		•		•
Strathcona Science	15	G-26			•							•		
Strawberry RA	75	VV-21,22	•											
Sulphur Gates RA	13	G-20	•	•								•		
Sulphur Lake RA	19	D-21	•		•				•	•		•		•
Sundance	14	G-22	•		•					•		•		
Swan Lake RA	14	H-24	•		•					•		•		
Sylvan Lake	14	H-25			•		•		•	•			•	
Syncline RA	8	K-25						•				•		•
Tay River RA	14	H-24	•						•	•				
The Narrows RA	15	H-26,27	•							•				
Thompson Creek RA	83	Q-11	•		•					•		•		
Thunder Lake	20	F-25	•		•	•	•	•	•	•	•		•	•
Tillebrook	9	J-28	•			•	•	•				•	•	
Trapper Lea's Cabin RA	20	F-24,25	•											
Travers Reservoir RA	9	J-27	•							•	•			
Trout Pond RA	75	WW-21			•							•		
Twin Lakes RA	26	C-22	•						•	•		•		
Two Lakes	19	F-20	•							•	•	•		
Vermilion	15	G-28,29	•		•	•	•			•		•	•	•
Wabamun Lake	14	G-25	•		•	•	•		•	•	•	•	•	•
Waiparous Creek RA	14	I-24,25	•							•		•		•
Waiparous Valley Viewpoint RA	14	I-24			•									
Wapiabi RA	14	H-23		•						•		•		
Ware Creek RA	75	YY-22										•		
Waskahigan River RA	20	F-22	•							•		•		•
Waterton Reservoir RA	8	K-26	•		•				•	•	•			
Watson Creek RA	13	G-22	•							•				
Weald RA	14	G-23								•				•
West Bragg Creek RA	8	J-25			•							•		
White Goat Wilderness Area	85	O-9,10		•								•		
Whitehorse Creek RA	87	H-7								•		•		
Whitehorse Wildland	87	H-6,7		•								•		
Whitemud Falls Wildland	21	D-29		•								•		
Whitney Lakes	15	G-29	•		•	•	•	•	•	•	•	•	•	•
Wild Horse RA	14	I-24										•		•
Wildhay RA	13	G-21,22								•				•
Wildhorse Lake RA	13	G-22	•		•					•	•			
Wildhorse RA	75	YY-21,22		•								•		
William A. Switzer	13	G-22	•				•		•	•	•	•	•	
Williamson	20	E-22	•		•	•				•	•	•	•	
Willmore Wilderness	13	G-20		•								•		

Park	Page Number	Coordinate	Vehicle / Tent Campsites	Wilderness Walk-In Camping	Picnic / Day Use	Sani-station	Showers	Wheelchair Access	Swimming	Fishing	Boat Launch	Hiking / Trails	Playground	Group Camping
Willow Creek	8	J-26								•				
Winagami Lake	20	E-23	•		•	•			•	•	•	•	•	•
Winagami Wildland	20	E-23		•								•		
Wolf Creek RA	75	XX-22		•								•		
Wolf Lake RA	21	F-29	•			•				•	•		•	
Wolf Lake West RA	14	G-23	•						•	•	•	•		
Woolford	9	K-26			•					•		•		
Writing-on-Stone	9	K-28	•		•	•			•	•		•	•	•
Wyndham-Carseland	8	J-26	•		•	•				•		•	•	•
Young's Point	20	E-22	•		•	•	•		•	•		•	•	•

NORTHWEST TERRITORIES

Park	Page Number	Coordinate	Vehicle / Tent Campsites	Wilderness Walk-In Camping	Picnic / Day Use	Sani-station	Showers	Wheelchair Access	Swimming	Fishing	Boat Launch	Hiking / Trails	Playground	Group Camping
Blackstone	29	B-5	•		•	•	•	•	•	•	•	•	•	
Cameron River Crossing	29	B-7			•				•	•		•		
Chan Lake	29	B-6			•									
Dory Point	29	B-6			•									
Fort Providence	29	B-6	•		•	•		•		•				
Fort Simpson	29	B-5	•				•	•				•	•	
Fred Henne	29	B-7	•	•	•	•	•	•	•	•		•	•	
Gwich'in	28	A-3	•		•					•	•			
Happy Valley	28	A-3	•		•	•	•	•		•		•		
Hay River	29	B-6	•		•	•	•	•	•	•		•		
Hidden Lake	29	B-7		•					•	•		•		
Jàk	28	A-3	•		•		•	•				•	•	
Kakisa River	29	B-6			•					•	•			
Lady Evelyn Falls	29	B-6	•		•		•	•		•	•	•		
Little Buffalo River Crossing	29	B-7	•		•					•	•			
Little Buffalo River Falls	29	B-7	•		•						•	•		
Madeline Lake	29	B-7			•					•	•		•	
McKinnon	29	A-4		•	•									
McNallie Creek	29	B-6			•			•				•		
Nitainlaii	28	A-2	•		•							•		
North Arm	29	B-6	•							•				
Pontoon Lake	29	B-7			•					•	•	•		
Prelude Lake	29	B-7	•		•	•			•	•	•	•		
Prosperous Lake	29	B-7						•		•	•			
Reid Lake	29	B-7	•	•	•	•			•	•		•	•	
Sambaa Deh Falls	29	B-6	•		•		•	•		•		•		
Sixtieth Parallel	29	B-6	•		•	•	•	•		•	•	•		
Tetlit Gwinjik	28	A-2						•				•		
Twin Falls	29	B-6	•		•	•	•	•				•	•	•
Yellowknife River	29	B-7			•					•	•	•		

YUKON TERRITORY

Park	Page Number	Coordinate	Vehicle / Tent Campsites	Wilderness Walk-In Camping	Picnic / Day Use	Sani-station	Showers	Wheelchair Access	Swimming	Fishing	Boat Launch	Hiking / Trails	Playground	Group Camping
Coal River Springs	28	B-4		•								•		
Fishing Branch Ni'iinlii'njik	28	A-2												
Tombstone	28	B-2	•	•								•		

Community Index

Note: Where there are duplicate listings, the first listing refers to the community's location on the provincial scale maps (pages 4 - 29) and the second refers to its location on the regional scale maps (pages 30 - 87).